KEYS TO MANAGEMENT

David Cotton

LONGMAN

Pearson Education Limited
Edinburgh Gate, Harlow,
Essex CM20 2JE, England

This edition published by Addison Wesley Longman Ltd 1996
Sixth impression 1999
ISBN 0-17-555825-6

Designed by Wendi Watson

Printed in Malaysia, ACM

Acknowledgements

Cover by SNAP Graphics

Illustrations by Phillip Burrows (pp. 32, 37, 41, 67, 74, 79 (the 2nd), 90, 103,
112,127 and 156), Martin Farrar (pp. 36, 66, 69, 73, 77, 79 (the 1st), 99, 129,
152, 164 and 167) and Peter Joyce (pp. 28, 39, 49, 86, 123, 124, 131, 136 and
145).

The publishers are grateful to the following for permission to reproduce
copyright material. They have tried to contact all copyright holders but
where they have failed will be pleased to make all the necessary
arrangements at the first opportunity.

Gower Publishing Company for the extract from *Working* by Studs Terkel on
p.30; William Heinemann (London) for the extract from *The Practice of
Management* by Peter Drucker on p. 43 and for the card from *How to
Manage*, Editor Ray Wild, on p. 81; Personnel Journal for Fig. 1 on p. 104;
Richard D. Irwin Inc. for Fig. 3 on p. 105, taken from *Personnel: a Diagnostic
Approach*, Third Edition, by William Glueck; McGraw-Hill Book Company
for Fig. 1 on p. 130, taken from *New Patterns of Management* by Rensis
Likert; CBS College Publishing for Fig. 2 on p. 132, taken from *Organizational
Behavior* by Richard M. Hodgetts and Steven Altman; Macmillan for Chart 1
on p. 143, taken from Handbook of Leadership by Ralph Stogdill; McGraw-
Hill Book Company for chart 2 on p. 144, taken from *A Theory of Leadership
Effectiveness* by Professor Frederick E. Fiedler, and Grid Publishing Inc. for
the examples on p. 156, taken from *International Business Blunders* by Ricks.
Fu and Arpan.

Photographs

The Times for p. 7; The Royal College of Art for p. 13; Barnaby's Picture
Library for pp. 30, 61, 141, 142 (the 1st), 154 and 170; Heals for pp. 42 and 43;
Yorkshire and Humberside Development Association for p. 47; Toshiba for
p. 51; Marks and Spencer for p. 53; BBC Hulton Picture Library for p. 119;
Camera Press for pp. 142 (the 2nd) and 178; Massey Ferguson for p. 157;
International Defence and Aid Fund for p. 171 and Rank Xerox for p. 173.

Contents

Introduction   4

1   The manager's role   6
2   Frederick W. Taylor: 18
      Scientific Management
3   The Quality of Working Life   30
4   Decision-making   41
5   Top management – planning and strategy   52
6   Goal-setting   67
7   The management of time   78
8   Motivation   90
9   Performance appraisal   103
10 Centralisation or decentralisation?   117
11 Communications   129
12 Leadership   142
13 Management in multinationals   156
14 Social responsibility   170

Tapescript and key   182

Introduction

General description

Keys to Management is a course in Business English which is intended for higher intermediate/advanced students wishing to increase their knowledge of management theory and practice.

The course consists of fourteen units, each dealing with a key management concept such as planning, motivation, appraisal and leadership, each of which is illustrated by real examples from the world of business. Thematically linked to the topic of each unit are a wide variety of language activities, designed to focus on business lexis and difficult points of grammar as well as developing reading, writing, listening and speaking skills. The main emphasis of *Keys to Management*, however, is to develop the students' oral fluency and their ability to communicate effectively in a wide range of management situations.

Keys to Management can be used either as a main coursebook or as supplementary material. It is also suitable for short courses, as each unit is entirely self-contained, allowing teachers to select material appropriate to the particular needs of their students.

Aims of the course

A   The business aims are:
  (i) to introduce students to the basic concepts of management;
  (ii) to stimulate students' interest in the subject and to encourage them to learn more about management;
  (iii) to present a range of management situations in the form of case studies, role-plays and discussions which familiarise students with the problems faced by managers and provide them with the opportunity to develop effective communication skills.

B   The language aims are:
  (i) to develop students' reading, writing, listening and speaking skills but, in particular, their ability to express themselves accurately and effectively in business situations;
  (ii) to focus on language functions and structures which are particularly useful for managers;
  (iii) to increase the students' knowledge of commercial vocabulary, specialist management terms and business idiom;
  (iv) to give students practice in writing business communications such as short reports, memoranda, advertisements and letters.

Organisation of the units

The units consist of the following sections:

DISCUSSION

This section serves as an introduction to the topic(s) of each unit and usually takes the form of a short reading passage, mini case study or dialogue, followed by a number of questions intended to generate discussion.

READING

The reading passages are generally between 800 and 1,000 words in length. They deal with key management ideas or practices and should therefore be of interest to business executives wishing to learn more about the theories of management.

Understanding the main points
The reading passages are followed by a variety of comprehension – checking devices to ensure that students have understood the most important ideas contained in the text. These include open-ended questions, true/false statements, sentence completion, note-taking, grid completion and identifying the order of the main ideas.

Vocabulary focus

Having demonstrated that they have grasped the main arguments put forward in the passage, students are then asked to work through an intensive reading exercise which requires them to examine the meaning of certain important vocabulary items. This exercise involves either finding words or phrases in the text which are similar in meaning to the synonyms or definitions given in the exercise, or using the context of the passage to help them to guess the meaning of vocabulary items taken from the text.

LANGUAGE STUDY

The aim of this section is to increase students' knowledge of management-related vocabulary, collocation, phrasal verbs and general business idiom, while at the same time providing the opportunity for remedial grammar work. The points of grammar are those which students at this level continue to find problematic, such as which prepositions follow which verbs, the inversion of subject and verb after certain adverbs and adverbial phrases, the differences between countable and uncountable nouns, the use of conjunctions and other linking devices, and reported speech.

COMMUNICATION SKILLS

This section usually begins with a dialogue (recorded and printed in the Student's Book) whose purpose is to present a variety of phrases and expressions which are used to express certain language functions such as introducing yourself, giving opinions, agreeing, making suggestions, giving advice, discussing possibility, persuading and giving warnings.

Role play

Following the presentation of examples of the language used to fulfil a particular function or functions, students take part in a simple role play activity in small groups. They are given a situation similar to the one in the dialogue and are asked to play a role requiring them to practise using certain key phrases and expressions, which are listed for easy reference.

Case study

The short role play activity is followed by one or more case studies presenting realistic management situations or problems. These allow the students to take part in small and large group discussions; simulated meetings; more involved, longer role play activities; problem-solving exercises and so on. All of the activities in this section aim to build up the students' confidence to communicate effectively in the type of business situations which managers regularly face.

WRITING

The exercises in this section give students the opportunity to practise writing various types of business letter, memoranda, reports, newspaper articles, minutes of meetings, advertisements and telexes. Students are generally provided with some guidance concerning the structure and style of the communication they are required to produce.

LISTENING

The listening passages include conversations between people in a wide variety of typical management situations such as board meetings, appraisal meetings, planning and strategy meetings and production meetings. In addition, there is a news broadcast, a conversation about stocks and shares, an assessment of their respective bosses by two secretaries and a series of conversations about the kidnapping of a top executive by terrorists.

Understanding the main points

The listening passages are followed by a variety of comprehension-checking devices to ensure that students have grasped the main points. These include sentence completion, note-taking, grid completion, open-ended questions and true/false statements.

Vocabulary focus

Following the listening-for-gist exercises, students are required to work through intensive listening exercises which focus their attention on specific phrases and expressions used by the speakers. Students must either fill in the gaps in sentences taken from the dialogue (and then discuss their meaning) or identify phrases or expressions which are equivalent in meaning to the ones printed in their books.

1 The manager's role

Look at the following lists of positions and organisations and answer the questions below. Then, in groups of two or three, compare your answers.

POSITION	ORGANISATION
manager	a famous pop music group
head of research and development	an oil company
supervisor (on an assembly line)	a car company
general manager	a fashion business
vice-chancellor	a university
chairman	a multinational company

1 What duties do all these people have in common?
2 What qualities and skills are required for each position?
3 Which of the positions would you prefer to have? Why?
  Are there any you would not want to hold? Why?

READING

Our society is made up of all kinds of organisations, such as companies, government departments, unions, hospitals, schools, libraries, and the like. They are essential to our existence, helping to create our standard of living and our quality of life. In all these organisations, there are people carrying out the work of a manager although they do not have that title. The vice-chancellor of a university, the president of a students' union or a chief librarian are all managers. They have a responsibility to use the resources of their organisation
10 effectively and economically to achieve its objectives.

Are there certain activities common to all managers? Can we define the task of a manager? A French industrialist, Henri Fayol, wrote in 1916 a classic definition of the manager's role. He said that to manage is 'to forecast and plan, to organise, to command, to coordinate and to control'. This definition is still accepted by many people today, though some writers on management have modified Fayol's description. Instead of talking about *command*, they say a manager must *motivate* or *direct and lead* other workers.

20 Henri Fayol's definition of a manager's functions is useful. However, in most companies, the activities of a manager depend on the level at which he/she is working. Top managers, such as the chairman and directors, will be more involved in long range planning, policy making, and the relations of the company with the outside world. They will be making decisions on the future of the company, the sort of product lines it should develop, how it should face up to the

competition, whether it should diversify etc. These strategic decisions are part of the planning function mentioned by
30 Fayol.

On the other hand, middle management and supervisors are generally making the day-to-day decisions which help an organisation to run efficiently and smoothly. They must respond to the pressures of the job, which may mean dealing with an unhappy customer, chasing up supplies, meeting an urgent order or sorting out a technical problem. Managers at this level spend a great deal of time communicating, coordinating and making decisions affecting the daily operation of their organisation.

40 An interesting modern view on managers is supplied by an American writer, Mr Peter Drucker. He has spelled out what managers do. In his opinion, managers perform five basic operations. Firstly, managers set objectives. They decide what these should be and how the organisation can achieve them. For this task, they need analytical ability. Secondly, managers organise. They must decide how the resources of the company are to be used, how the work is to be classified and divided. Furthermore, they must select people for the jobs to be done. For this, they not only need analytical ability but also
50 understanding of human beings. Their third task is to motivate and communicate effectively. They must be able to get people to work as a team, and to be as productive as possible. To do this, they will be communicating effectively with all levels of the organisation – their superiors, colleagues, and subordinates. To succeed in this task, managers need social skills. The fourth activity is measurement. Having set targets and standards, managers have to measure the performance of the organisation, and of its staff, in relation to those targets. Measuring requires analytical ability. Finally, Peter Drucker
60 says that managers develop people, including themselves. They help to make people more productive, and to grow as human beings. They make them bigger and richer persons.

In Peter Drucker's view, successful managers are not necessarily people who are liked or who get on well with others. They are people who command the respect of workers, and who set high standards. Good managers need not be geniuses but must bring *character* to the job. They are people of integrity, who will look for that quality in others.

'A manager develops people, including himself or herself . . . (and) helps them to grow and become bigger and richer persons.'

Peter Drucker

Understanding the main points

1 According to the writer, what is the main duty of the head of any organisation?
2 Why do some people disagree with Henry Fayol's definition of the role of management?
3 In what ways are the functions of a company director, for example, different from those of a middle manager?
4 In Peter Drucker's opinion, which of the following things should a manager be?

exceptionally intelligent ☐

keen to improve people's lives ☐

interested in other people ☐

popular ☐

able to give clear orders ☐

honest ☐

admired by others ☐

able to examine carefully and make judgements ☐

Vocabulary focus

1 *Find words or phrases in the text which mean the same as the following:*

1 carefully, not wastefully (paragraph 1)
2 expand the range of products (paragraph 3)
3 operate (paragraph 4)
4 resolving (paragraph 4)
5 said in a clear, detailed way (paragraph 5)

2 Managers set *objectives* (line 43)

What is an *objective*?
Give examples of objectives that sales, production and personnel managers might set.

LANGUAGE STUDY

1 *Complete the following sentences using suitable words or phrases from the box below.*

managing director	junior executive	colleague
director	supervisor	staff
senior executive	superior	employee
middle manager	subordinate	work-force

1 The group of executives working below the top managers are generally called ....
2 Valerie is an important person in our company. She is a member of the Board of ....
3 Peter, a recent university graduate, has been with the firm for a year. He is at present a .... and is being trained for a managerial position.
4 Their .... is expanding rapidly. They now have over 5,000 employees.
5 At least 50% of our .... have been with the company over ten years.

6 .... in an organisation generally have more fringe
benefits than lower-level managers.

7 We are a small group in the Research and Development
Department. Fortunately, I get on well with all my
....

8 Our telephone operators work under the direction of a
....

9 I work under Mr Brown. He's my ....

10 Sheila and Tom work under my authority. I am their boss and
they are my ....

11 I am responsible for .... training and development.

12 A .... is a person of high rank in an organisation,
usually next in importance to the Chairman.

2 Word building
*Complete the following sentences with the correct form of the
words in italics.*

1 *produce*
   a Our .**production**... of washing-machines increased by 5% last
   year.
   b We have recently put on the market two new ....
   c .... per worker will increase with the introduction
   of the new machines.
   d Word processors have helped to make office workers more
   ....
   e The company is well known in the agricultural industry. It
   sells mainly farm .... – eggs, butter, milk, etc.

2 *compete*
   a Coca Cola's main .... is the Pepsi-Cola company.
   b We try to stay .... by investing heavily in
   advertising and promotion.
   c Our company's main objective is to keep ahead of the
   ....

3 *plan*
   a The meeting did not go as ....
   b Some projects take years of ....
   c Before asking a bank manager for money, it is wise to show
   him a business ....

4 *analyse*
   a Managers needs to have an .... mind.
   b Our .... showed that we needed to put more
   emphasis on marketing.
   c We must look at the problem ....

3 Complete the following sentences with the correct word or phrase (a, b, c or d).

1 Nowadays, I eat out at restaurants regularly and often go
abroad for holidays. My .... is much higher than it
used to be.
   a standard of living   b cost of living   c lifestyle
   d way of life

2 Writing reports is not a .... that everyone enjoys.
   a duty   b work   c job   d function

3 This machine uses much less fuel than the previous one. It is far more ....

   a sparing **b** economic **c** effective **d** economical

4 The management has worked out a .... to improve our market share.

   a strategy **b** policy **c** target **d** planning

5 Many of the .... in the Personnel Department are part-time workers.

   a staff **b** staffs **c** employers **d** personal

6 One of the company's main .... is to increase sales by 10% per year.

   a designs **b** plans **c** purposes **d** objectives

7 Several machines have broken down. We won't be able to .... an important order.

   a fill **b** meet **c** make **d** do

4 Phrasal verbs with *out*

sort out (line 36)
spell out (line 41)

Complete the following sentences, using suitable forms of the verbs in the box below.

sort out	make out	bring out	pull out
spell out	buy out	carry out	
sell out	sound out	turn out	

  1 The firm .... about five hundred sports cars a year.

  2 We hope to .... our production problems soon.

  3 If the firm doesn't make a profit, the owners will probably ....

  4 I'm willing to consider introducing flexitime, but would you first .... the advantages of the system, please?

  5 Givenchy have .... an exciting new perfume.

  6 Would you .... the cheque to David Cotton, please?

  7 In order to develop new products, pharmaceutical companies have to .... a lot of research.

  8 Several leading banks such as Barclays have .... of South Africa.

  9 A group of senior managers want to take over the firm by .... it ....

10 We're looking for a new chief executive. I understand one or two possible candidates have already been ....

In pairs, use some of the verbs above in sentences of your own.

COMMUNICATION SKILLS

FUNCTIONS

Introducing yourself
Giving brief details about yourself and the organisation you work for

Dialogue

Listen to the following conversation, which takes place at a conference.

BRIAN How do you do? My name's Brian Robinson.

JOAN How do you do? I'm Joan Knight.

BRIAN Who do you work for then?

JOAN I'm with the Palmer Reece Group. You may have heard of us. We design and manufacture electronic equipment. I'm the Finance Manager.

BRIAN I see.

JOAN How about you?

BRIAN I work for a firm of kitchen designers. Kitchen Interiors, we're called. We install fitted kitchens, mostly in private houses. I'm Area Sales Manager.

JOAN That's interesting. Where are you based?

BRIAN Our head office is in Colchester. We've got branch offices all over the country. Where's your head office?

JOAN We're in the Midlands. In Leicester, actually. But I work in our London office. Have you been with your company long?

BRIAN Fairly long. I've worked for them for five years now. Before that, I was a salesman for a department store. I must say, I prefer what I'm doing now. You get out and meet all kinds of people. And I enjoy all the driving too. Your company's pretty big, isn't it?

JOAN Mm. I'd say so. Our turnover's almost £50m. And we've got a work-force of over 1,000. Yes, we *are* big.

BRIAN My firm's much smaller. Our turnover's roundabout £5m.

JOAN How about staff?

BRIAN Oh, about seventy or eighty people – full-time staff, that is. We're a private company, by the way. Still family-owned. But I reckon we'll go public in a few years' time.

JOAN Really? Your firm must be doing well. We're a public company, of course. We have been for the last thirty years.

BRIAN Ah, I thought I'd noticed your firm's name when I was looking at the share prices recently in the newspaper.

INTRODUCING YOURSELF		
	FIRST SPEAKER How do you do? My name's Brian Robinson.	SECOND SPEAKER How do you do? I'm Joan Knight.
FORMAL	Hello. Let me introduce myself. I'm Brian Robinson. Hello. Allow me to introduce myself...	How do you do? Pleased to meet you.
INFORMAL	Hello. I'm Brian Robinson. Hi! I'm Brian Robinson.	Oh hello. I'm Joan Knight. Oh hello. Joan Knight.
GIVING DETAILS ABOUT YOUR ORGANISATION		

I'm with the Palmer Reece Group.
I work for Kitchen Interiors.

We make/manufacture/sell/deal in $\begin{cases} \text{electrical products.} \\ \text{fitted kitchens.} \end{cases}$

My company's based in ...
Our head office is in ...

I've $\begin{cases} \text{been with} \\ \text{worked for} \end{cases}$ the company for five years.

We have branch offices/subsidiaries in ...
Our turnover is ...
We've got a work-force of ...

Role play

Situation

You are a manager attending an exhibition of office equipment. In the hospitality lounge you start talking to some other business people who are at the exhibition.

Instructions

Working in groups of two or three, improvise a conversation similar to the one in the dialogue on page 11.
Before starting the conversation read the following:

1 Choose a company or business organisation. It may be real or imaginary.
2 Introduce yourself; say who you work for, what your position is in the organisation and how long you have worked for it.
3 Give the following information:
 a what kind of business organisation it is (e.g. private, public, sole trader, partnership)
 b its main business activities
 c location of its head office, branches/subsidiaries
 d turnover, profits, size of work-force etc.
4 Give any other information about yourself, your job and the organisation.

Case study

Anyone who is interested in sports cars will know all about the Victor Motor Company (VMC). For those who don't, here are some brief facts:

VICTOR MOTOR COMPANY M⎰V⎰C

LOCATION:	Maybury
SIZE:	medium-sized– 1987 turnover £50m
MAIN PRODUCTS:	a range of high-performance sports cars
MAIN MARKETS:	exports 60% of its output to USA and Canada, plans to increase sales to W. Germany, Switzerland, Sweden and the Middle East
NEW PROJECT:	super sports car, using latest advanced technology; to sell at £100,000+, aim to launch in 1993
MAIN OBJECTIVE:	to treble turnover by 1995
FUTURE:	VMC face tough competition from rivals; labour relations could become strained

MEMORANDUM

M⎰V⎰C

To: All board members

From: Brian Lockley
      Personnel Director

Date: 25-09-88

Subject: Appointment of a new General Manager

As I am sure you are all aware by now, Anthony Hiller will be retiring at the end of this year, which leaves us a little over two months in which to appoint a new General Manager.

The post is currently being advertised in both the national press and the leading trade magazines and I intend to begin the first round of interviews in mid October. The advertisements contain the following description of the General Manager's duties:

* to have overall responsibility for the running of the plant;

* to coordinate the work of the management team so that the company's targets and objectives are met;

* to advise on new product development;

* to negotiate with trade union representatives;

* to accompany the Sales Manager on overseas sales trips, whenever possible;

* to represent the company when the Managing Director is unavailable.

The right man for the job

The problem

Two candidates, Jim Collier and Bernard Wheeler, are being considered for the position. The two men have been interviewed by
 (i) The Managing Director and a team of senior executives;
(ii) An industrial psychologist, who has carried out a number of tests.

The candidates have also had lunch with the interviewing team and the industrial psychologist. The wife of Bernard Wheeler was present at the lunch.

Below are the candidates' curricula vitae, extracts from the psychologist's reports and the interviewing team's notes.

```
                    CURRICULUM VITAE

                    PERSONAL DETAILS


    Name:    Jim Collier          Date of birth:  21-10-50

    Address: 18 Acacia Drive      Marital status: divorced

             Cheadle Hulme        Nationality:    American

             Manchester


                    EDUCATION

QUALIFICATION          ESTABLISHMENT               DATES

Diploma in Business    Los Angeles Adult Training  1973 - 74
Administration         College


                    WORK EXPERIENCE

POSITION               COMPANY                     DATES

Formula One mechanic   Lotus Racing Team           1969 - 70

Formula One driver     McClaren Racing Team        1970 - 73

Sales representative   Houseman Automobiles        1976 - 78
                       (car dealers)

Sales Manager          Houseman Automobiles        1978 - 80

Assistant Production   Vauxhall Motors UK          1981 - 84
Manager

Head of Production     Vauxhall Motors UK          1985 -
Control
```

EXTRACT FROM PSYCHOLOGIST'S REPORT ON JIM COLLIER

```
Mr Collier is a man of very high intelligence. He is creative,
imaginative, and good at problem-solving. When put under pressure,
he kept cool and showed a sense of humour. Although he appears to
be calm and cheerful, he is an emotional person. He is deeply
dissatisfied with his personal life. He is still upset and shaken
by the breakdown of his marriage to his English wife. Note: during
interview it came out that he had been expelled from two schools
for indiscipline.
```

EXTRACT FROM INTERVIEWING TEAM'S NOTES ON JIM COLLIER

Super-confident – at times almost aggressive; extremely ambitious – wants to have own car manufacturing company one day; frank and outspoken in opinions; believes that "winning is the only thing that matters in life"; seemed to be a relaxed, calm personality; but admitted he could "blow his top" if people didn't do their job properly; in a letter of reference, a previous employer suggested he was "charming, but could be very moody when he didn't get what he wanted – not an easy person to work with".

Curriculum Vitae

SURNAME	Wheeler	AGE	42
FIRST NAMES	Bernard Martin	MARITAL STATUS	Married
		DEPENDANTS	Three children

ADDRESS   229 Station Road
           Solihull
           Warwickshire

TELEPHONE   056 45611511 (home)
             021 656222 (work)

Education

M.A. in Engineering from Cambridge University	1968
Post-graduate Diploma in Management from	1979
The London School of Economics.	

Work History

Executive in Research and Development Department, Philips (electrical appliances)	1968 – 70
Production trainee, Volkswagen (Birmingham)	1971 – 73
Production Supervisor, Volkswagen (Birmingham)	1974 – 78
Project Coordinator in Volkswagen/Nissan joint-venture project in Tokyo and Birmingham	1978 – 82
Assistant Works Manager, Volkswagen (Birmingham)	1982 –

EXTRACT FROM PSYCHOLOGIST'S REPORT ON BERNARD WHEELER

Mr Wheeler has above-average intelligence. He is a logical person, with good powers of reasoning. He has planned his life carefully and knows where he is going. He is not particularly creative. When put under pressure, he became ill-at-ease, and finally lost his temper. He is devoted to his family. As he says, "They come before everything." He is serious, with no apparent sense of humour. Perhaps this is because he was an only child, and his parents separated when he was young, *gave long, thoughtful replies; knew a great deal about Victor- well prepared for interview; a patient man, polite but didn't take to him very much – not particularly likeable, but showed strength of character; wishes to leave Volkswagen because of personality clash with his Works Manager; when questioned on this he said, "I prefer not to discuss the matter"; main ambition: to become a company director; in letters of reference, described as "efficient", "dependable" and "self-reliant". Note: At the lunch, wife did not shine – nervous, unsure of herself and of limited conversation.*

Instructions

Working in groups of two or three, analyse the strengths and weaknesses of the two candidates. Decide who should be offered the position, noting the reasons for your choice. Compare your decision with that of the other groups. One of you should chair the discussion.

WRITING

You see the following advertisement in a national newspaper. *Write a suitable letter in reply to it and enclose your curriculum vitae.*

VICTOR MOTOR COMPANY

ARE YOU INTERESTED IN A CAREER IN THE MOTOR INDUSTRY?

Owing to the expansion of our UK operations, we have the following vacancies:

Area Sales Manager (S.W. England)
Publicity Officer
Sales Representatives (Scotland and Wales)
Accounts Executives
Production Controller

We offer competitive salaries and fringe benefits such as company cars, pension schemes, profit-sharing and generous relocation allowances.
Write to us saying what position you are interested in and why we should employ you. Include your curriculum vitae and current remuneration details.

M V C

David Jenkins, Chief Personnel Officer,
Victor Motor Company, Victor House, 117 High Street,
Maybury, Surrey, KT36 5NB

LISTENING

Understanding the main points

Listen to the following conversations and complete the sentences below. (You may wish to make notes as you listen.)

1 Mervyn is not satisfied with Peter Martin's work because ....
....

2 Brian is extremely surprised when Mervyn tells him about Peter Martin because ....
....

3 Peter Martin's problem is that ....

....

4 Brian telephones the Chief Personnel Officer to ....

....

Vocabulary focus

1 *Listen again and fill in the gaps in these sentences from the three conversations.*

   1 He's been here almost three months now, so his ....
.... 's almost over.

   2 I can't really .... my .... on it.

   3 He ought to be able to cope. It should be a .... of
.... for him.

   4 We've got to .... to the .... of this.

   5 How are you .... , Peter?

   6 To tell the truth, I don't .... very well
with the others.

   7 The work's interesting – right .... my .... ,
really.

   8 No, there's nothing we can do about it, nothing at all. He's
.... his ....

2 *In pairs, discuss the meaning of the words and phrases above.*

2 Frederick W. Taylor: Scientific Management

DISCUSSION

*Read the following information about IBM's methods of work and·
then discuss the questions below.*

In his book *Management* Peter Drucker makes some comments
about the workers who produce IBM's equipment. He says that IBM
made a conscious effort to make their jobs *big*. Take, for example,
the machine operators. Although the operations they perform are
designed to be simple, the workers do a number of different tasks,
of which at least one requires skill and judgement on the worker's
part. Also, because of the range of his/her tasks, the worker is able
to change the pace at which he/she works.

Drucker says interesting things about other IBM methods. The way
the company develops new products is worth noting. Before the
engineering of the new product is finished, the project is given
over to one of the foremen, who then manages it. So, the final details
of the engineering design are worked out on the shop floor with the
engineer and workers who will make the machine.

IBM production workers are not told what production rate they must
achieve. They work out a rate with their foreman. IBM says that
'there is no such thing as a production norm. Each man works out
for himself, with his superior's help, the speed and flow of work that
will give him the most production.'

1 What are the advantages of making the jobs of production
  workers *big*? Are there any disadvantages?
2 Why, do you think, does IBM develop new products in the
  manner described?
3 What do we learn about
  (i) IBM's attitude towards its production workers?
  (ii) the company's style of management?

No one has had more influence on managers in the twentieth century than Frederick W. Taylor, an American engineer. He set a pattern for industrial work which many others have followed, and although his approach to management has been criticised, his ideas are still of practical importance.

Taylor founded the school of Scientific Management just before the 1914–18 war. He argued that work should be studied and analysed systematically. The operations required to perform a particular job could be identified, then arranged in a logical
10 sequence. After this was done, a worker's productivity would increase, and so would his/her wages. The new method was scientific. The way of doing a job would no longer be determined by guesswork and rule-of-thumb practices. Instead, management would work out scientifically the method for producing the best results. If the worker followed the prescribed approach, his/her output would increase.

When Taylor started work at the end of the nineteenth century, the industrial revolution was in full swing. Factories were being set up all over the USA. There was heavy investment in
20 plant and machinery, and labour was plentiful. He worked for twenty years (1878–1898) with the Midvale Steel Company, first as a labourer, then as a Shop Superintendant. After that, he was a consultant with the Bethlehem Steel Company in Pennsylvania.

Throughout this time, he studied how to improve the efficiency of workers on the shop floor. He conducted many experiments to find out how to improve their productivity. His solutions to these problems were, therefore, based on his own experience. Later, he wrote about his experiments. These writings were collected and published in 1947, in a work entitled *Scientific*
30 *Management*.

When he was with Bethlehem Steel, Taylor criticised management and workers. He felt that managers were not using the right methods and that workers did not put much effort into their job. They were always 'soldiering' – taking it easy. He wanted both groups to adopt a new approach to their work, which would change their thinking completely. The new way was as follows:

1 Each operation of a job was studied and analysed;
2 Using this information, management worked out the time and
40   method for each job, and the type of equipment to be used;
3 Work was organised so that the worker's only responsibility was to do the job in the prescribed manner;
4 Men with the right physical skills were selected and trained for the job.

Observing; analysing; measuring; specifying the work method; organising and choosing the right person for the job – these were the tasks of management.

Taylor's approach produced results! For example, at Bethlehem Steel, he did an experiment with shovels, the tool
50 used for lifting and carrying materials. He studied the work of two first-class shovellers and then changed their working procedure. In the beginning, the men used their own shovels for all the types of materials they handled, whether coal or

iron ore. The average load was 38 pounds, and each lifted 25 tons of material a day. By experimenting, Taylor found out that if the men used smaller shovels and carried 21 pounds per load, their daily output increased to 30 tons. As a result, at the beginning of each shift, workers were given different sized shovels, depending on the type of material they loaded, but

60 the load was still 21 pounds. Other workers meeting the standards set by the two shovellers had their wages increased by 60%. Those who could not reach the standard were given special training in shovelling techniques.

By introducing methods like these, Taylor and his colleagues greatly increased productivity at Bethlehem Steel. After a few years, the same amount of work was done by 140 workers instead of 500. Handling costs of materials were halved, which led to annual savings of $80,000.

Taylor made a lasting contribution to management thinking.

70 His main insight, that work can be systematically studied in order to improve working methods and productivity, was revolutionary. Also, he correctly emphasised that detailed planning of jobs was necessary.

The weakness of his approach was that it focused on the system of work rather than on the worker. With this system the worker becomes a tool in the hands of management. It is assumed he/she will do the same boring, repetitive job hour after hour, day after day while maintaining a high level of productivity. Another criticism is that it leads to de-skilling –

80 reducing the skills of workers. Because the tasks are simplified, workers become frustrated. And with educational standards rising among factory workers, dissatisfaction is likely to increase. Finally, some people think that it is wrong to separate doing from planning. The two tasks can, and should, be done by the same person. A worker will be more productive if he/she is engaged in such activities as planning, decision-making, controlling and organising. For all these reasons, a reaction has set in against the ideas of Frederick W. Taylor.

Understanding the main points

1 *Complete the following sentences, using your own words.*

1 Taylor's method of management was revolutionary because

....

2 Companies which adopted this new approach to management would benefit because ....

3 Scientific Management would also be a good thing for workers because ....

4 At Bethlehem Steel Taylor decided to give workers smaller shovels so that ....

5 As a result of the new working procedures introduced at Bethlehem Steel, within a few years the company ....

....

2 *Complete the following table.*

Frederick W. Taylor: *Scientific Management* (1947)	
ADVANTAGES	DISADVANTAGES
1	1 ....
2	2 ....
3	3 ....

Vocabulary focus

1 *Find words or phrases in the text which mean the same as the following:*

  1 making a judgement without being certain (paragraph 2)
  2 calculate (paragraph 2)
  3 quantity of goods produced (paragraph 2)
  4 established (paragraph 3)
  5 amount to be carried (paragraph 6)
  6 fixed period of time worked each day, especially for factory workers (paragraph 6)
  7 perception, clear realisation, deep understanding (paragraph 8)

2 What is the meaning of *the shop floor* (line 25)?

LANGUAGE STUDY

1 *Complete the following chart.*

PERSON	NOUN	VERB	ADJECTIVE
manager	management	manage	managerial or managing
		criticise	
performer			
	science		
	training		
			analytical
	industry		
		observe	
			engineering
			revolutionary
		consult	

2 Phrasal verbs and compound nouns with *set*

set up (line 19)
set in (line 88)

A *Match the following verbs and nouns with the correct definitions.*

1 set up (v.)	**a** keep for a special purpose
2 set-up (n.)	**b** establish a business or organisation
3 set back (v.)	**c** something that slows or impedes
4 set-back (n.)	progress
5 set about (v.)	**d** an organisation or arrangement
6 set in (v.)	**e** start to do, or deal with, something
7 set out (v.)	**f** put back or delay the development of
8 set against (v.)	something
9 set aside (v.)	**g** begin an undertaking of some kind, e.g.
10 set down (v.)	a journey
	h start and probably continue
	i balance against
	j write, make a record of

B *Complete the following sentences, using suitable verbs and nouns from the list above.*

1 When the Managing Director .... to change the management structure, no one thought he had a chance of succeeding.
2 The strike of our shop floor workers .... production at least three months.
3 It looks as if a recession is about to .... No one seems to have any money at the moment.
4 The new Marketing Manager doesn't understand the .... of our department yet.
5 It is a common practice of companies to .... certain business losses .... taxes.
6 One of our competitors has .... a distribution network covering the whole country. How annoying!
7 How on earth are we going to .... reducing our costs?
8 Most companies .... a part of their profits for future investment. The money is kept in their reserves.
9 We had a big .... last year when our warehouse caught fire and our stock was destroyed.
10 If an employee has an accident at work, he or she has to .... what happened in a report.

3 *Complete the following passage, using suitable words and phrases from the box below.*

assembly line	foreman	schedule	quality control
bonus	lay off	incentive	robot
capacity	layout	overtime	
component	redundant	shift	

'I used to work in a company which made .... (1) for cars. Things like spark plugs, carburettors, and so on. We were well paid and we had a productivity .... (2) too. And if you needed extra money for a holiday, you usually had the chance to do a bit of .... (3). The management was generous. They gave prizes, such as car radios, to workers who attended regularly. That was a real .... (4) for us not to be sick! We worked two .... (5) at the factory – I usually worked at night. I liked the .... (6) a lot. He let you get on with the job.

Things changed two years ago. We got several big orders at once and just couldn't cope. The Production Manager got really upset when we got behind .... (7). The .... (8) people weren't too pleased either because a number of carburettors had faults, so they were thrown away. In the end, the company brought in some management consultants. They studied our methods of work, then recommended automating part of the plant. That meant changing the whole .... (9) of the factory.

Well, we did as they said. I must say, our production .... (10) did increase and stock levels became high again. The trouble is, the management decided to cut down the work-force. At first, only a few workers were .... (11), but later staff from all departments were made .... (12).

Nowadays, I'm working on an .... (13) in a car manufacturing factory. I spray the car bodies. Would you believe it, I hear they're bringing in .... (14) to do my job! So I'll be out of a job again soon.'

COMMUNICATION SKILLS

FUNCTION

Expressing points of view

*Study the following list of words and phrases and then look at the statements in **Discussion** on page 24.*

GIVING OPINIONS

I think/believe/feel . . .   In my opinion/view . . .
It seems to me . . .

ASKING FOR OPINIONS

What do you think?   What's your opinion/view?
How do you feel about this?   I'd like to hear your view on this.

AGREEING

I agree (with you).   True.
Yes (indeed).   Quite.
You're/That's right.   Absolutely.

DISAGREEING

I disagree (with you).
I'm not sure (about that).

PARTIALLY AGREEING

Up to a point I agree with you.
I agree with you to some extent.

EXPRESSING UNCERTAINTY

I don't know about that.   Hm . . . maybe.
I'm not too sure really.

Discussion

Working in groups of two or three, discuss the following statements, using the expressions on page 23 to help you.

1 No person should be allowed to smoke at his/her workplace.
2 Production work is more satisfying than office work.
3 After having worked for a company for twenty years, every person should be allowed one year's paid holiday.
4 Men make better managers than women.
5 Nowadays, in *most* countries, women have as much chance of getting to the top in business as men.

Case study

The Kellerman process

CIAO! makes stylish clothes for teenagers and the under-twenty-fives. The company supplies the New York fashion trade, and it operates in competitive conditions. To survive, it has to react quickly to changes in consumer taste, produce goods lightning fast for clients, and keep costs low.

Life has been hard these last five years. During this time, the firm's pre-tax profits have fallen from $4.5 million to $200,000. Cheap foreign imports have been partly to blame, but another reason is that the management have been unable to control production properly. Because of this, stocks have built up to high levels. And there have been bottlenecks in production, leading to cancelled orders.

Lily Jacobavitz, Chief Executive of the company, has thought a lot about the problem of rising production costs. Now she thinks she has the answer. Recently she held a meeting to discuss her ideas with two colleagues, Sydney Gorman, her Production Manager, and Gloria David, Personnel Director. 'I think we ought to buy the Kellerman process,' she told them. 'I've talked to Kellerman's Sales Director. He reckons we could have the electronic machines and the computer system for $150,000 to $200,000. What do you think?'

THE
KELLERMAN
PROCESS
The leading edge in textile technology

The two managers looked at her in surprise. Gloria David was the first to speak. 'Do you have that kind of money to throw around?' she asked.

'We have for the Kellerman system,' Lily Jacobavitz replied, just a little coldly. 'It'll increase the productivity of our machine operators by 30%–50% and cut costs. That's what we want, isn't it?'

At this point, Sydney Gorman cut in.' I think we'd better talk about your proposal at our next management meeting, don't you?'

'Sure,' answered Lily Jacobavitz. 'But I'll want a decision on this one – fast.'

The Kellerman process consists of electronic machines which are linked to a computer system. The sewing-machine operators key in their daily output on their own machine as soon as they've finished their batch of materials. The output is displayed on a small screen opposite their target production figure. The screen shows what percentage of the target they have achieved, and also if they have produced more than their target. All the information from the machines is fed into a computer, so management know exactly what is going on in the production process at any time.

The manufacturers claim that operators using Kellerman machines work harder. Also, because of improved production control, management can step in if there are problems like bottlenecks or high stock levels.

'It should make things easier for the Accounts Department as well,' thought Lily Jacobavitz. The sewing-machine operators – a hundred and fifty in all – were paid a certain amount for each garment produced. At present, operators filled in work sheets which were attached to bundles of materials. The job of collecting and recording the information on these 'work tickets' was time consuming for the accounts staff. 'If we get the Kellerman system,' Lily said to herself, 'the operators may get off my back about getting them a new canteen. They might even start meeting their targets for a change.'

Instructions

Working in groups, enact the management meeting. Each member of the group should take one of the roles which follow. The Chief Executive should act as Chairperson.
The purpose of the meeting is:

1 to discuss thoroughly the proposal to introduce the Kellerman process;
2 to decide whether or not to buy the system.

Study your own role-card only, and prepare carefully for the meeting.

Note: The role of Chief Executive may be played by a male. For smaller groups, roles such as the non-union representative, the Operations Manager and the Warehouse Manager may be omitted.

CHIEF EXECUTIVE

As Chairperson, you must ask for the opinions of all the members of the meeting. However, you will try to persuade everyone that the Kellerman process should be bought. The manufacturers of the system have assured you that it will reduce costs and increase productivity. You think that, with the new system, the operators will be motivated to exceed their targets, probably by as much as 30%–50%. If the process isn't introduced, you might have to think of hiring a more efficient Production Manager!

PRODUCTION MANAGER

You are against buying the Kellerman process. In your opinion, this is the wrong time to spend such a large sum of money. There is no guarantee the system will work well. If it is introduced, the production process may become disorganised and the workers unhappy – especially the older ones. You want more money to be spent on improving working conditions. You've been trying for months to persuade the Chief Executive to repaint the interior of the factory. Relations between you and the Chief Executive are not good at present.

PERSONNEL DIRECTOR

You are not certain what to think about the proposal. Manufacturers always say that their new process is wonderful, but do the systems always work well in practice? In your opinion, the company should get some sort of guarantee from the manufacturers. For example, if productivity did not increase by 20% within six months, they should take back their equipment. You are also worried about how the older workers will react to the Kellerman system. They are generally suspicious of new technology.

UNION REPRESENTATIVE (SEWING-MACHINE OPERATORS)

You want to buy the Kellerman process. Most of the operators in your union are young. They think that, with the new system, they would be able to earn a lot more money. Some of them should be able to earn even more than their supervisors! Production will be more efficient, so the company's financial situation will improve. The process is easy to install and run, so there will be no bad effects on production.

REPRESENTATIVE (NON-UNION SEWING-MACHINE OPERATORS)

You are strongly against buying the Kellerman system. You represent about seventy non-union operators – all older women. You and the other workers like the present system of production. You can work at your own pace, and, whenever you like, go outside to have a cigarette or cup of coffee. The 'work ticket' procedure is easy to understand and carry out. You are all suspicious of the Kellerman system. The management just want to squeeze more work out of you. The factory is becoming more like a sweatshop every day.

SALES MANAGER

You are against the proposal. If the company is going to spend $200,000, the money should go to the Sales Department. You need at least three more sales staff, but you have not been allowed to hire them. In your opinion, CIAO! needs to increase sales greatly if it is to survive. Actually, you think the firm should forget about teenagers and start producing fashions for the well-off, thirty-year-old executive market.

OPERATIONS MANAGER

You are responsible for scheduling and processing orders. You may make up your own mind about the new process. However, what worries you is that, with the new system, the machine operators may earn more than you do! You work like a slave meeting deadlines and dealing with difficult customers. The job's tough, but you work for peanuts!

WAREHOUSE MANAGER

The Kellerman process will make your work a lot easier, so you're in favour of it. All you want is an easy life. You're tired of hearing the production workers complaining about their working conditions. They should see the tiny office you work in! If the new system is introduced, output will be much higher. Therefore, you will expect a large salary increase.

FINANCIAL DIRECTOR

You have a difficult decision to make. On the one hand, you hate to see the company spend any money at all in the present financial situation. On the other hand, you think the system might benefit the firm. Perhaps CIAO! should wait for a year or two until the process has been used by more organisations. It would be clearer then how efficient it was. You may prefer to listen to the opinions of other members before giving your own.

WRITING

Recently, information about the company's fashion designs has been leaking out to competitors. As a result, copies of CIAO!'s exclusive dresses have been appearing in clothes shops *before* the company has finished manufacturing them.

Imagine that you are the Personnel Manager of CIAO! Send a memo to all staff in which you give practical advice about how to prevent details of the company's designs from being leaked in the future.

Below is the beginning of the memo. Complete it, using the structure suggested.

CIAO!
MEMORANDUM

To: All staff

From: Gloria David

Subject: Trade secrets   Date: 5 June 1988

As I am sure most of you are aware, a number of our exclusive fashion designs have recently been copied by competitors and sold to the retail trade. As a result of this pirating CIAO! has suffered considerable financial loss. It is vital that our fashion designs should not be allowed to fall into the hands of our competitors again.

Below are a number of steps I suggest that we all take in order to protect our trade secrets:

Firstly, ...

....

....

Secondly, ...

....

....

Another way of safeguarding company secrets ....

....

....

Finally, ...

....

....

Gloria David

LISTENING

Understanding the main points

Listen to the following conversation and complete the sentences below and the table on page 29. (You may wish to make notes as you listen.)

1 Just over a year ago IC Electronics decided to ....
....

2 The core period is the time when ....
....

3 If staff work more than, say, thirty-five hours during a week, they are allowed to ....
....

THE ADVANTAGES OF FLEXITIME	
BENEFITS TO STAFF	BENEFITS TO COMPANY
(i)	(i) ....
(ii)	(ii) ....
(iii) *can arrive at work later, avoiding rush hour*	(iii) ....
(iv)	(iv) *increased productivity*
(v)	(v) ....

Vocabulary focus

1 *Listen again and fill in the gaps in these sentences from the conversation.*

   1 You must .... !
   2 If my memory .... me .... , it was twelve to four o'clock.
   3 ... the staff can start and finish when they want – it's .... them.
   4 So then they can .... a couple of mornings .... , or leave work early one week.
   5 That's quite useful, from the firm's .... of .... , I mean.
   6 The staff have been .... a lot more work.
   7 It seems they feel more responsible, and that the management's .... them .... mature people.
   8 Maybe ... well, it might just be .... trying flexitime here.
   9 Actually, that's why I .... the subject ...
   10 ... I was .... you ....

2 *In pairs, discuss the meaning of the words and phrases above.*

3 The Quality of Working Life

DISCUSSION

An American writer, Studs Terkel, has written a book entitled *Working*. In it, he describes the working lives and feelings of all kinds of American people. In this extract, a spot welder[1] at a Ford assembly plant in Chicago, USA, is talking about his job.

Read the extract and then answer the questions below.

'I stand in one spot, about two- or three-feet area all night. The only time a person stops is when the line stops. We do about thirty-two jobs per car, per unit. Forty-eight units an hour, eight hours a day. Thirty-two times forty-eight times eight. Figure it out. That's how many times I push that button.

The noise, oh it's tremendous. You open your mouth and you're liable to get a mouthful of sparks. (shows his arms) That's a burn, these are burns. You don't compete against the noise. You go to yell and at the same time you're straining to maneuver the gun to where you have to weld.

You got some guys that are uptight, and they're not sociable. It's too rough. You pretty much stay to yourself. You get involved with yourself. You dream, you think of things you've done. I drift back continuously to when I was a kid and what me and my brothers did . . .

It (the production line) don't stop. It just goes and goes and goes. I bet there's men who have lived and died out there, never seen the end of that line. And they never will – because it's endless. It's like a serpent. It's just all body, no tail. It can do things to you . . . (laughs)

I don't understand how come more guys don't flip. Because you're nothing more than a machine when you hit this type of thing. They give better care to a machine than they will to you. They'll have more respect, give more attention to that machine. And you know this. Somehow you get the feeling that the machine is better than you are.' (laughs)

1 How does the man feel about his job?
2 Do you think that many workers today feel as he does? *Explain your answer.*
3 What examples can you find in the text of non-standard English?

---

[1] To *weld* is to join metals together by pressure or by melting them when they are hot. A spot welder is a person who welds parts of the body of a car before the car goes to another production line where the floor, roof, bonnet and doors are fitted.

Over the last thirty years, a new approach to management has been developing. Those favouring it say that the way to increase workers' efficiency is to improve their job satisfaction and motivation. Followers of the Quality of Working Life movement (QWL) have been trying out various methods of making work more interesting. These include job enlargement, job enrichment and new forms of group work.

With job enlargement, the worker is given additional tasks to perform. Thus, the operator of a word-processor may be
10 asked to do filing duties as well. Job enrichment involves giving extra responsibilities to workers such as production planning, quality control and technical development of equipment. In some organisations, special types of work groups have been formed where workers share responsibility for certain tasks. For example, at the Volvo car plant in Kolmar, Sweden, assembly workers do not work on a moving production line. They are organised into thirty teams of fifteen to twenty members. They have their own tasks, like assembling heating and electrical systems, and they work in
20 their own part of the factory.

As can be seen, the basic idea of QWL is that a worker should have an interesting, even challenging job. QWL encourages managers, therefore, to be sensitive to the needs of employees.

The roots of the QWL movement can be traced back to the 1920s and 1930s. It was at this time that the famous Hawthorne Studies were carried out. These were held at the Hawthorne plant of the Western Electric Company in Chicago, USA, from 1927–32. Most of the studies were directed by Professor Elton
30 Mayo, a Harvard University psychologist. Their aim, initially , was to evaluate the factors influencing productivity. However, the researchers soon directed their attention towards studying people, especially their social relationships at work.

It all began when the Hawthorne Company investigated the effect of factory lighting on production and workers' morale. They found out that the groups of workers who were studied increased their output whether the lighting was improved or not. This led them to look for the human factor influencing efficiency. To help them in their search, they brought in
40 Professor Elton Mayo and his colleagues.

He directed a series of experiments on how working conditions affected output. In the early experiments, his subjects were a group of girls who assembled telephone equipment. Such things as lighting, lunch times, rest periods, wall colours, pay and temperature were varied to see how they affected productivity. The researchers generally discussed the changes with the girls before putting them into effect. Once again, it was found that there was an increase in productivity whether conditions were made better or worse.

50 The researchers began looking for other factors which would explain the increased productivity. They realised that their study was also about workers' attitudes and values. It was clear that the girls had developed a high morale during the

experiment and had been motivated to work hard. This high morale was put down to several factors. First, the girls had enjoyed feeling they were especially selected for the study and were receiving a lot of attention from management. Secondly, they had developed good relationships with each other and with their superior during the experiment. This was because they had been fairly free to work at their own pace and to divide their work up amongst themselves. Lastly, the good relationships and social contacts had made their work more enjoyable.

This experiment was followed by many others. The researchers came to the conclusion that social relations, among workers and between workers and their bosses, affect output, the quality of work and motivation. Another important finding was that a worker needs more than money and good working conditions to be productive. The feeling of belonging to a group, and his/her status within that group, strongly affect his/her behaviour – even if the group is an unofficial or informal one.

It is said that Elton Mayo founded the Human Relations school whose offspring is the Quality of Working Life movement. He directed and publicised the Hawthorne experiments which have been so influential to this day. The conclusions of the study challenged the theory of Scientific Management put forward by Frederick W. Taylor. Both men, however, changed the course of management thinking.

Understanding the main points

1 *Decide whether the following statements are true or false.*

	True	False
1 Managers who believe in QWL are experimenting with new ways or organising work.	☐	☐
2 The idea of job enlargement is to make work more satisfying for an employee.	☐	☐
3 Job enrichment involves giving workers more tasks of the same level of difficulty.	☐	☐
4 The Kolmar car plant is efficient because workers specialise in one task.	☐	☐
5 The QWL approach makes managers more aware of their workers' interests.	☐	☐

2 In what way did the Hawthorne experiments change direction?

3 In Mayo's experiments how did changes in working conditions affect the workers he studied?

4 Why did the group of girls become more efficient?

5 According to the researchers, what other factors, besides money, affect a worker's productivity?

6 Why have Mayo's experiments been so influential?

Vocabulary focus

Explain the meaning of the following words and phrases.

1 *motivation* (line 4)
2 *assembly workers* (line 16)
3 *production line* (line 17)
4 *challenging* (line 22)
5 *carried out* (line 27)
6 *evaluate* (line 31)
7 *morale* (line 35)
8 *brought in* (line 39)
9 *putting them into effect* (line 47)
10 *at their own pace* (line 60)
11 *status* (line 70)
12 *challenged* (line 77)

LANGUAGE STUDY

1 *Complete the following sentences with the correct word or phrase (a, b or c).*

1 People work harder if they know that someone is .... in their progress.
   a enthusiastic **b** interesting **c** interested

2 Nothing has been announced but we've heard .... that the Company Secretary has resigned.
   a formally **b** officiously **c** unofficially

3 Friendly .... no longer exist between members of the sales department because some got bonuses and others didn't.
   a relations **b** contacts **c** connections

4 .... in the Production Department is low because the workers have heard about the plans to reduce the work-force.
   a morale **b** feeling **c** moral

5 This is a useful ....
   a equipment **b** machine **c** machinery

6 We have carried out .... into the effect of lighting on our workers' productivity.
   a a research **b** some research **c** researches

7 Strikes can be avoided if managers are .... to the feelings of their employees.
   a aware **b** sensible **c** sensitive

8 Some people like to work at their own ....
   a beat **b** motion **c** pace

9 We have several proposals for increasing sales. We must .... the merits of each of them.
   a cost **b** value **c** evaluate

10 Has the change in exchange rates had any .... on the cost of your raw materials?
   a result **b** affect **c** effect

2 Phrasal verbs and idiomatic expressions with *put*

put down to (line 55)
put forward (lines 77–8)

put down to	attribute, e.g. I put his mistake down to inexperience.
put forward	suggest, propose (an idea, scheme)
put across	explain or communicate clearly
put back	move to a later date
put off	postpone or delay
put on to	give someone information about, e.g. You need expert advice about this. I can put you on to a very good lawyer.
put through	connect by telephone
put up	invest, provide money for, e.g. They've put up £50,000 for the project.
put out	**a** put *someone* out – inconvenience him or her. **b** put *oneself* out – make a special effort
put up with	tolerate, endure
put one's finger on	find the cause of the trouble
put one's foot in	say the wrong thing or make an awkward mistake
put paid to	destroy, ruin completely, e.g. His accident put paid to his chances of being promoted.
put in a good word for	recommend someone

A *Rewrite the following sentences, replacing the words in italics with phrasal verbs or idiomatic expressions from the list above. Make any other necessary changes.*

1 I think we'd better *hold* the meeting a week *later*.
2 Apparently a foreign investor has *provided* $1m to finance the project.
3 At such short notice, I can't *postpone* my visit.
4 My boss won't *accept* any inefficiency from his staff.
5 She knows a lot about the use of computers but she can't seem to *express* her ideas *clearly* to the rest of us.
6 Our chairman has *presented* a proposal for a profit-sharing scheme.
7 I'm not surprised by our poor financial performance. I *think it was caused by* ineffective leadership.
8 I've been trying to discover why the morale of the sales department is so low but I just can't *understand what the problem is.*

B *Complete the following sentences with phrasal verbs and idiomatic expressions from the list above. Make any other necessary changes.*

1 Our sales have been low this quarter. That's .... to my chances of a bonus.
2 (on the phone) Hello ... yes, it is ... Mr Smith? Certainly. Hold on a second. I'll .... you ....

3 It's very kind of you to ask me to dinner. I hope I'm not
.... you ....

4 When senior managers from head office come to visit us we
really .... ourselves .... to make their stay
enjoyable.

5 You want to know the prices of houses in the United States?
Sorry, I can't help, but I can .... you .... to
someone who can.

6 I .... it when I asked Mr Johnston how his wife was.
Apparently, she's just left him!

7 You'd like to transfer to the Personnel Department, would you?
Perhaps I can .... for you when I see the Personnel
Manager.

**COMMUNICATION
SKILLS**

FUNCTIONS

Asking about problems
Expressing worries
Reassuring

Managers need to be sensitive and understanding. They have to be
sympathetic when people have problems, and offer reassurance
and encouragement.

Dialogue

*Listen to the following conversation, which takes place in the
Advertising Sales Department of a newspaper.*

ANGELA   You don't look too happy. What's the problem?

JANE   It's just that I've been phoning people for three days now
but I haven't sold a single space. No one seems to want to
place an advertisement. I'm really worried. I'm beginning
to wonder if I'm in the right job.

ANGELA   Oh, come on now. This sort of thing often happens.
Everything'll be all right soon, I'm sure.

JANE   I don't know. When you're paid on commission, like I am,
you start to get a bit panicky.

ANGELA   Don't worry. Things will improve soon. It's not very easy
this time of the year.

JANE   I suppose you're right.

ANGELA   Don't be so pessimistic. Everything will work out, you'll
see. Just ... try to take it easy!

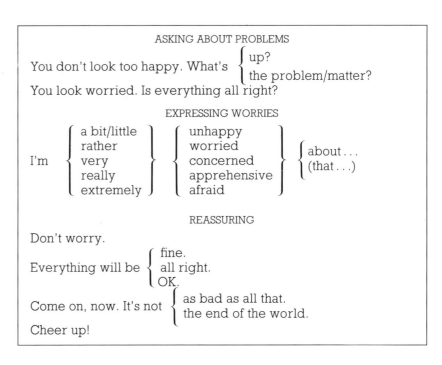

ASKING ABOUT PROBLEMS

You don't look too happy. What's { up?
{ the problem/matter?

You look worried. Is everything all right?

EXPRESSING WORRIES

I'm { a bit/little / rather / very / really / extremely } { unhappy / worried / concerned / apprehensive / afraid } { about... / (that...) }

REASSURING

Don't worry.

Everything will be { fine. / all right. / OK.

Come on, now. It's not { as bad as all that. / the end of the world.

Cheer up!

Role play

The following situations take place in a newspaper office. Some of the employees have worries concerning their work.

In groups of two or three, act out the situations, using some of the expressions above.

Situations

1 You are the editor of a newspaper. In recent months, the paper's profits have been falling and its circulation has been decreasing. The owner of the paper visits you one day. He/She is sympathetic and understanding, offering you reassurance and encouragement.

'You look worried. Is everything all right?'

2 You are a newspaper reporter. The editor of the paper has just asked you to go to the Middle East to report on a war there. You are worried – you've never done this kind of reporting before. And, having just got married, you know your wife will not want you to go. When you return to your typewriter in the general office, some of your colleagues ask you what the problem is.

3 You are a well-paid printer for the newspaper. You've heard a

rumour that the management are going to invest in new printing machinery. If they do this, half the printers will be made redundant. During the morning break, some of the other workers notice you look upset.

4 You are a junior reporter. Last week, you wrote an article which strongly criticised a local chemicals company for causing pollution. This morning, the Managing Director of the company phoned you. He threatened legal action if you continued to write about his company's pollution problem. The General Manager of the office passes by and comments that you look unhappy.

Case study 1

The Open Door policy

The American company, IBM, believes in creating good working conditions for its employees and in building up employee–manager relationships. One of its key policies is its Open Door programme.

This policy was started by IBM's founder and first Chairman, T. J. Watson, about fifty years ago. Watson had close contacts with staff working in the plant and field offices. Therefore, staff often brought their problems to him. Using telephone broadcasts, Watson told his staff that they should go first to their plant or branch manager if they felt they were being unfairly treated. But if they were still not satisfied, they should come to him.

Many of his staff took advantage of his offer. Some would take a day off work, leaving the plant in Endicott to go to see Watson in his office in New York City. He would give them a sympathetic hearing, often deciding in favour of the employee who had complained. By the time he left the company, Watson had become a trusted friend to thousands of IBM employees.

Today, the Open Door policy is still practised by IBM. The programme works like this: if employees think they have been unfairly treated by their immediate manager, they can appeal to a higher level of management to solve the problem. In fact, they can go to higher and higher levels of management if they wish. Alternatively, they can take their case directly to an executive director. In practice, some cases are taken to senior management and executive management level; others are resolved by the immediate manager's manager. Staff may raise any subject they wish. Generally, appeals are about promotions, relations with immediate managers, and assessments of staff performance.

In recent years, there have been 20–25 Open Door appeals dealt with by executive management annually. The employee's appeal has been favourably received in a quarter of those cases.

Instructions

Working in groups of two or three, consider the following questions.

1 What benefits do IBM probably obtain from the programme?
2 What sort of problems could arise from such a policy? Consider the problems from the point of view of managerial and non-managerial staff.
3 What is your opinion of this employment practice? Should all companies have this kind of programme?

Now, compare your answers with those of the other groups.

Case study 2

The employee who worked too hard

When Paula, aged twenty-five, joined the Packing and Despatch Department, she was determined to do a good job and get on in the company. There were six other women in the department, mostly older women. Paula, being young and keen, worked harder than all of them. Soon, in fact, her work-rate was double that of everyone else. About a year after she joined the company, the supervisor of the department retired. Paula was offered the job, which she accepted with delight.

From the very beginning she had problems. For one thing, she wasn't popular with the other women. They made jokes about her to her face, saying that she was trying to impress the management by working so hard. And, whenever she tried to persuade them to increase their work-rate, they said that the department was becoming a 'sweat shop'. Another thing that annoyed them was Paula's attitude to life. She made no secret of the fact that she had several different boyfriends. She was a 'liberated woman' wanting to get the most out of life. 'You only live once' was her favourite expression. The other women didn't like her attitude at all, and made this clear to her.

One day, Paula criticised one of the women for taking an unofficial fifteen-minute tea break. A little later, the group of women came to Paula. One of them, Eileen – a sort of leader of the group – told Paula they were stopping work for the day. 'We're not putting up with this kind of treatment,' Eileen told her.

After this incident, relations between Paula and the women became worse. A month later, the women went on a three-day strike, insisting that they wouldn't work with Paula a day longer.

Instructions

Working in groups of two or three, consider the following questions.

1 Was Paula a suitable person to be a supervisor?
2 Was she to blame for the problems that arose in the department?
3 What should the management do now to solve the problem?
4 What lessons can be learned from this case?

WRITING

You work for an electrical goods company which has a 'Go to the top' policy. This means that an employee can write to a senior manager or even the Chairman about any subject he/she wishes to raise. The employee always receives a reply within a reasonable period of time.

Imagine that you are involved in one of the situations described below. Write an appropriate memo to the person indicated.

1 You have worked in the Overseas Sales Department for the last fifteen years. Your work has always been good. In spite of this, you have never received a promotion. You work long hours and sometimes come in at weekends if there is an important order to be dealt with. Your salary is below average for the industry and you haven't had a proper holiday for years. You are dissatisfied, and rapidly losing your motivation for the job. Write to the Marketing Director about this situation.
2 You are an employee in the Accounts Department. You come to work by car. Recently, you have had to park your car in the

streets outside the factory because there has been no space in the company car park. Sometimes, it has taken you fifteen or twenty minutes to find a space in the streets. When this has happened, you have been late for work. As a result, half an hour's pay has been deducted from your salary and your supervisor has given you a hard time. Write to the General Manager about this situation.

```
MEMORANDUM

To:

From:

Subject: _____
```

LISTENING

Understanding the main points

Listen to the following conversation and complete the minutes below, in note form.

ELM ELECTRONICS

Minutes of Senior Management Meeting - 2/4/88 - 11.30

Subject: ..:.......................

Present: Don Aiken, Patricia White, Jonathan Laidlaw,
         William Cooper

D.A. wanted to know if the staff were happy; and, if not, what could be done about it?

P.W. thought that morale was very low at present. Some people were worried that.. .

J.L. pointed out another problem affecting morale — ....
....

D.A. added that last year the company lost ....
.... because of ....

W.C. reminded us that in his department ....
....

P.W. suggested ....
with questions such as ....
....

W.C. agreed with P.W. He said it would show that management were concerned about staff feelings and problems— so it would be good for morale.

J.L. also liked P.W.'s idea, but stressed that ....
....
If not, ...

D.A. noted J.L.'s point and said that we must bear it in mind when the survey is prepared.

Vocabulary focus

1 *Listen again and fill in the gaps in these sentences from the conversation.*

1 .... the .... , I'd say that morale's very low at the moment.
2 You .... , the .... that we've just laid off two hundred or so workers?
3 What are you .... , Jonathan?
4 Mm . . . that's .... for .... , I must admit.
5 I think I'm .... the .... now, and it's not a very pretty one.
6 And you know, I may have .... the answer.
7 A survey could tell us what's .... in this firm.
8 Everybody must feel free to speak the truth, or else the data won't be .... to us.

2 *In pairs, discuss the meaning of the phrases and expressions above.*

4 Decision-making

DISCUSSION

Read the following case study. Then, working in groups of two or three, answer the questions below. Finally, compare your answers with those of the other groups.

The time is almost midnight. Sheldon, Chief Executive of Reprox, a photocopying equipment firm, sits in an armchair, looking shocked. He has just had a phone call from Donald, his Marketing Manager, and what Donald has told him is very worrying. Sheldon pours himself out a stiff whisky and considers the facts.

Apparently, the previous night, Donald had gone to a local restaurant with his wife. There, he had seen the firm's top salesman, Melvin, having dinner with a woman. Donald had been amazed at Melvin's choice of a dining companion, for the woman was Lois Markham, an executive from Hitex, one of their main competitors.

The next day, Donald called Melvin to his office, intending to give the top salesman a quiet warning about mixing with the enemy. However, the conversation did not go as planned.

'If you must know, I've been living with Lois for about a year now. And I might very well marry her,' Melvin said, 'but I don't see that it's any business of this company's.'

'Come on now, don't be so naïve,' Don answered. 'Think of the security aspect. We're in a competitive business – it's dog eat dog.'

'I haven't done anything wrong. You've got no right to interfere in my private life. And if you start doing so, maybe I'll have to look for another job.'

Sheldon considered the problem. Should he turn a blind eye to what was going on? Or was some sort of action needed on his part?

1 Summarise briefly the problem that Sheldon must solve.
2 What factors should he take into account before taking a decision?
3 How should he deal with the situation?
4 Can firms do anything to avoid this type of problem?

In carrying out management functions, such as planning, organising, motivating and controlling, a manager will be continually making decisions. Decision-making is a key management responsibility.

Some decisions are of the routine kind. They are decisions which are made fairly quickly, and are based on judgement. Because a manager is experienced, he knows what to do in certain situations. He does not have to think too much before taking action. For example, a supervisor in a supermarket may decide, on the spot, to give a refund to a customer who has brought back a product. The manager does not have to gather a great deal of additional information before making the decision.

Other decisions are often intuitive ones. They are not really rational. The manager may have a hunch or a gut feeling that a certain course of action is the right one. He will follow that hunch and act accordingly. Thus, when looking for an agent in an overseas market, a sales manager may have several companies to choose from. However, he may go for one organisation simply because he feels it would be the most suitable agent. He may think that the chemistry between the two firms is right. Such a decision is based on hunch, rather than rational thought.

Many decisions are more difficult to make since they involve problem-solving. Very often, they are strategic decisions involving major courses of action which will affect the future direction of the enterprise. To make good decisions, the manager should be able to select, rationally, a course of action. In practice, decisions are usually made in circumstances which are not ideal. They must be made quickly, with insufficient information. It is probably rare that a manager can make an entirely rational decision.

When a complex problem arises, like where to locate a factory or which new products to develop, the manager has to collect facts and weigh up courses of action. He must be systematic in dealing with the problem. A useful approach to this sort of decision-making is as follows: the process consists of four phases: i) defining the problem; ii) analysing and collecting information; iii) working out options and iv) deciding on the best solution.

As a first step, the manager must identify and define the problem. And it is important that he does not mistake the *symptoms* of a problem for the *real* problem he must solve. Consider the case of a department store which finds that profits are falling and sales decreasing rapidly. The falling profits and sales are *symptoms* of a problem. The manager must ask himself what the store's *real* problem is. Does the store have the wrong image? Is it selling the wrong goods? Or the right goods at the wrong prices? Are its costs higher than they should be?

At this early stage, the manager must also take into account the rules and principles of the company which may affect the final decision. These factors will limit the solution of the problem.

One company may have a policy of buying goods only from home suppliers; another firm might, on principle, be against making special payments to secure a contract; many enterprises have a rule that managerial positions should be filled by their own staff, rather than by hiring outside personnel. Rules and policies like these act as constraints, limiting the action of the decision-taker.

The second step is to analyse the problem and decide what additional information is necessary before a decision can be taken. Getting the facts is essential in decision-making. However, as already mentioned, the manager will rarely have all the knowledge he needs. This is one reason why making decisions involves a degree of risk. It is the manager's job to minimise that risk.

Once the problem has been defined and the facts collected, the manager should consider the options available for solving it. This is necessary because there are usually several ways of solving a problem. In the case of the department store, the management may decide that the store has the wrong image. A number of actions might be possible to change the image. New products could be introduced and existing lines dropped; advertising could be stepped up; the store might be modernised and refurbished or customer service might be improved.

It is worth noting that, in some situations, one of the options may be to take no action at all. This is a decision just as much as taking a more positive course of action. Peter Drucker, in his book *The Practice of Management*, gives a good example of the no-action option. He writes about a shipping company which, for twenty years, had problems filling a top position. Each person selected got into difficulties when doing the job:

> In the twenty-first year, a new President asked, 'What would happen if we did not fill it?' The answer was 'Nothing'. It then turned out that the position had been created to perform a job that had long since become unnecessary.

Before making a decision, the manager will carefully assess the options, considering the advantages and disadvantages of each one. Having done this, he will have to take a decision. Perhaps he will compromise, using more than one option. Thus, the manager of the department store may solve his problem by making changes in the product range, increasing advertising and improving the interior of the store.

DECISIONS

Understanding the main points

Decide whether the following statements are true or false.

	True	False
1 Before taking a routine decision managers must collect a great deal of information.	☐	☐
2 When choosing an overseas agent most managers rely on their intuition.	☐	☐
3 When a firm dismisses one of its junior managers it is making a strategic decision.	☐	☐

4 Managers cannot always wait until they have all the □ □
necessary information before taking important
decisions.

5 The first thing managers must do when solving a □ □
problem is to collect all the facts.

6 Because of their company's rules and policies □ □
managers may not be able to take certain actions
in order to solve a problem.

7 After collecting all of the necessary information □ □
managers have to identify the various actions
they could take to solve a problem.

8 When important decisions have to be made □ □
managers need to use a systematic process of
decision-making.

Vocabulary focus

*Find words or phrases in the text which mean the same as the
following:*

1 very important (paragraph 1)
2 immediately, without hesitation (paragraph 2)
3 occurs, appears (paragraph 5)
4 put, build, establish (paragraph 5)
5 consider carefully, assess (paragraph 5)
6 bear in mind, consider, remember (paragraph 7)
7 succeed in getting, win (paragraph 7)
8 choices, possible courses of action (paragraph 9)
9 increased (paragraph 9)
10 take a middle course of action (paragraph 11)

**LANGUAGE
STUDY**

1 Collocation

make a decision (lines 12–13)
take a decision (line 92)
take into account (line 51)
solve a problem (line 71)

The phrases above are examples of collocation. This refers to
words which are frequently grouped together.

Complete the following sentences with appropriate verbs.

1 Although our company wants to expand rapidly, we must
.... in mind that we have limited cash to do so.

2 It is important to .... into account all options before
.... a decision.

3 The Financial Director has .... the conclusion that we
must reduce costs by 10%.

4 Finally, the Chairman .... his opinion about the
matter. After we had listened to him, we were able to
.... to an agreement.

5 Patricia .... an interesting suggestion at the meeting.

6 If we don't come up with new products, we .... the
risk of falling behind our competitors.

7 Our chairman is too old for the job. Some of the directors have
.... pressure on him to resign.

8 The writer has .... some recommendations in his
report.

9 What conclusion have you .... from the facts given in his letter?
10 I have .... a great deal of thought to our financial problems.
11 After five hours' negotiation, we finally .... agreement.
12 I don't want to .... action until I've heard everyone's opinion.

2 Idiomatic uses of *spot*
on the spot (line 10)

A Below are some phrases each containing the word *spot*.
Match the phrases with the correct definitions.

1	on the spot	**a**	at the centre of public attention
2	in the spot	**b**	quick, random examination
3	in the spotlight	**c**	cash on delivery
4	spot-on	**d**	aspect of a character, situation or organisation that can be criticised
5	spot-check		
6	put someone on the spot	**e**	immediately or at the place of action
7	spot-cash		
8	high spot	**f**	outstanding moment
9	weak spot	**g**	ask someone a difficult question or put someone in a difficult situation
10	knock spots off		
		h	be much better than
		i	in a difficult situation
		j	exactly right

B *Complete the following sentences with suitable phrases from the list above.*

1 We're .... at the moment because one of our biggest customers has gone bankrupt. He owed us a lot of money.
2 Recently, The Distillers company has been .... Two companies have been fighting to take it over, and everyone has been talking about the takeover battle.
3 The forecasts of our Marketing Department have been .... I don't know how they manage to be so accurate.
4 Our terms for this consignment of rubber are ....
5 I don't want to wait for an answer. Can't you give me a decision .... ?
6 Can we give you twenty machines for immediate delivery? Mm ... Now, you're really .... me .... I don't know how many we have in stock.
7 The income tax officials often do a .... on taxpayers to make sure they are giving accurate information.
8 The .... of our year is our staff party. Even the Chairman lets his hair down.
9 Our distribution system doesn't cover certain areas of the country. It's the .... in our business.
10 In my opinion, our computer products .... those of our competitors.

3 *Complete the following passage with the correct forms of the words in the box below.*

arise (v.)   rise (n.)   rise (v.)   raise (v.)

A serious problem has .... (1) in my company. Because the cost of living .... (2) by 6% last year, management decided to .... (3) the salaries of all the staff. For this reason, they gave everyone a .... (4) of £10 a week. However, later on, they had to pay for this by .... (5) the prices of all our products by 10%. Such a large .... (6) in prices made our products uncompetitive. So now, management is talking of lowering our salaries again!

4 Phrasal verbs with *up*

weigh up (line 35)
step up (line 75)

Replace the words in italics in the following sentences with phrasal verbs from the box below.

weigh up   take up (three meanings)   step up
bring up   draw up   pick up

1 Before *preparing* the contract, may I go over one or two points again, please?
2 We have to *increase* our work-rate if we are going to get the accounts finished in time.
3 If I'm going to have any chance of becoming a member of the Board, I'll have to *start playing* golf.
4 I'd like to *mention* the subject of expense claims at our next meeting.
5 (Chairman, at a meeting) Your point is interesting, Donna, but I'd like to *discuss* it later, if I may.
6 We must *consider* all the possibilities before we decide which market to enter.
7 I *start* my new appointment next month.
8 We didn't get many orders last quarter but now sales have *improved*.

COMMUNICATION SKILLS

FUNCTION

Making a presentation

David Sibley is the new Executive Director of The Yorkshire and Humberside Development Association in the north of England. The work of the Association is to encourage British and overseas companies to set up factories in the area. This region of England needs more business and industry so that more employment opportunities will be provided for young people living in the area.

In David Sibley's office at the moment are the Managing Director and Production Manager of a company. They are about to tell Sibley about their company's activities.

Dialogue

Listen to their conversation.

YHDA
The Regional Specialists

MANAGING DIRECTOR	Before I tell you a little about our company, could I first thank you for seeing us at such short notice – it was very good of you.
SIBLEY	Please, don't mention it.
MANAGING DIRECTOR	Now about our company, Surefire Heating. We're a public limited company based in Wokingham. We've been in business some thirty years now. In the beginning, we made only heating and ventilation units – they're still our main product lines, actually. But recently we've moved into the field of kitchen equipment for the hotel and catering trade.
SIBLEY	Interesting. You should find plenty of customers for that equipment up here. I'm sure you're aware of that.
MANAGING DIRECTOR	Oh yes, we're not short of customers in northern England. Now, I should tell you that our most exciting new product line is micro-wave ovens. We've got big plans for these. More about that in a moment.
SIBLEY	Right.
MANAGING DIRECTOR	Let me give you some idea of the company's size now. Our turnover last year was close to £30m, our pre-tax profits around £4.5m. We've got a work-force of approximately 300 employees. We're expanding fast, I'm happy to say. Our growth rate – in terms of turnover – has been almost 10% a year.
SIBLEY	Very impressive.
MANAGING DIRECTOR	Thank you. Now Bob will say a word about our labour relations. He has more to do with that side of things than I do.
PRODUCTION MANAGER	Thanks Ian. Well, in a word, Mr Sibley, our relations with the union are first class. We've never had a strike at the plant and obviously we're very proud of that record. It's probably because we treat our employees well. We listen to what they have to say about their work, and they've plenty of opportunities to give their opinion. Mind you, we're not complacent. I'm not saying we'll never have a strike.
SIBLEY	Mm, nothing's certain in life, is it?
PRODUCTION MANAGER	Right.
MANAGING DIRECTOR	I think that gives you some idea of our business, Mr Sibley. Let me tell you now why we wanted to meet you. You see, we're planning to produce 30,000 micro-wave ovens next year. And we expect our output to rise to 60,000 or even 70,000, in two or three years' time. For that, we need a factory, say 40,000 square feet, and more workers. Eighty to a hundred employees at least.
SIBLEY	We can certainly help you there. Let me tell you what the north of England can offer you.

DECISIONS

47

Role play

The Yorkshire and Humberside Development Association have decided to give a substantial development grant to *one* of the companies which are currently interested in opening a factory in the region.

Instructions

Work in groups of four or five. Each group consists of
1 a managing director and production manager
2 members of the Development Association

MANAGING DIRECTOR AND PRODUCTION MANAGER

You represent either a British or foreign company. You must make a presentation of your company to members of the Development Association. Be prepared to answer any questions they may ask you. Use the headings below as a guide and prepare your presentation. Remember that there is only *one* grant available.

Yorkshire & Humberside Development Association
Westgate House, 100, Wellington Street, Leeds LS1 4LT.
Tel: Leeds (0532) 439222 Telex: 55253 YHDA G Fax: (0532) 431088

CANDIDATE INFORMATION

name of company: .... type: ....

head office: .... no. of years in business: ....

existing product(s) or service(s): ....

new product(s) or service(s): ....

turnover 1987: .... pre-tax profits 1987: ....

work-force: .... growth-rate: ....

management style: ....

labour relations: ....

reason(s) for requiring new factory: ....

....

size: .... employment created: ....

other information: ....

....

....

MEMBERS OF DEVELOPMENT ASSOCIATION

First, listen to the presentation by the company representatives and make notes about the company. Then, using the headings above to help you, ask them for any further information which you may require. Next, tell the other members of the Development Association (from the other groups) all about the company which you have interviewed. Finally, decide together which company should be offered the grant.

Case study

Executive relocation

John Grigg is Personnel and Training Manager for a US-based food company which sometimes transfers executives to its overseas subsidiaries, either because they are needed for a particular job, or because the overseas posting will give them useful experience.

Transferring staff overseas is costly for the company and can be a traumatic experience for the executives. Nevertheless, John Grigg is disappointed with his company's experience in relocating executives. In the past two years, there have been ten postings and five of these have been unsuccessful. Two staff had insisted on returning to head office after a few months abroad; two had left the company soon after their posting had ended and one man had had a nervous breakdown during the posting.

Listen to some of the comments made to John Grigg by three of the dissatisfied executives.

Food technologist posted to Montreal, Canada:

'Nothing went right from the start. We spent the first nine months in a hotel because we couldn't get suitable accommodation. My wife never stopped complaining. She hated the cold winter and the Canadian way of life, ''All they ever think about is ice-hockey,'' she used to say. She never really wanted to come to Montreal anyway. She had to give up a great job as Office Manager when I was transferred. I didn't enjoy the job there much because I didn't get on with my colleagues. My French isn't bad, but I certainly couldn't understand the sort of French they spoke.'

Marketing executive posted to an African subsidiary:

'I'd say my overseas posting cost me over $50,000. I had to sell my house at a loss because property prices were low at the time of my transfer. When I got there, I was amazed at the cost of living. I tell you, I couldn't save a cent. And living conditions were unbelievable. One time, I had to go without a bath for a month because of a water shortage. The job was awful. My African boss obviously didn't want me there – or any American for that matter. When I got back to head office three years later, I expected to become Marketing Manager. But someone else got the job.'

Financial Director posted to the Middle East:

'Don't talk to me about foreign postings. You disrupt your family life, sell your house, and they send you off to some country which is either boiling hot or freezing cold. You try to adapt to the way of life in the country, which is often completely alien to you, and to do a good job. Then you come back after a few years and nobody wants to know. They look at you as if you're a ghost!'

Instructions

You are all members of the Personnel and Training Department.

First, working in groups of two or three, suggest a number of ways in which the company could make overseas postings more acceptable to its executives.

Your proposals should include suggestions as to what type of financial payments the company should make towards relocation expenses.

Finally, meet as one group, with one person acting as Manager of Personnel and Training. Try to agree on a set of proposals which would be presented to the Board of Directors for approval.

WRITING

The Executive Director of the Devon and Cornwall Development Bureau (a development agency in Southern England) has received a letter from an American company based in Houston, Texas.

Read the letter and then write an appropriate reply.

KNOX ELECTRONICS Inc.

Carlton Square
Houston (Texas)
USA
Tel. (713) 439-8884
Telex KNOXEL 84798

January 29 1988

Executive Director
Devon and Cornwall Development Bureau
Phoenix House
Notte St
Plymouth PL1 2HF
England

Dear Sir,

I have recently been talking to a business colleague who spent some time in your area last summer. He was full of praise for the natural beauty of Devon and Cornwall, and mentioned that you were seeking to attract foreign investment to the region.

My company is planning to set up an overseas plant in Europe, which will manufacture micro-chips. It is possible that we might include Devon and Cornwall in our list of suitable locations. Before doing so, however, I would like to obtain some information on certain specific points. Once I have the answers on these matters, I will perhaps write to you for further documentation.

We would require information about the following:

i) the size of factories available, financial terms, leasehold or freehold etc. ;
ii) the possibility of obtaining a custom-built plant;
iii) the financial or other incentives offered to firms setting up in your area;
iv) the average wage rates of factory workers in the area;
v) labour relations in similar high-technology firms operating in the region.

Please let us have any further data you think may be relevant.

Cordially yours

Jim Bowman

Jim Bowman
President

1 *Work in groups of two or three. Read the newspaper article below and discuss any problems of vocabulary.*

TOSHIBA SETS UP MICROWAVE FACTORY IN PLYMOUTH

THE JAPANESE manufacturing giant, Toshiba, has just opened a microwave oven plant in Plymouth, Devon.

The new factory cost just under £3 million and will eventually produce ovens for all of the major European markets. Toshiba say that in its second year it will be producing at least 20,000 units per year.

Toshiba are, of course, very well known in the Plymouth area, having already established a TV and video facility there. This has shown steady growth since being set up five years ago.

This morning's ceremony to mark the opening of the microwave plant was remarkably informal. There was just one speech, given by Dr David Owen, the local Member of Parliament.

Following the ceremony, Eric Hammond, General Secretary of the Electrical, Electronic, Telecommunications and Plumbing Union (EETPU), spoke about the agreement his union had made with Toshiba's management. Both sides had agreed that strikes would only be allowed in exceptional circumstances.

With regard to Toshiba's much publicised system of open management, Mr Hammond explained that there was a Company Advisory Board where employees and managers regularly meet to discuss sales results, company finances, productivity, quality control etc. However, only the most senior managers were allowed to see important documents.

Toshiba is doing extremely well in Great Britain. Their profits for last year were approximately £200 million. Labour relations are excellent and people obviously enjoy working for the company. Toshiba's aim now is to achieve an average growth rate of 30% for its UK companies in the next two years.

2 *Now listen to the following extract from a news broadcast about the opening of the Toshiba factory.* You will notice that there are several mistakes in the *newspaper article*.

3 *Listen to the news broadcast again. As you do so, identify the mistakes made by the writer of the article.*

4 *Compare your findings with the other members of your group.*

5 Top management – planning and strategy

Read the following case study and then answer the questions below.

Richard Thomas, a brilliant electronics engineer, left the company he had worked with for ten years in order to set up his own business. He felt there was a gap in the market for low-priced computer components.

Richard's bank manager was impressed by his experience and by the business plan he presented. An overdraft facility of £25,000 was quickly arranged. This, together with Richard's savings of £15,000, provided the start-up capital for the firm, Computex.

He began by hiring another person to help him develop the components. The two of them spent the next six months producing the type of products they felt the market needed. When they had built up a good supply of components, they set about trying to sell them. To Richard's surprise, however, this proved very difficult. Many potential customers seemed to be suspicious of the low prices of the products. Why were they so much cheaper than those of more famous, well-established competitors, they wanted to know. Other customers clearly saw Richard's company as a newcomer not to be trusted – a cowboy outfit who would be here today and gone tomorrow.

It was over a year before Richard got his first order. By that time, he had an overdraft of £40,000 and no more money to make further supplies of components. He was spending all his time advertising the products, running round to meet customers and trying to persuade them to buy.

Three months later, a few large orders were received, but Richard realised that he would have to wait two months or so before being paid.

At that point, the bank manager lost confidence in the business. He informed Richard that he was calling in the overdraft. 'Give me some time to look around for more capital,' Richard said. 'All right, I'll give you a month, but no more,' was the bank manager's reply.

After rushing around and talking to a lot of people, Richard received firm offers from two venture capital companies. The first was prepared to invest £200,000 in return for an 80% share of Richard's business; the second was willing to put up £250,000 for a 90% share.

This was the situation facing Richard Thomas fifteen months after he had set up his high-technology enterprise.

1 Could Richard have avoided the situation he now finds himself in? If so, how?

2 What should he do now?
3 What advice would you give him about how to run the company in the future?
4 What problems can arise when someone starts up a high-technology enterprise?

The top management of a company have certain unique responsibilities. One of their key tasks is to make major decisions affecting the future of the organisation. These strategic decisions determine where the company is going and how it will get there. For example, top managers must decide which markets to enter and which to pull out of; how expansion is to be financed; whether new products will be developed within the organisation or aquired by buying other companies. These and other such decisions shape a company's future.

10 Before doing any kind of strategic planning, the management must be sure of one thing. They must decide what is the mission and purpose of their business. They also need to decide what it should be in the future. In other words, they must know why the business exists and what its main purpose is. Deciding the mission and purpose is the foundation of any planning exercise.

Two examples will make this point clear – one British, the other American. Most people have heard of Marks and Spencer, one of the biggest and most successful retailers in the 20 world. Michael Marks opened his first penny bazaar in 1884, in Leeds, England. Ten years later there were nine market stores, and Marks had taken into partnership Tom Spencer, the cashier of one of his suppliers. In 1926 Marks and Spencer

became a public company. At that point, they could have rested on their laurels! However, around that time, they developed a clear idea of Marks and Spencer's mission and purpose. Their later success was founded on this idea. They decided that the company was in business to provide goods of excellent quality, at reasonable prices, to customers from the working and middle classes. Providing value for money was their mission and purpose. One of the strategies they used was to concentrate on selling clothing and textiles. Later on, food products were added as a major line of business.

The second example concerns the American Telephone and Telegraph Company. They decided on their mission some sixty or so years ago. The head of the organisation at that time, Theodore Vail, realised that a privately-owned telephone and telegraphic company might easily be nationalised. If the company didn't perform well, the public would call for its nationalisation. To avoid this fate, it had to give efficient service to its customers. Vail and his colleagues decided that giving service would be the mission and purpose of the organisation. This became the overall objective of the company, and has remained so ever since.

Having decided on its mission and purpose, an organisation will have worked out certain more specific objectives. For example, a car firm may have the objective of producing and marketing new models of cars in the medium-price range. Another objective may be to increase its market share by 10% in the next five years. As soon as it has established its more specific, medium-term objectives, the company can draw up a corporate plan. Its purpose is to indicate the strategies the management will use to achieve its objectives.

However, before deciding strategies, the planners have to look at the company's present performance, and at any external factors which might affect its future. To do this, it carries out an analysis, sometimes called a SWOT analysis (strengths, weaknesses, opportunities and threats). First, the organisation examines its current performance, assessing its strengths and weaknesses. It looks at performance indicators like market share, sales revenue, output and productivity. It also examines its resources – financial, human, products and facilities. For example, a department store chain may have stores in good locations – a strength – but sales revenue per employee may be low – a weakness. Next, the company looks at external factors, from the point of view of opportunities and threats. It is trying to assess technological, social, economic and political trends in the markets where it is competing. It also examines the activities of competitors. The department store chain, for example, may see the opportunity to increase profits by providing financial services to customers. On the other hand, increasing competition may be a threat to its very existence.

Having completed the SWOT analysis, the company can now evaluate its objectives and perhaps work out new ones. They will ask themselves questions such as: Are we producing the right products? What growth rate should we aim at in the next five years? Which new markets should we break into?

The remaining task is to develop appropriate strategies to achieve the objectives. The organisation decides what actions it will take and how it will provide the resources to support those actions. One strategy may be to build a new factory to increase production capacity. To finance this, the company may develop another strategy, the issuing of new shares to the public.

Company planning and strategic decision-making are key activities of top management. Once they have been carried out, objectives and targets can be set at lower levels in the organisation.

Understanding the main points

1 *Number the following ideas 1–8, depending on the order in which they appear in the text.*

a The American Telephone and Telegraph Company decided that its principal objective was to provide customers with an efficient service. ☐

b The first step in planning the (long-term) future of a company is to decide on its overall objective. ☐

c After analysing its strengths, weaknesses, opportunities and threats, an organisation may re-consider its objectives. ☐

d The purpose of a corporate plan is to state how management intends to achieve the objectives. ☐

e The second planning stage is to establish more specific (medium-term) objectives.

f Finally, management needs to decide what actions it should take in order to achieve its objectives. ☐

g It is necessary for management to analyse the company's current performance as well as external factors affecting its future before they can draw up a corporate plan. ☐

h Marks and Spencer's aim to provide excellent value for money has led to their becoming one of the world's most successful retailers. ☐

2 *Consider Computex, the high-technology company mentioned in the discussion on page 52. Note down some of its strengths, weaknesses, opportunities and threats.*

STRENGTHS	WEAKNESSES	OPPORTUNITIES	THREATS
1	1	1	1 ....
2	2	2	2 ....
3	3	3	3 ....
4	4	4	4 ....

3 What, in your opinion, is the *mission and purpose* of the following organisations?

1 Coca Cola
2 International Business Machines (IBM)
3 Sony
4 American Express
5 Rolls Royce
6 Mcdonald's
7 Yves St Laurent (perfumes)
8 Walt Disney Productions

Vocabulary focus

*Explain the difference between a **strategy** and an **objective**.*

LANGUAGE STUDY

1 *Complete the following sentences using suitable items from the box below.*

> product range   sales revenue   growth-rate   product-line   market share   production capacity   resources   productivity

1 A well-known advertising agency aims to achieve a .... of 20% a year.
2 This .... is unprofitable. We'll have to discontinue it.
3 Companies like Unilever and IBM have huge financial ....
4 By re-organising the work of office staff, you can often increase their ....
5 We're a small firm, so we aren't able to offer a wide ....
6 Most of Shell Oil's .... comes from overseas subsidiaries.
7 By extending our factory, we have been able to expand our ....
8 With the help of their cheap, high-quality word-processor, the Amstrad company were able to greatly increase their .... in the UK.

2 Phrasal verbs

> *pull out* (line 6)   *carry out* (line 57)   *work out* (line 46)
> *break into* (line 77)   *draw up* (line 51)

Answer the following questions in any way you wish using the verbs in brackets.

1 What does a firm often have to do if it is not successful in a market? (pull out)
2 What do you do if your main competitor is doing better than you in the market? (work out)
3 After you have made a deal with an overseas agent, what do you usually do? (draw up)
4 How can you find out if there will be a demand for a product you wish to develop? (carry out)
5 What can you do if the demand for your products in your home market is saturated? (break into)

3 *Complete the following passage with the correct form of the words in the box below.*

strategy	right	venture	personnel	finance
skill	planning	drawback	expertise	set up
delegate	innovative	trust	segment	

The problems of small high-tech firms have attracted a lot of attention recently. Research shows that many of these firms are .... (1) by talented, creative scientists. Their owners have no trouble coming up with .... (2) products but they often can't build on their early success.

One reason for this is that they don't have much management .... (3). Therefore, they are unable to develop the .... (4) which are necessary for their company's growth. They are in a rush to develop products, and don't think enough about how to market them. When they do try to sell their products, they spend too much time trying to gain the .... (5) of potential customers. Another mistake they make is to underprice their products so that they have no .... (6) for future development.

Once the firms begin to grow, their owners underestimate the future costs of developing and marketing new products. Lack of financial .... (7) is a major weakness of such companies. It is difficult for the high-tech firm to attract the right .... (8) because it cannot offer the same job security as a large organisation.

The high-tech firm can get round some of these problems by developing a specialist image. It can aim at a particular .... (9) of the market. Customers then start seeking out the firm, so its marketing costs are reduced. The only .... (10) is that it may take some time before customers accept the firm's new technology.

As soon as the high-tech business has reached a certain size, it will be a good idea to bring in professional management. The founder of the firm can then .... (11) responsibility for activities like marketing and finance. If a high-tech firm needs money very badly, it may arrange a link-up with a larger company. It will offer that company exclusive .... (12) to its technology.

Enthusiasm, bright ideas, ... (13) capital and technology are not enough to ensure success. Basic management .... (14) – especially financial and marketing ones – are also vital.

4 Verb constructions

One of the strategies they used was to *concentrate on* selling clothing and textiles. (lines 31–2)

Rewrite the following sentences without changing their meaning. Use the verbs or phrases in italics followed by the correct prepositions and make any other necessary changes.

e.g. We think you ought to change your pricing policy.
suggest

We suggest { changing / (that) you change / (that) you should change } your pricing policy.

1 We always try to give good service to our customers.
make a point
2 'I'm delighted you have kept within your budget,' said the Chairman to our Advertising Manager.
congratulate
3 The Managing Director said, 'The new product must be launched by January.'
insist
4 Marks and Spencer are making a special effort to sell fashionable clothes for young people.
concentrate
5 We are pleased when our customers are satisfied.
take pleasure
6 The owner doesn't want to sell the business at the moment.
interested
7 I don't agree with our Chief Executive when he says we should expand the range of our products.
wrong
8 We are considering breaking into new markets.
think
9 He is sure that the bank will lend him the money for future development.
depend
10 Marks and Spencer have always been able to forecast accurately what their customers want.
succeed

COMMUNICATION SKILLS

FUNCTION
Exchanging information

Case study

The Benson group is a chain of department stores in the USA. Its chief competitors are Hi-Mark and Levinson Brothers.

Work in pairs. One of you should read article A, the other article B. Then, each person should fill in as much of the company profile on page 60 as possible, using the information in his/her article. Finally, find out from your partner the information about Benson which you are missing and complete the company profile.

BENSON FACES UNCERTAIN FUTURE

BENSON Inc., the department store group, announces this year's annual results on Wednesday. Once again, profits are expected to be well below expectations.

Benson built its first store in 1952. It now owns ten stores in the southern region of the United States, and two in Ontario, Canada. All the stores are on prime sites in the high streets of major cities. The Group's head office is in Petersville.

Recently, Benson's performance has been extremely disappointing. Two years ago, pre-tax profits had fallen to just $8.3m on a turnover of $225m. This year, profits are expected to be down yet again. Sales per employee is also much lower than the industry's average.

Fortunately for Benson, it still has a number of loyal customers who would not think of shopping elsewhere. However, the Group is facing fierce competition from Hi-Mark and up-and-coming Levinson Brothers. Hi-Mark

are well established, with a clearly defined up-market image. It has a reputation for selling good quality merchandise but at high prices. Levinson Brothers set up its first store seven years ago. Since then, it has expanded fast. It now has eight stores located in big cities. Levinson Brothers' target consumer is the 16-25 wage-earner. Nevertheless, it attracts to its stores people of all ages and from all income groups.

Levinson Brothers' marketing is more aggressive and effective than that of its two main competitors. It often cuts prices, and even offers goods at give-away prices to get people into its stores. It advertises heavily in local newspapers, and on local television. Its special promotions are always accompanied by a great deal of razzmatazz. Levinson Brothers' share price stands at $12 – its highest rating this year. Even so, the share is still probably a good buy for investors.

In order to compete more effectively, Benson changed its business strategy about eighteen months ago. It began to rent space to outside firms on a concessionary basis. Almost 20% of its stores' space was rented to selected companies from outside the organisation. Unfortunately, this strategy has not been too successful. Several firms renting space complain that their sales have been poor.

Benson's stores were redecorated recently. This 'facelift' has met with mixed reactions from its customers. The layout of the stores continues to confuse customers. The customers complain that departments are not grouped together in a logical manner. As a result, shoppers get tired out looking for the goods they want.

At present, it looks very much as if Benson has lost its dynamism and sense of purpose. Investors holding shares in the group might be well advised to sell.

TROUBLED TIMES FOR BENSON GROUP

When Benson announces its annual results on Wednesday, it is expected that the group's profits will be around $6m. This will mean a drop of some 25% compared with the previous year. Today, Benson's share price fell to just under $7 in anticipation of the results. Two or three years ago, it will be recalled, the share price stood at $10.

One of Benson's biggest problems is that it lacks a clear image. Although some well-off customers have stuck to Benson through thick and thin, many others have moved on and now shop at Hi-Mark. These customers seem to prefer Hi-Mark's tasteful decor and high-priced, exclusive goods. Another of Benson's disadvantages is that its

merchandise does not particularly appeal to younger buyers. These prefer the self-service, down-market approach of Levinson Brothers – Benson's other main rival. Both Hi-Mark and Levinson Brothers are profitable organisations. Hi-Mark's strategy is, essentially, to maintain good profit margins on all its merchandise. Levinson Brothers, on the other hand, aim for high volume and lower margins.

All three organisations – Benson, Hi-Mark and Levinson Brothers – face a common problem. They are all aware of the threat coming from the new multiple stores – retailers like Klassic, Marginal and Clique. These are 'muscling in' on the other groups' traditional markets of clothing, home decoration and food. The new multiples have been very successful at attracting to their stores fashion-conscious customers, both

young and old. They seem to have the knack of offering exciting, stylish goods at prices people can afford.

Rising costs have been the main cause of Benson's low profits. Stock levels tend to be high, but very often goods are not available when required by customers. At present, goods are kept in warehouses at each store. Benson are considering changing this system. It may build one or two huge distribution centres which will supply all the stores. This could be a less costly way of organising its warehousing facilities. In addition, it has been suggested recently that service at Benson's stores is not what it used to be. It is believed, also, that staff turnover and absenteeism is too high.

Unless Benson's management take action soon to revive the group's fortunes, it would seem that the outlook for the organisation is bleak.

COMPANY PROFILE – Benson Inc.

	MOST RECENT YEAR	PREVIOUS YEAR
Turnover Pre-tax profits Share price		
No. of stores		
Major strengths		
Major weaknesses		
Opportunities		
Threats		
Image and business strategy		
Recent and future developments		

The Benson Group

The Benson Group is a chain of department stores in the south of the USA. Its performance over the last five years has been poor. It has lost market share to its two main rivals, Hi-Mark and Levinson Brothers. This year's annual results, just announced, have again been bad. Its pre-tax profits have fallen to $6.6 million, causing the share price to drop to $7. When David Klein, Group Chief Executive, holds his next management meeting, the atmosphere is gloomy.

Klein comes straight to the point: 'I don't need to tell you how serious the situation is. We're losing market share, our profits are down two million, sales per employee are far too low, and our profit margins are declining over a whole range of merchandise. Frankly, we're in a mess.' He looked grimly at his management team. Then his eyes fell on Sally Blake, the group's Marketing Director. 'What are we doing wrong, Sally?' he asked her.

'As I see it,' she answered, 'our turnover hasn't been rising fast enough. We should be achieving sales of 300–400 million by now, then it wouldn't matter if our profit margins were low. But in fact our turnover was just over 200 million this year.'

'So what's our real problem?'

'The market's become too competitive. Levinson are taking away a lot of our younger customers, and Hi-Mark seem to be appealing more to our older ones. And then of course, there are these specialist stores springing up all over the place. They're under-cutting us half the time and often offering better goods – or at least more fashionable ones.'

David Klein looked thoughtful. 'Up until recently, I always thought we had the loyal support of the middle-class buyer, the 30–45-year-old man or woman, with a good income and a family to look after. Surely, that's our target buyer, isn't it? What do you think, Dan?' Klein turned to Dan Rozell, his Financial Director.

Rozell had been waiting to be asked his opinion. 'Our problem is we've no real image. The public have no idea what Benson really represents. And let's be honest, David, we've no clear idea where we're trying to go. Should we compete against Levinson or Hi-Mark or even against both? On the one hand, we know that young people are pouring into our sales areas because business is booming. So, should we try to grab a share of that market, or leave it to Levinson Brothers? On the other hand, would it perhaps be better to compete more aggressively against Hi-Mark?'

David Klein nodded in agreement. 'An interesting contribution, Dan, thanks. Let's hear what you have to say now, Sonia.'

Sonia Liebermann, head of the Corporate Strategy Unit, was one of the youngest and newest members of the management committee. 'It's true we've got no image, but that's not our only problem. I mean, have we ever really worked out our strategy properly? We always seem to be reacting to what our competitors are doing.'

'How do you mean?' asked Klein, a little puzzled.

'Well, if Levinson or Hi-Mark have a carpet sale, then we do the same. We seem to have a me-too approach; we never take the initiative.'

David Klein frowned, but admitted to himself that there was truth in what she had said. 'Go on,' he said.

'There are so many other things I could mention. We spent a million on re-decorating the stores. But I still think our colour scheme is wrong. Cream and brown is . . . so safe, so traditional.'

'Maybe,' said David Klein coldly. He could see that nothing would stop Sonia from making her points.

'Anyway,' she said, 'what's the use of re-decorating if customers can't find their way round the store, and when they can't get decent service from any of our staff?'

'Absolutely, Sonia,' cut in Des Morris, Company Secretary. 'And may I say, we ought perhaps to try to find some way of persuading customers to go up to the higher floors of our stores. I've no need to remind everyone, sales revenue per square foot decreases sharply, the higher the floor.'

At that point David Klein looked at all the members of the management committee. An idea came to him. 'OK everyone,' he said. 'May I suggest that we adjourn this meeting today, and that we meet again first thing Monday morning. I'd like you to think carefully about the position of our group, and about the problems we face. I would ask you also to come up with ideas for our future strategy. We can't go on as we have done in the past – that's clear. The question is, where do we go from here? I look forward to hearing your views on Monday morning.'

Instructions

You are directors of the Benson Group. Each of you plays one of the roles described below. (If there are not enough roles for all the members of your group, some of you can act as assistants to directors.)

The purpose of the meeting is to decide:

(i) how Benson can improve its performance and increase its market share;
(ii) what its future strategy should be.

The Chief Executive will chair the meeting.
Prepare for the meeting by studying your role-card only.

Note: These are given as a guide to how you should act in the meeting. You may, however, add any information you wish.

CHIEF EXECUTIVE

You will chair the meeting. You must ask people for their opinions and encourage them to discuss fully the questions on the agenda. At the end of the meeting, you and your board of directors must try to agree on the future strategy of the company. Personally, you are not sure what to do in the present situation. You are retiring in five years' time and you hope there will be no big changes in the organisation before you go.

DEPUTY CHIEF EXECUTIVE

You think that Benson should compete strongly against the Hi-Mark stores, and forget about Levinson Brothers. Therefore, Benson should make every effort to up-grade the quality of its goods. By doing this, it will be able to create an image of quality and luxury. It should also concentrate more on fashion clothing. The stores could sell more designer clothes and well-known brands which appeal to young people. They could buy high-quality goods and sell them under the Benson brand name, too.

COMPANY SECRETARY

In your opinion, Benson cannot complete successfully against Levinson Brothers and Hi-Mark. You would like the company to join with Levinson Brothers to form a merger. Suggest that your Chief Executive meets the President of the Levinson organisation as soon as possible to discuss this possibility. A merger is a good idea because (i) the new organisation – Benson-Levinson – would appeal to all age and income groups (ii) Levinson's cash resources could be used for Benson's future development (iii) Levinson would bring to Benson new ideas, management expertise and dynamism.

DIRECTOR – CORPORATE STRATEGY

In your view, the present Chief Executive is no longer suitable to lead the Benson Group. He's too old and has 'lost his touch'. Try to suggest – in a diplomatic way – that he should give up the job. You would like to bring in someone from outside to run the Group. This person would probably be the successful head of another organisation. To attract the right candidate, Benson should offer a top salary, a share in profits, and other benefits. As a long-term strategy, the company should consider building huge stores in out-of-town locations where customers would have a lot of parking space.

DIRECTOR – PUBLIC RELATIONS

You feel strongly that Benson must go down-market and compete directly with Levinson Brothers. Young people are pouring into the South, so Benson must aim its marketing at the 15–25-year-old consumer. After all, these days, young people have plenty of money to spend. Therefore, you want Benson to (i) redecorate the stores in bright colours, blue and yellow perhaps (ii) change its sales approach by gradually offering more goods appealing to young people (iii) introduce new types of racks and counters which allow self-service (iv) have eye-catching window displays to attract teenagers and young adults. You will, of course, have other suggestions for attracting young people.

DIRECTOR – CORPORATE FINANCE

You have no doubt that the company must cut costs and increase its cash flow as quickly as possible. Benson needs cash to reduce its loan capital – this is much too high – and to finance its future development. To cut costs, the company must reduce its work-force by 20%. The Group must also have a new distribution system, with one or two large centres supplying goods to all the stores. This will reduce stock levels. You have plenty of ideas for improving the cash flow. For example, the stores could increase the profit margins on goods which were selling well. In addition, they should be ready to buy up cheap, good-quality merchandise. This could be sold in a special part of the stores, known as The Market Place.

DIRECTOR – MARKETING

You want the company to bring in specialist management consultants to do a study of Benson. They could work with the Marketing Department and Corporate Strategy Unit. Their job would be to analyse the organisation, and make recommendations about future strategy. It might be a good idea, too, if Benson developed new activities. For example, they could open an optician's service – very profitable – or offer financial services. A Financial Department could trade in stocks and shares, offer credit facilities, store credit cards, etc. You have several other ideas for new activities.

DIRECTOR – PERSONNEL AND STAFF DEVELOPMENT

For some time, you have wanted to have a three-week training programme for all sales staff. After the programme, they would be allowed to choose which department they wished to work in. Whenever you have suggested this scheme, the Finance Director has opposed it. 'We can't afford it,' he always says. Try once again to persuade the board to agree to the proposal. You think, also, that Benson should stop all its concessions. Outside firms renting space in the stores should be encouraged not to renew their contracts. The company must sell its *own* goods and build up its *own* image. In the long run, you would like an architectural solution to Benson's problems. Stores should have a central elevator system and an ultra-modern shopping arcade on the top floor, under a giant glass dome.

NON-EXECUTIVE DIRECTOR

Discuss Benson's problems with your colleague, the other non-executive director on the board. You are both advisers to the board. You may, therefore, make any suggestions or comments you wish concerning Benson's strategy. Be ready to criticise proposals made by other directors.

NON-EXECUTIVE DIRECTOR

Your role is as described above.

DISCUSSION

1 *Choose some companies or service organisations that you know well. Then, in each case, discuss:*

(i) what the *objectives* of each business are;
(ii) what *strategies* the management are using to achieve their objectives.

Are all the businesses using the right strategies?
If not, what changes should they make?

2 *Work individually or in groups of two or three. Give a short oral presentation of any organisation you are familiar with. Try to point out its strengths, weaknesses, opportunities and threats (SWOT). Talk about its objectives and strategies, and say what you think its future prospects are.*

WRITING

Imagine that you are the Chief Executive of the Benson Group. Write a letter to the President of Levinson Brothers, suggesting that Benson and Levinson Brothers should merge and form one group. Explain why you think the merger is desirable and how it would benefit both store groups. Finally, invite Levinson Brothers' President to meet you to discuss your proposal.

Understanding the main points

Listen to the following conversation and complete the company profile below.

```
_____
                          COMPANY PROFILE
_____


NAME OF COMPANY  ...........................................

INDUSTRY         Business Machines


PROFITS          MOST RECENT YEAR        PREVIOUS YEAR

                 £ ...........           £ ...........


SHARE VALUE      PRESENT        - 6 MONTHS        - 12 MONTHS

                 ...... pence   ....... pence     ....... pence


REASONS FOR CURRENT SUCCESS    1 .............................

                               2 launching high number of new products

                               3 .............................

LATEST PRODUCT                 TYPE: .........................

                               BRAND NAME: ...................

                               PRICE: £ ........

                               COMPONENTS: computer, ..........

                               ...............................

                               STRENGTHS:  cheaper than competition, .......

                               ...............................
```

Vocabulary focus

Listen again and identify the phrases or expressions in the conversation which mean the same as the following:

1 I've just made a large amount of money.

   ‘ ....’

2 I'm glad you've been lucky.

   ‘ .... !’

3 It's very easy to operate.

   ‘ ....’

4 ... (he told me) Futura were going to become very successful.

   ‘ ....’

5 I think the price is very reasonable.

   ‘ ....’

6 Goal-setting

DISCUSSION

Listen to the following conversation and then discuss the questions which follow.

Jack Macdonald is Sales Manager of a leather goods company. Brenda Cole is a sales representative. Each January, Jack writes a report on her work performance during the previous year and discusses it with her. Below is an extract from one such meeting.

MACDONALD	I've said in my report that I'm fairly happy with your work, Brenda. I set you a sales target of £150,000. And, in fact, you had sales of roughly £118,000 – a reasonable effort on the whole.
COLE	Thanks. I'd have liked to have reached my target, but to be honest, I never thought I had much chance.
MACDONALD	Really? You didn't say anything when we set the target last year. How come?
COLE	Oh, I didn't want to sound too gloomy, I suppose. No one else was complaining, so why should I? I didn't want to rock the boat.
MACDONALD	Mm, I see. Still, results are what count here, and yours are quite good, I suppose. There are one or two things I'd like to mention, though.
COLE	Uh huh?
MACDONALD	About the way you dress for work. One of our customers mentioned it. He said you looked rather ... er ... casual when you last visited him. It seems you were dressed in jeans and a jumper. That's no good for our image, surely?
COLE	Oh ... er ... no. I did dress casually once or twice, when I visited a customer on a Saturday morning. But usually ...
MACDONALD	All right. But don't let it happen again, will you?
COLE	Of course not.
MACDONALD	Another thing. I've noticed there are quite a few slow payers among your customers. Can't you do something about that?
COLE	I could chase them up a bit. Put some pressure on them.
MACDONALD	Do that. You're expected to get on to slow payers, you know, and find out what's going on. Don't you ever read your job description?
COLE	Job description? I haven't looked at it for years. And I bet no one else has around here either.
MACDONALD	You may be right. But it's no excuse. You know perfectly well, Brenda, that I set the highest standards for all my sales staff. And I expect you to meet them. Right?
COLE	Yes, O.K.

'He said you looked rather... er... casual when you last visited him.'

1 How well do you think Macdonald dealt with this part of the discussion? Explain your answer, with examples.
2 If you were Brenda Cole, what would you have said to make the discussion more effective?

READING

Management by Objectives (MBO) is a system which was first described by the American Peter Drucker, in 1954, in his book *The Practice of Management*. Since then, MBO has attracted enormous interest from the business world, and its principles have been applied in many of the world's largest companies.

In his book, Peter Drucker emphasised that an organisation and its staff must have clear goals. Each individual must understand the goals of the enterprise he/she works for, and must make a contribution to them. It is also vital, in Drucker's
10 view, that the individual knows what his/her manager expects of him/her. He/She must know what sort of results he/she is expected to achieve.

If an organisation uses the Management by Objectives approach, it must pay careful attention to planning. This is because each individual has clearly defined objectives. And these will contribute to the overall objectives of the enterprise. With MBO, individual and organisation objectives are linked. A special feature of MBO is that the subordinate participates with his/her manager in developing objectives. After these
20 have been worked out, his/her performance, in relation to the goals, can be assessed. MBO, therefore, focuses on results. The subordinate's performance is judged in terms of how well or badly he/she has achieved his/her goals.

Various kinds of MBO systems are used in organisations. Here is an example of how a programme might work in a company:

The programme consists of several stages. First, the subordinate's job is defined. Next, his/her current performance is evaluated. Then, new objectives are developed by the subordinate and his/her manager. Finally,
30 the programme is put into action. Later, there are periodic reviews of the person's performance, and his/her progress is checked.

Let us consider these phases in more detail. At the first stage, the subordinate and his/her manager define the job separately. They also rank the tasks in order of importance. Both parties then meet and discuss the statements they have made in writing. It is quite possible that they will not agree about certain aspects of the job. They discuss their differences of opinion. In the end, they both have a clearer idea of what
40 the job involves.

At stage two, the subordinate and his/her manager examine each task. They try to decide how well or badly it is being performed. Again, they do this evaluation separately. They meet and discuss their assessments. All being well, the manager will have the chance to praise the subordinate for some of his/her work. On the other hand, the subordinate or the manager – or even both parties – may point out areas where there are problems – tasks which are not performed properly.

50 Developing objectives comes next. The subordinate and his/her manager try to develop goals which are challenging but realistic. The manager may set performance standards which can be measured or quantified. But this is not essential. The objectives probably spell out results that must be achieved. There will be dates by which the subordinate must achieve his/her goals.

In the table below, Figure 1, you can see examples of objectives for an MBO programme.

Figure 1

SUBORDINATE	OBJECTIVES
Sales representative	Increase sales of video-recorders in the Chicago area by 5%, by 1 June. Obtain five new accounts by 1 January. Send sales reports in on time.
Chief Accountant	Reduce bad debts from 8% to 4% of sales turnover by 1 January. Introduce new computer systems in Accounts Department by 1 January.
Marketing Manager	Complete test marketing of PX hi-fi units by 1 January. Increase market share of home computers by 3% by 1 January.
Production Manager	Meet 90% of all delivery dates. Reduce cost of bought-in materials by 5%. Reduce the number of units rejected by quality control. Increase number of quality control circles meeting each month. All goals to be achieved by 1 January.
Personnel Manager	Complete training programme for shop-floor workers by 1 January. Present bonus scheme for Board approval by 1 June. Make suggestions for improved selection procedures by 1 June.

'But you guys don't understand. I gotta increase my sales by 5% before June!'

60 The subordinate and the manager discuss the objectives and make plans for achieving them. The manager may have to help in some way, perhaps by providing more training for the subordinate or buying more modern machines.

Finally, the subordinate sets about achieving the goals. From time to time, the subordinate and the manager meet to discuss progress. It is vital that the manager receives feedback from the subordinate on performance and achievements. (The documents used for the last two stages of the MBO programme are shown in Figure 2.)

70 There are many benefits of Management by Objectives. The system helps the subordinate to see clearly his/her role in the organisation and the tasks he/she must carry out. He/She has a say in how his/her job is performed, and what his/her goals should be. As a result he/she feels more responsible and motivated and is therefore likely to be more committed to the objectives of the organisation.

MBO is a good technique for assessing an individual's performance. He/She is judged on results, rather than on the personal feelings or prejudices of the manager. An MBO programme should lead to better coordination and 80 communications within an enterprise. The subordinate must liaise closely with his/her manager. The manager acts as teacher and guide. The individual is encouraged to identify with the goals of the organisation. Most important of all, MBO makes the individual think of results, of the contribution he/she is making – or should make – to the enterprise. The main limitations of the system are that it is time-consuming and may create a lot of paperwork. In practice, MBO programmes are often not fully supported by managements. This could be because managers are not always skilled at interviewing and 90 giving guidance.

A few years ago, it was discovered that 70% of the 500 biggest companies in the USA were using MBO. However, a later survey showed that only 15% of the programmes were considered successful. In spite of this finding, there is little doubt that MBO has helped to increase the efficiency of both subordinates and their managers.

Figure 2   Goals Sheet – Performance Evaluation – Achievement

GOALS SHEET

Name   David Jeffries

Position   Research and Development Manager

Date   5 January, 1988

Goals for the current year	Goals for the next year	Performance Indicator
Design, develop and produce a prototype of product BLP-2 within a budget of $500,000	Attract more money from government agencies to develop new products	Prototype of product BLP-2 by the end of the year
Complete modifications to Antisneez	Re-launch Antisneez by September	Achieve sales of $50,000 by year end

```
PERFORMANCE EVALUATION

Name     David Jeffries

Position  Research and Development Manager

Date    5 January, 1989
```

Goals for the current year	Goals for last year	Results achieved
Attract more money from government agencies to develop new products	Design, develop and produce a prototype of product BLP-2 within a budget of $500,000	Prototype of product BLP-2 produced by the end of October at a cost of $450,000

ACHIEVEMENT

UNSATISFACTORY	FAIR	GOOD	VERY GOOD	OUTSTANDING
☐	☐	☐	☐	☒

Understanding the main points

1 How does a manager evaluate the performance of a subordinate under the MBO system?

2 *Note down the five stages of the programme given as an example of an MBO system.*

Stage 1	....
Stage 2	....
Stage 3	....
Stage 4	....
Stage 5	....

3 *Note down some of the advantages of MBO for each of the following:*

THE BENEFITS OF MANAGEMENT BY OBJECTIVES		
COMPANY	MANAGER	SUBORDINATE
1	1	1 ....
2	2	2 ....
3	3	3 ....
4	4	4 ....

4 In your opinion what is the manager's role in an MBO programme?

a judge **b** observer **c** motivator **d** critic

Vocabulary focus

Explain the meaning of the following words and phrases.

1 *goals* (line 7)   6 *challenging* (line 51)
2 *vital* (line 9)   7 *realistic* (line 52)
3 *linked* (line 17)   8 *sets about* (line 63)
4 *focuses* (line 21)   9 *committed* (line 74)
5 *reviews* (line 31)   10 *liaise* (line 81)

LANGUAGE STUDY

1 *Complete the following passage, using suitable forms of the words in the box below.*

achieve	reach	report	feedback	objective
progress	performance	role	stage	view

My boss called me into his office to discuss my .... (1) during the last six months. She said that I had made good .... (2) and had had no difficulty in .... (3) my goals. She made it clear that she was going to give me a good .... (4) .

I suppose I should have been grateful to her. However, one thing bothered me. I wondered why she didn't ask me what *I* felt about the job. Why didn't she get some .... (5) from me? I thought that was one of the main .... (6) of the interview.

Since my .... (7) was obviously to sit quietly and say nothing, I did just that. At this .... (8) of my career, I can't afford to upset my boss. But if I ever .... (9) her position, I shall handle these interviews differently. In my .... (10), it's vital to listen to employees.

2 More phrasal verbs with *out*

point out (line 47)

Complete the following sentences, using suitable forms of the verbs in the box below.

point out	hold out	make out (two meanings)
have out	stand out	cut out (two meanings)

1 Sheila wants to .... the training sessions she runs on Friday afternoon. She's too busy to hold them then.
2 When reviewing my performance, Mr Jones .... several weaknesses.
3 I'm a valuable member of the organisation, so at my next salary review, I shall .... for a lot more money.
4 I think I .... among all the candidates because my qualifications for the job were so good.
5 How did you .... in the interview, Patricia?
6 He said that I was not .... for a career in banking.
7 I'm fed up with my boss criticising me all the time. I'm going to .... it .... with him.

8 Can you read David's writing? I can't .... what he's put on this report.

3 *Rewrite the following sentences without changing their meaning. Use the verbs or phrases in italics and make any other necessary changes.*

e.g. We cannot supply you on time because there has been a fire in our factory.
explain
He explained that they could not supply us on time because there had been a fire in their factory.

1 I said to her, 'Why don't you log my use of time?'
suggest
2 The Research and Development Manager said, 'This product has got to be taken off the market.'
demand
3 The new Chairman said it was essential to reorganise the board of directors.
insist
4 I said, 'Let's interview the other candidates tomorrow.'
propose
5 I have to finish this report by the end of the week.
It's vital
6 You should stop working now – it's almost midnight.
It's time
7 The management should realise we are human beings, not machines.
It's essential
8 He said, 'Would you like me to help you write the report?'
offer

COMMUNICATION SKILLS

FUNCTION

Making suggestions

Dialogue

'I name this racket Boris…'

Listen to the following conversation, in which four executives discuss when to put a new tennis racket on to the market.

ALAN In my opinion, the best time would be just before the summer season. I suggest we launch the racket in May.

MARY I'd say that's a bit late. Why don't we introduce it in March or April? That would give people time to see it in shop windows and get used to its new design.

DAVID Don't you think we should launch it even earlier than that? Don't forget, retailers will need time to study our sales literature. And we'll have to set up a lot of point-of-sale display material – that'll take time too. I propose we start supplying our sales outlets at the beginning of the year.

JOHN I agree. But it might also be worthwhile getting a few people to play with it in indoor courts. Then, re-launch the racket with a big bang later in the summer.

Case study

Make or break

Your company has been developing an ultra-modern product which has several revolutionary features. You are confident it will be a world-beater!

Unfortunately, you have spent a fortune on the development costs of the project. Because of this, the company is on the verge of going bankrupt. You need a lot more money to finance the final stage of the project and to ensure that the launch of the product will be successful.

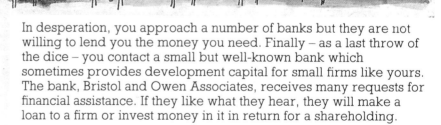

In desperation, you approach a number of banks but they are not willing to lend you the money you need. Finally – as a last throw of the dice – you contact a small but well-known bank which sometimes provides development capital for small firms like yours. The bank, Bristol and Owen Associates, receives many requests for financial assistance. If they like what they hear, they will make a loan to a firm or invest money in it in return for a shareholding.

Instructions

Three or four members of the class should play the roles of executives from Bristol and Owen Associates. The rest of the class should divide into groups of three or four, each group representing a company which is desperately seeking a loan from the bank.

Study your respective role-cards and then do the following:

The executives from Bristol and Owen Associates should meet each of the companies in turn and listen to their presentations. The bank's executives should then ask relevant questions. Finally, the bank's executives should discuss the merits of each company's application and then choose **one** *company to whom it will lend the money.*

THE COMPANIES

You work for a company which is developing an exciting and revolutionary new product. You may choose any product you wish. Your job is to make a convincing presentation of your product to Bristol and Owen Associates.

Prepare your presentation carefully.

Your presentation should take the following form:

1 Introduce the members of your management team (Managing Director, Financial Director, Marketing Director, Technical Director, Production Director etc.)
2 Give a brief presentation of your company: location, company mission, business strategy, product range, markets, turnover, pre-tax profits, size of work-force etc.
3 Give details about the new product you are developing: general description, technical specifications, revolutionary features, target consumer, price, marketing plans, production targets etc.
4 Explain to the bank how you see your company developing in the future.
5 Tell the bank how much money you need and on what terms.

Be prepared to answer questions from the bank's executives.

BRISTOL AND OWEN ASSOCIATES

You work for Bristol and Owen Associates. It is your job to listen to each company's presentation and to question each team about their project, either during and/or after their presentation. Remember, your bank is not a charity (an organisation which gives away money)!

Before you meet the companies, choose one of the members of your group to be Chairman of the bank and to lead the discussion. Discuss together how you are going to conduct the meetings. After meeting all the companies, decide which one you are going to lend the money to. Finally, make a formal announcement to the class, giving the reasons for your choice.

WRITING

In the role-play exercise above, some of you gave details of ultra-modern products which your companies were developing. Let's suppose that those products are ready to be put on to the market. The marketing departments of each company have to devise suitable advertisements for the products, which will be placed in newspapers and/or specialist magazines.

Work in groups of two or three, each group consisting of the marketing and advertising executives of each company. Plan an advertisement for the product you are responsible for. Draft the written text of the advertisement, and if possible provide some rough artwork. Try to give a clear impression of how it will look when it is presented in printed form. When you have finished, present your advertisement to the rest of the class.

Finally, examine the other groups' advertisements critically and discuss whether or not they are effective. Suggest any changes to the advertisements which you feel would increase their impact.

LISTENING

Understanding the main points

Listen to the following conversation and complete the memorandum below.

memorandum

To: George Holbrook

From: Vanessa McIntyre

Subject: ....

Ralph Harris has just informed me that ....
....
Apparently, this regrettable delay has been caused by ....
....
Ralph says they still haven't managed to develop a biscuit which
crackles when you bite into it.

Ralph now estimates that his department will not have solved this
problem satisfactorily until ....
.... Naturally, this will make it impossible
for us to ....
....

In view of these unfortunate circumstances I would suggest that our
best course of action would be to postpone the launch ....
....
Could we meet to discuss this as soon as possible?

Vocabulary focus

1 *Listen again and fill in the gaps in these sentences from the conversation.*

  1 We're .... some
    problems, I'm afraid.
  2 And they've taken it home and .... it ....
    on their children.
  3 Good heavens! That means we'll never................... it
    .... the market by June. .... !
  4 Even so, I'm not going to .... ,
    Vanessa.
  5 OK. I'll .... a meeting ....
    George.

2 *In pairs, discuss the meaning of the phrases and expressions
above.*

7 The management of time

DISCUSSION

John Midgley is General Manager of a medium-sized engineering company. He decided to keep a diary of his activities for one day. These are noted below. For your information: Shirley is the company's Sales Manager; Penny is John Midgley's secretary and Don is the Production Manager.

Look at the diary and then discuss the questions which follow.

7.30–8.00	arrived at office – had coffee – checked to see if any telexes – read newspapers
8.00–8.15	chatted to Shirley – looks as if marriage is on the rocks
8.15–8.45	Don dropped by – talked about England–Brazil game – then discussed Fritz Muller order for Switzerland
8.45–9.45	looked through mail – answered urgent letters – interrupted twice by telephone calls from customers
9.45–10.45	interview with applicant for position of Assistant to Chief Buyer – interview started 15 mins late because of telephone calls (see above)
10.45–11.15	answered more letters
11.15–11.25	phone call from Chamber of Commerce – agreed to give talk at next Wednesday's lunch
11.25–11.45	discussed Penny's maternity leave and arrangements for replacing her
11.45–12.15	worked on drafting Strategy report
12.15–12.30	Shirley dropped by – talked about Sales trip to Egypt. Fascinating stuff about Pyramids

12.30–12.55	continued report
12.55–3.25	met Ms. Ito from Japan – took her to lunch
3.25–4.00	weekly supervisors meeting – started 25 mins late
4.00–4.10	Dick phoned – arranged tennis for weekend
4.10–4.20	wife phoned – Jamie hurt leg at school – nothing serious
4.20–4.45	another phone call – argument with supplier over invoice
4.45–5.45	visited bank manager to discuss loan for company – arrived 15 mins late – manager NOT pleased – miserable old devil!
5.45–7.20	gave talk at local Technical College – arrived 30 minutes late – but talk went like a bomb!
7.20–8.00	returned to office to collect report to work on at home – chatted to Tom, our caretaker – what a talker!
8.00	arrived home – had a row with Jenny in kitchen – went to meet dinner guests

1 **a** Judging by this diary, do you think John Midgley is using his time effectively? *Explain your answer.*
b If not, how could he become more effective?

READING

In any business, it is important that managers should be effective. They must be able to achieve their objectives, and to 'get the right things done'. For most executives, being effective is easier said than done. The problem is that there are so many pressures on managers, reducing their efficiency. For one thing, their work is fragmented. Most days, they are doing a number of tasks, some fairly trivial, others highly important. They find that they do not have enough time to devote to the really important jobs. Besides, sometimes they are under such pressure that they forget which jobs are important.

The manager also faces another difficulty. He finds that other people take up a lot of his time, so that he has little time of his own. Just as he is ready to tackle that report, a customer will ring up unexpectedly. No sooner has he hung up than Bill, from Sales, drops by his office for a chat. He works on the report for a few minutes, then the Personnel Manager calls him. Could he interview someone tomorrow afternoon? And so it goes on. The manager must constantly respond to the demands that others make on his time.

Things do not get better as he climbs higher in the organisation. In fact, they get worse. The higher he goes, the more demands will be made upon his time.

Because of the nature of the manager's work, it is not easy for him to be effective. He will have difficulty distinguishing between important and less important tasks. He will often feel that he has too many demands on his precious time and at times will find it difficult to turn people away. There will always be someone – or something – to divert him from what he should really be doing.

Effective managers learn how to manage their time. They cut out unproductive activities. They never forget that time cannot be replaced.

Before being able to control his time, the manager must find out how he is actually using it. He must know where it goes. The best way to do this is to record how he uses time. The usual method is to log the tasks he performs. Either he or his secretary keeps an exact record of how he spends his working

day, or week. The manager should not rely on memory when
logging time. Not many executives can remember, at the end
of the day, all the things they did during the day – all the
telephone calls, chats, interruptions, work on the computer,
letter-writing and so on. One way of logging time is to note
down all the activities and indicate how long they took. Thus,
the log of an executive could look something like this:

START	ACTIVITY	TIME TAKEN (MINUTES)
0830	Arrive. Make coffee.	5
0835	Read through files.	10
0845	Check diary.	10
0855	Telephone call from Bob.	5
0900	Wife phones.	5
0905	Chat with secretary.	7
0912	Read mail.	4
0916	Peter says hello. Talks about last night's TV programme on Aids.	5
0921	Read mail.	10
0931	Dictate letters to secretary.	15
0946	Telephone call from supplier.	12
0958	Telephone call to Accounts Department to follow up supplier's complaint.	7

This logging of time should be done once or twice a year. It
shows the executive how he actually spends his time at work –
not how he thinks he spends it.

Once the manager has an accurate picture of how he uses
time, he can analyse the time log. This will help him to re-think
and re-plan his work schedule. He can ask questions such as:
Are some of the things I'm doing wasting time? Should I be
spending more time on certain activities? Could other people
do some of the tasks? Am I wasting the time of my colleagues?

As a result of this analysis, the effective manager will start
getting rid of unproductive, time-wasting activities. He will
learn to say 'No' more often to people demanding his time. He
will start turning down some of those requests to give
speeches and attend luncheons. He will, in short, be more
discriminating in using time.

He will also get rid of some activities which can be done just as
well by someone else. Knowing how to delegate is an essential
skill of a manager. This does not mean, of course, that he will
be forever 'passing the buck' to subordinates! But, where
possible, he will try to create more time so that he can attend
to important tasks.

Having recorded and analysed time, he can now re-shape his
schedule. It is up to him how he does this. Some managers like
to set aside certain times for important tasks. For example,

70 they may work at home one day a week. Others earmark certain days of the week for particular activities, e.g. management meetings, production scheduling, staff appraisal sessions etc. One manager is known to spend ninety minutes at home, in his study, before setting off to work. A common method of managing time is as follows. The manager works out all the jobs he must do in the coming day or week. Then he lists the tasks in order of priority. He also sets deadlines for carrying out the more important activities.

80 Peter Drucker, the American expert on management, believes that effective executives work systematically to manage time. They must acquire this 'habit of mind', this ability to use time efficiently. Below, you can see an example of how Mr Drucker manages his own time.

> MR. PETER F. DRUCKER
> GREATLY APPRECIATES YOUR KIND INTEREST, BUT IS
> UNABLE TO: CONTRIBUTE ARTICLES OR FOREWORDS;
> COMMENT ON MANUSCRIPTS OR BOOKS; TAKE PART IN
> PANELS AND SYMPOSIA; JOIN COMMITTEES OR BOARDS OF
> ANY KIND; ANSWER QUESTIONNAIRES; GIVE INTERVIEWS;
> AND APPEAR ON RADIO OR TELEVISION.

taken from *How to Manage*, Editor Ray Wild, William Heinemann London.

Understanding the main points

1 *Complete the following sentences, using your own words.*

1 Because the work of a manager is 'fragmented' ....
....

2 As executives take up more senior positions within a company they often find that ....
....

3 A time log is useful to a manager because ....
....

2 *Note down the ways in which managers can make sure that they have enough time to carry out their most important functions.*

1 ....
2 ....
3 ....
4 ....

3 *Note down the three stages of the system used by some executives in order to manage their time effectively.*

1 ....
2 ....
3 ....

Vocabulary focus

Find words or phrases in the text which mean the same as the following:

1 ordinary, unimportant (paragraph 1)
2 deal with (paragraph 2)
3 pays a casual visit (paragraph 2)
4 claims, requirements (paragraph 3)
5 valuable (paragraph 4)
6 get rid of, omit (paragraph 5)
7 depend (paragraph 6)
8 refusing (paragraph 8)
9 able to choose the best (paragraph 8)
10 keep for a special purpose (paragraph 10)
11 needing attention before other things (paragraph 10)

1 Compound nouns and phrases with *time*
What do the following mean?
Each member of your group should choose one of the compound nouns or phrases and explain what it means.

1 time-card
2 time-lag
3 time-and-motion study
4 time-zone
5 time-switch (referring to a machine)
6 time-limit
7 time-sharing (referring to a computer)
8 timekeeper
9 to be on time
10 to be in time

Now, if you are still unsure of the meanings of any of the above, check them in your dictionary.

Make sentences of your own using five of the above.

2 *Rewrite the following sentences, replacing the words in italics with words and phrases from the box below. Make any other necessary changes.*

for the time being	in no time at all	in good time
ahead of its time	at one time	from time to time
work against time	before one's time	

1 The salesman decided to get to the meeting *fairly early* so that he could prepare his presentation.
2 I can get these brochures and price lists off to you *almost immediately*.
3 I must stay with my company *for the moment* because jobs are hard to find.
4 We *have little time left* to complete the project.
5 I am going to retire *earlier than expected*.
6 The technology used in the Lotus car is *very advanced indeed*.
7 *Formerly* I worked on the shop floor of the factory. Now, I'm Managing Director. Times have changed!
8 We check the machines *at intervals*.

3 *Complete the following sentences with the correct word or phrase (a, b, c or d).*

1 It is only a .... before the firm closes down.
   a matter of time **b** course of time **c** length of time
   d stage of time
2 There is usually a .... between when you sell goods and when you get paid by your customer.
   a time-log **b** time-delay **c** time-hold **d** time-lag
3 Meetings are necessary, but they can be very ....
   a time-consuming **b** time-saving **c** time-losing
   d time-costing
4 The fact that many small shops are closing down is a .... of the times.
   a mark **b** image **c** sight **d** sign
5 It is important that we get the .... of our sales campaign right. We must not have it too early or too late.
   a moment **b** point **c** timing **d** time
6 Some workers like to .... doing a job.
   a wait their time **b** spare their time **c** spend their time
   d take their time
7 When I visited our subsidiary in West Germany, I had .... – everyone was most hospitable.
   a wonderful experiences **b** the best of times **c** good times
   d the time of my life
8 I bumped into a former colleague recently. We had a drink together ....
   a for the sake of good times **b** for old times' sake
   c in memory of good old times **d** for the good old days

4 Inversion

No sooner has he *hung up* than Bill drops by his office ... (line 15)

When the following words and phrases *begin* a sentence, the subject and verb are inverted.

> under no circumstances   no sooner   at no time
> not until   hardly   scarcely   rarely   seldom
> never (before)   only   little

Study the following pairs of sentences.

1a You should not smoke in this area under any circumstances.
  b *Under no circumstances should* you *smoke* in this area.
2a The company has never had such a successful year.
  b *Never has* the company *had* such a successful year.

Note that the second sentence of each pair is more emphatic than the first and that the subject and auxiliary verb are inverted. Inversion is used mainly in formal English.

A *Make all the changes and additions necessary to produce correct sentences from the following sets of words and phrases.*

e.g. No sooner/I start/write/report/someone/telephoned/me.
   No sooner had I started to write the report when someone telephoned me.

1 Hardly/I finish/phone/my boss/drop into/my office.
2 Under no circumstances/manager/rely on/memory/log/time.

3 Not until/two years ago/company/begin/make/profits.
4 Only/after three hours' negotiations/we succeed/reach agreement/the final contract.
5 Rarely/our company/fail/meet/delivery dates.

B *Put the following words in the correct order, so as to make correct sentences. Begin each sentence with the word* underlined.

e.g. have efficient I met a more <u>rarely</u> manager
Rarely have I met a more efficient manager.

1 been <u>seldom</u> after so I meeting have tired a
2 I my office sooner <u>no</u> in arrive rang did telephone the than
3 disturbed no I be must circumstances <u>under</u>
4 on did a <u>only</u> of lot the market put research after they the product
5 any to relax does she <u>rarely</u> have time
6 1986 <u>not</u> factory our able to until were we buy own
7 <u>little</u> redundant that soon he be made he realise does will
8 by boss dropped my <u>hardly</u> report started had the I when

COMMUNICATION SKILLS

FUNCTIONS

Stating priorities
Giving advice

Dialogue

Listen to the following conversation, in which an executive discusses a business trip to England with a colleague.

MIKE   It's not going to be easy to plan the trip, you know. I've only got four days there, and a lot to pack in during that time.
PAUL   Like what?
MIKE   Well, for one thing, it's essential that I spend at least a day in Sheffield – with our associate company.
PAUL   Uh huh. And what else?
MIKE   I must spend another day at the National Exhibition Centre in Birmingham. It's one of the main purposes of my visit.
PAUL   Of course. That should give us a good idea of what the competition will be bringing out in the fall.
MIKE   Exactly. And then I should spend a morning in London. I'd like to visit the Design Centre, among other things.
PAUL   Interesting. While you're there, it would be helpful if you could see Jim Seymour. You *did* promise you'd visit him if you were in London.
MIKE   Right, it might be a good idea to drop in on him, I agree.
PAUL   If I were you, I'd try to stay an extra day or two. There are plenty of things you could do for us there.
MIKE   Oh, I don't know, I'm really busy here at the moment, you know.
PAUL   Yes, I know you are. I think you ought to talk to Dan. I'm sure he'd do some of your work while you're away.

```
                    STATING PRIORITIES
                Saying what it is essential to do

I've got to  ⎫
I must       ⎬  visit the National Exhibition Centre.
I have to    ⎪
I need to    ⎭

It's essential   ⎫   ⎧ I go          ⎫
It's vital       ⎬   ⎨ for me to go  ⎬  to Sheffield.
It's important   ⎭   ⎩               ⎭

                Saying what it is desirable to do

I should     ⎫
I ought to   ⎬  spend a morning in London.

It would be a good idea to     ⎫
It would be helpful/useful to  ⎬  talk to Jim Seymour.

                     GIVING ADVICE

If I were you, I'd              ⎫
I think you ought to/should     ⎬  try to stay a day longer.

You could always get Dan to do some of your work.

I would advise you to        ⎫
I think it would be best to  ⎬  talk to Dan. (formal)
It might be advisable to     ⎭
```

Role play

Instructions

Work in pairs.

One of you has to make a business trip to France next week. You will fly to Paris, arriving at 8 a.m. on 5 June and flying back from either Paris or Nice at approximately 8 p.m. on 7 June. While in France you will have a number of things to do – activities which fall into one of the following categories:

(i) essential
(ii) desirable
(iii) non-essential

You must plan the trip and work out a schedule for the three-day visit. You are not sure whether you will be able to fit in all of the activities you have planned for the visit and so you ask a colleague for advice and help in drawing up a schedule.

EXECUTIVE TRAVELLING TO FRANCE

Read the notes on page 86 and then explain to your colleague what you wish to do in France, indicating which activities have priority (essential, desirable or non-essential?).

When your colleague has completed the table on page 87, work out a schedule for the trip together, deciding which activities (if any) should be dropped.

Finally, compare your schedule with those of the other groups.

Executive travelling to France – Notes for visit

The list of activities is given below, with their order of priority. This is shown as follows:

    *** essential
    ** desirable
    * non-essential

The city where the activity takes place, and the time required for it, are also indicated.

*** meeting with an agent to finalise a contract	Nice	3 hours
** visit to a department store to buy gifts for the family	Paris	2 hours
* visit to a trade fair	Paris	½ day
* lunch at the French Chamber of Commerce	Bordeaux	2½ hours
** Social visit to the company's biggest customer – game of golf perhaps?	Lyon	½ day
*** visit to a glassware firm to discuss product range, price lists, terms of payment etc.	Nice	1 day
*** meetings with customers	Paris	6 hours
*** meeting with the Mayor of Lyon	Lyon	1 hour

Table (to be completed by colleague)

ACTIVITY	PRIORITY	PLACE	TIME REQUIRED
		Bordeaux	
Visit to trade fair			
		Lyon	
			3 hours
	essential		
			1 day
	desirable		
			2 hours

PRIORITY CLASSIFICATION
essential
desirable
non-essential

Case study

The burnt-out manager

Brian is Advertising and Promotions Manager for Interior Design Concepts, a firm specialising in home improvement products. About a month ago, he became worried about his health. He had not been sleeping well and was tired and depressed. He went to see the company doctor who encouraged him to talk about his work. This is what Brian said.

'Somehow I never seem to get on top of my work. Like yesterday, I had three really important things to do: a contract with the Hussein brothers, that had to be ready for typing; then there was the mobile sales display, that still needed to be set up properly; and the other big job was the work assessment report for a new member of staff – that was already overdue. Do you know, I never finished any of them? The day was a nightmare, from start to finish.

To begin with, we couldn't find the contract. My secretary – Sheila – and I spent over half an hour looking for it. I was going out of my mind! Imagine the fuss if we'd lost it. We found it in the end, hidden under a huge pile of documents on my desk. I can't blame Sheila, she's only been in the job a couple of months. She's still getting used to the office routine.

Anyway, I got started on the contract, then I needed to check some financial details. I tried to call Julia, our accountant. Just my luck, she was out of her office. Do you know, I must have called her at least five times that morning – nothing doing. I suppose I could have carried on with the contract but I was really fed up. I called my assistant – Ralph – to my office and we started putting together the mobile sales display.

We were doing well, actually, till my boss dropped in unexpectedly. Well, obviously, I stopped what I was doing – he is the boss, after all. He talked about his trip to Saudi Arabia and Oman, he's going there at the end of next week. Then he asked about the contract for the Hussein brothers, reminding me that I'd promised to have it ready for him yesterday. He's taking the contract with him next week. Why did I promise to have it ready so early?

I never did finish the mobile display. I had to rush over to the printers to pick up some catalogues. I suppose I could have sent Ralph, but he would have taken all day. I dropped work on the display and started the assessment report. After four interruptions from phone calls, I told Sheila not to put any more calls through *under any circumstances*. Well, I ended up taking the assessment report home and working on it until midnight. No wonder I'm worn out today, doctor.

This morning, one of our sales people phoned. Absolutely furious because he couldn't get through to me yesterday afternoon. Where was the mobile sales display I'd promised him? What a nerve! Some people expect miracles, don't they?'

Instructions

In groups of two or three, discuss the following questions.

1 What mistakes is Brian making in his use of time?
2 What can he do in order to become a more effective manager?
3 An expert on time management has listed a number of major timewasters – things that hold executives back and cause them to waste time. What do you think were the main items on this list?

WRITING

Interior Design Concepts – the firm which Brian works for – recently organised a one-day management training course entitled 'Time Management'. It was highly successful and led to a lively discussion among the company's executives.

Unfortunately, a number of managers were unable to attend the course. For this reason, the Personnel Department prepared a short report summarising the main points of the course. The document was intended to give executives advice on how to manage their time more effectively.

Imagine that you have been asked to prepare the report. Complete the memorandum below.

INTERIOR DESIGN CONCEPTS

MEMORANDUM

To: All managers

From: Personnel Department   Date: 5 August 1988

Using your time more effectively

Following our one-day course on Time Management, we thought it might be useful to outline the main points which were made during the various sessions. I hope the information given below will be useful to you.

....

....

Understanding the main points

Listen to the following conversation and answer the questions below.

1 What is Marion unhappy about?
2 Why was last Friday such an important day?
3 What did Marion have to do last Sunday?
4 According to Polly, Gerald is extremely good at planning his time.
5 *Note down the things he does to make the most effective use of his time.*

1 ....
2 ....
3 ....
4 ....
5 ....

Vocabulary focus

Listen again and identify the phrases or expressions in the conversation which mean the same as the following:

1 Edward's really irritating me!

'.. !'

2 He never seems to have enough time.

'.. .'

3 He wouldn't listen to me.

'.. .'

4 Perhaps I could give Edward some useful pieces of advice?

'.. ?'

5 He doesn't postpone them (the important jobs) until later.

'.. .'

6 Gerald never leaves a job until he's finished it.

'.. .'

7 Only a fool would dare to interrupt him then!

'.. !'

8 He's good at delegating responsibility to subordinates.

'.. .'

TIME MANAGEMENT

89

8 Motivation

DISCUSSION

Answer the following questions, then, in groups of two or three, compare your answers.

1 What sort of things motivate people to do their job well?
   List all the things you can think of.

2 If you won a great deal of money, for example in a lottery, would you continue working?
   If not, do you think you would lose anything by giving up work?

READING

The work of managers is to ensure that staff work efficiently in an organisation. To achieve this, it is clear that managers must know what motivates people. By understanding the factors influencing motivation, they can create the conditions in which employees will perform to their maximum potential.

One of the best known theories of motivation was put forward by an American psychologist, Abraham Maslow, in a book entitled *Motivation and Personality* (1954). In his theory, he presents a hierarchy of needs. He identified certain basic human needs and classified them in an ascending order of importance. Basic needs were at the bottom of the hierarchy, higher needs at the top. His classification is shown below:

10

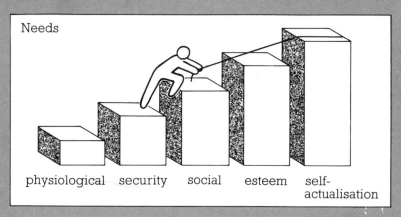

Needs

physiological security social esteem self-actualisation

Physiological needs
These were things required to sustain life like food, water, air, sleep etc. Until these needs are satisfied, Maslow believed, other needs will not motivate people.

Security needs
They are the needs to be free from danger, physical pain and loss of a job. They include the need for clothing and shelter.

Social needs
A human being needs to belong to a group, to be liked and loved, to feel accepted by others and to develop affiliations.

Esteem needs
After people have satisfied their social needs, they want to have self-respect and to be esteemed by others. They have a need for power, status, respect and self-confidence.

Self-actualisation needs
These are the highest needs, according to Maslow. They are the desire to develop, to maximise potential and to achieve one's goals.

Maslow said that people satisfied their needs in a systematic way. When a need had been met, it stopped being a motivating factor. For example, if a person was starving, he would not be too concerned about security and social needs. But once he had enough food, he would start thinking about those other needs.

Research into Maslow's theory has not been very conclusive. Studies have tended to show that needs vary greatly among individuals. At the higher levels in a company, self-actualising needs may be very strong whereas at lower levels, social and security needs may be dominant.

Another theory of motivation, which has been very popular with managers, is Frederick Herzberg's 'two-factor' theory. Herzberg conducted a number of studies in the region of Pittsburg, USA, in the late 1950s. He concluded that at work there are certain factors which cause job satisfaction while others lead to dissatisfaction.

The group of factors bringing about satisfaction were called 'motivators'. They include things like a challenging job, responsibility, advancement, recognition etc. These factors give rise to positive satisfaction. Herzberg called the other group of factors 'hygiene' or 'maintenance' factors. These include company policy and administration, salary and fringe benefits, job security, status and personal life. These factors are considered to be only 'dissatisfiers', not motivators. If they do not exist, they cause dissatisfaction. If they do exist in quality and quantity, they do not, however, give increased satisfaction.

Herzberg's two-factor theory is shown in the following diagram. It is worth noting that the hygiene factors refer to the *context* of the job – the conditions of work – while the motivators refer to job *content.*

Herzberg's motivation-hygiene theory

motivators	achievement challenging work the work itself career prospects responsibility recognition
hygiene factors	company policy and administration salary and fringe benefits quality of supervision relationship with colleagues job security status personal life work conditions

Hygiene factors are essential if workers are to be motivated. As one writer has aptly put it, they deal with the question 'Why work here?'. The motivators deal with the question 'Why work harder?'.

If Herzberg's theory is true, it means that managers must pay great attention to job content. They must find ways of making jobs more challenging and interesting. As a result, managers
70 in the USA and elsewhere have recently been showing great interest in job enrichment programmes. The idea of such programmes is to make jobs more challenging and to give the worker a sense of achievement.

Sweden has been leading the way in this respect. At one car plant, for example, Volvo workers assemble the whole of a car rather than do a few simple operations. In a glass factory, production workers have complete control over the work process in the grinding and polishing department. Other workers have helped to build and design paper mills. Job
80 enrichment is undoubtedly catching on fast in Sweden.

Understanding the main points

Decide whether the following statements are true or false.

		True	False
1	According to Maslow people are not concerned about achieving their personal goals in life unless they have satisfied their physiological needs.	☐	☐
2	Senior managers who want to become company directors have self-actualisation needs which they wish to satisfy.	☐	☐
3	Herzberg, like Maslow, believes that people satisfy their needs systematically.	☐	☐
4	Herzberg believed that workers would not necessarily work harder if they earned more money.	☐	☐
5	Job security is one of the most important factors which motivates employees.	☐	☐
6	The purpose of job enrichment programmes is to increase worker motivation.	☐	☐

Vocabulary focus

Find words or phrases in the text which mean the same as the following:

1 the most somebody or something is capable of (paragraph 1)
2 system of lower and higher ranks (paragraph 2)
3 respected, admired (paragraph 2, *Esteem needs*)
4 a person's position in relation to others (paragraph 2, *Esteem needs*)
5 final; putting an end to uncertainty (paragraph 4)
6 feeling (paragraph 9)
7 becoming popular or fashionable (paragraph 10)

LANGUAGE STUDY

1 Opposites

Complete the following sentences with words opposite in meaning to the words in italics.

e.g. *interesting* He does not like his job because it is **uninteresting** .

1 *satisfied*   Workers become .... if their jobs offer no challenge.
2 *conclusive*   Since the report was so .... , no recommendations were made.
3 *responsible* .... behaviour by staff can be costly to an organisation.
4 *popular*   Managements become .... if they fail to pay bonuses.
5 *respect*   No manager likes a subordinate to be ....
6 *secure*   A worker who feels .... in his job will probably not be committed to the firm he works for.
7 *social*   People who work .... hours, for example at night-time, generally receive extra pay.
8 *efficient*   Nowadays, it is not easy to get rid of an employee who is ....

2 Idiomatic uses of *catch*
catch on (line 80)

A *Match the following with the correct definitions.*

1 catch sight of (v.)   a attract attention
2 catch on (v.)   b pleasant and easily remembered
3 catch out (v.)
4 catch up with (v.)   c draw level with
5 catch one's eye (v.)   d start to burn
6 catch (n.)   e notice suddenly
7 catch-phrase (n.)   f a hidden or unexpected difficulty
8 catchy (adj.)
9 catch fire (v.)   g become popular or fashionable
10 become caught up in (v.)   h trap someone in an error; show someone to be at fault; find someone unprepared
                               i become involved in
                               j a phrase which becomes popular for a while

B *Complete the following sentences with suitable words and phrases with **catch** from the list on page 93.*

1 Everyone liked the .... tune of that TV commercial.
2 Do you think such an extraordinary style of dress will .... ? I can't believe it will.
3 At the car exhibition, that ultra-modern car – like something from outer-space – really .... everyone's ....
4 In the field of high-technology electrical goods, the Koreans are rapidly .... with the Japanese.
5 This business is being sold far too cheaply. I smell a rat somewhere. There must be a ....
6 'Put a tiger in your tank' was a popular .... a few years ago.
7 We were .... a few weeks ago when our main competitor suddenly lowered the prices of their products by 10%.
8 Management buy-outs are becoming more and more common these days. Obviously, the habit is ....
9 While I was going round the factory, I .... a worker who was smoking in a non-smoking area.
10 During one of our tests the prototype of our new hair-drier overheated, causing it to ....

3 Uncountable nouns

Research into Maslow's theory has not been very conclusive. (line 37)

Research is a noun which is usually uncountable. We do *not* say:
    *He carried out *many* research*es*.
    or
    *They have done *a* research into motivation.
Instead, we say:
    He carried out *a great deal of/a lot of* research.
    They have done *some* research into motivation.

Other uncountable nouns
accommodation   advice   experience   equipment
information   knowledge   luggage   machinery   news
progress   travel   weather   damage   work

Notes

1 Uncountable nouns are not used with the indefinite article *a/an*. We can make some of these words countable, however, by saying *a piece of* advice/equipment/research/machinery etc.
2 Uncountable nouns are singular, e.g. the news *is* bad; the advice *was* useful.
3 We do *not* say *some* information*s*/advice*s*/equipment*s* etc.
4 *travel* (noun) means 'the act of travelling',
    e.g. I enjoy foreign travel.
    Use *journey* or *trip* when you mean 'movement from one place to another',
    e.g. I had an interesting trip to Spain recently.

A *Make all the changes and additions necessary to produce correct sentences from the following sets of words and phrases.*

e.g. We buy/new machinery/last week/Japanese manufacturer.
We bought some/a lot of/a great deal of new machinery last week from a Japanese manufacturer.

Note that in some of the sentences below, no article is necessary.

1 Our Production Department/do/research/recently/job enrichment programmes.
2 The management consultants/give us/advice/how to improve/labour relations/the shop floor.
3 We/look/someone/experience/sell/IBM computers.
4 She has/knowledge/hotel industry.
5 It will be difficult/him/find/cheap accommodation/New York.
6 This is/fascinating/research.
7 This morning/supervisor/receive/bad news/important supplier.
8 That was/invaluable/advice.

B *Complete the following sentences in any way you wish, using the words in brackets.*

1 Maslow carried out .... (research)
2 I asked my boss .... (advice)
3 Is it true that .... ? (travel)
4 Have you made .... ? (progress)
5 I went to a business library .... (information)
6 I looked out of my office window and said,
'What .... !' (weather)

COMMUNICATION SKILLS

FUNCTIONS

Describing trends in graphs and charts
Expressing figures approximately

The graph below presents the sales of Trafalgar Products Ltd, a British company which makes hi-fi equipment and whose main markets are Great Britain, the USA and Europe. The graph shows the company's performance over the period 1984–88 and includes estimated sales for 1989 and 1990.

TOTAL SALES IN GREAT BRITAIN, USA AND EUROPE

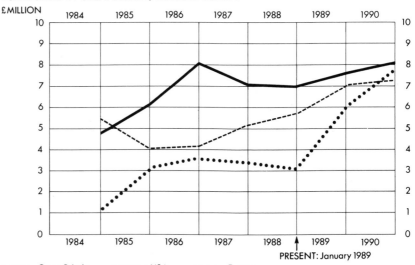

PRESENT: January 1989

—— Great Britain •••••• USA ------- Europe

Listen to the following passage, in which the Overseas Sales Manager describes the trend of sales in the USA to a group of managers:

'As you can see from the graph, results have been good during the five-year period. We're extremely satisfied with our growth in the area. Sales rose from just under £1m in 1984 to £3m in 1988 – that's an increase of 200%.

Looking at the trend in sales during that time, you can see that during 1984, they stayed roughly at the same level. Then, during 1985, they increased sharply to £3m. We continued to do well in 1986 when our sales reached a peak of just over £3½m. In 1987 they levelled off and last year dropped back to £3m.

The future in the USA looks very bright for us. We've got a new distributor there – a company with a nation-wide sales network. We estimate that sales will double, and even treble in the next two years. By the end of 1990 – this is an optimistic forecast – they should be in the region of £8m.

Role play 1

Instructions

Work in pairs. Take it in turns to play the role of the Overseas Sales Director and describe to each other the company's performance in Great Britain and Europe. Use the words and phrases in the tables below to help you prepare what you are going to say.

Describing trends in graphs

UP ↗		DOWN ↘	
NOUN	VERB	NOUN	VERB
an increase	to increase	a fall	to fall
a rise	to rise	a drop	to drop
an improvement	to improve	a decline	to decline
a growth	to grow		to go down
	to go up		to fall off
	to take off		
	to shoot up		

NO CHANGE →
to remain stable
to level off
to stay at the same level

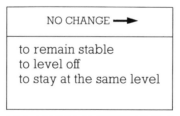

to peak
to reach a peak

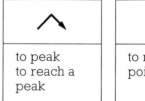

to reach a low point

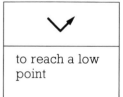

KEY PHRASES
to rise *from* £1m *to* £3m
to fall *from* £5m *to* £4½m
to increase *by* 50%
to drop *by* 10%

USEFUL PHRASES	
WITH NOUNS	a rapid/sharp/dramatic/substantial (increase) a slow/gradual/steady (decline) a great/large/considerable (rise) a small/slight (drop)
WITH VERBS	to (increase) rapidly/sharply/dramatically/ substantially/slowly etc. to double/triple/quadruple

Role play 2

You are a Sales Manager in Trafalgar Products. You and your sales team are responsible for England and Scotland. This memo has just arrived on your desk.

 Trafalgar Products Ltd

MEMORANDUM

To: Sales Manager   Date: 9 January 1989
     (England and Scotland)
From: Chairman

Sales presentation: 20 January 1989

Following our telephone conversation, I confirm that you - and members of your sales team - will be making a sales presentation to members of the Board at 2p.m. on 20 January. As agreed, your presentation will take the following form:

    1 Total sales (England/Scotland) for the year ending 1988

    2 The trend in total sales over the period 1984-88

    3 The regional distribution of sales, with indications of areas of growth and 'problem' areas

    4 Sales forecasts

I hope you and your team will give the Board a clear picture of our sales performance in England and Scotland.

May I remind you, finally, to provide 12 copies of any graphs or other visual material which you may wish to circulate to Board members.

Instructions

Divide into four groups. Groups 1 and 2 should prepare sales presentations, as instructed in the memo from the Chairman. See also the table on page 98. Groups 3 and 4 are going to play the roles of members of the Board of Directors. (See page 98.)

CHART A
Sales of hi-fi equipment in England and Scotland (£,000)

	1984	1985	1986	1987	1988	FORECAST 1989	FORECAST 1990
A	175	195	250	320	410	450	500
B	750	800	875	825	780	900	1,000
C	1,200	1,850	2,550	2,375	2,220	2,500	2,600
D	900	1,275	1,770	1,410	1,500	1,600	1,750
E	620	890	1,380	990	1,000	1,100	1,150
F	660	635	625	615	480	500	525
G	510	495	595	605	610	625	650
TOTAL	4,815	6,140	8,045	7,140	7,000	7,675	8,175

A South-West England
B South-East England (excluding London)
C London
D The Midlands
E North-West England
F North-East England
G Scotland

Case study

Shaking up the sales force

Jill Alexander joined Trafalgar Products just six months ago. As Sales Manager for England and Scotland, she led a team of sales people covering seven sales areas. Each salesperson was responsible for one of the areas.

When she arrived, Managing Director Don McCaul was clear about what he expected from her. 'Your job is to get the sales force moving again,' he said. 'And to halt the decline in sales. If you can organise the sales effort properly, and motivate the staff, there's no reason why we can't get back to where we were two years ago.' And he added confidently, 'We've got high-quality products – as good as, if not better than, the stuff coming in from Japan.'

After a few weeks in the job, Jill realised she had taken on a tough assignment. The morale in the sales force was rock-bottom. For the last two years, sales revenue had been dropping sharply. And that meant lower commissions for the sales staff. Salesmen are ambitious people – they're never happy when their earnings drop.

A short while ago, Jill had an unpleasant conversation with Jim Braddock, one of the top salesmen. Jill had queried an item on Jim's expense account – a high-priced dinner – and Jim had got rather hot under the collar. 'Why are you going on and on about one lousy dinner?' he had shouted at her. 'I'm not exactly earning a fortune here. I reckon I could earn twice as much if I were somewhere else.' 'That's up to you,' Jill had replied, though she had no wish to lose a salesman of Jim's ability.

Jill had an unpleasant surprise just after that when she received a memo from Frank Collins, the company's Finance Director. Frank had pointed out to her that the number of unpaid customer accounts was high. 'Can't you tell your sales staff to get on to slow-paying customers and put pressure on them to settle their bills?' he asked her.

'Can't you tell your sales staff to get on to slow-paying customers and put pressure on them to settle their bills?'

Something had to be done to improve the performance of the sales team. After thinking carefully about the problem, Jill came up with the following proposals:

1 Shake-up the sales force
   Sales staff who were mobile would be moved to new areas. By 'exchanging' areas they would face a new sales challenge. Because of this, they should get back their energy and enthusiasm for the job.

2 Cash bonuses
   All sales staff would receive the same basic salary. In addition, they would earn cash bonuses every three months when they exceeded the sales target for their area. The size of the cash bonus would depend on the percentage increase in sales over and above the target. The Sales Manager, together with the Managing Director, would agree the targets for each area.

3 Prizes
   Each quarter, the top sales representative would receive a prize. This would be an all-expenses-paid weekend holiday anywhere in Britain.
   Each year, the top three sales representatives would be given prizes. The top salesperson would have a holiday for two in a foreign country; those in second and third place would get cash

prizes. When selecting the winners, the Sales Manager would take into account factors such as volume of sales, number of sales calls per week and success in chasing up slow payers.

4 New customer accounts
Cash bonuses would be paid for all new customer accounts.

5 Slow payers
A cash bonus would only be paid to a sales representative when the customer had settled the invoice. In other words, unpaid orders would not be taken into account when a cash bonus was calculated.

Instructions

The Sales Manager has called a meeting to hear the sales representatives' reactions to the proposals.

One of you should play the role of the Sales Manager. Another acts as Assistant Sales Manager. The other members of the class are the sales representatives. First study your role-card and then prepare for the meeting.

SALES MANAGER AND ASSISTANT SALES MANAGER

Discuss together how you think the sales representatives will react to the proposals. Prepare some arguments to persuade them that they should accept the proposals. Remember that the company is in a difficult financial situation and radical changes *must* be made.

SALES REPRESENTATIVES

In groups of two or three discuss the proposals. Decide which ones are useful and which ones would not be effective. Note down the reasons for your views. Also, make your own suggestions for improving sales. Finally, express your views at the meeting with the Sales Manager and Assistant Sales Manager. Argue your case as firmly as possible!

WRITING

You are the Sales Manager of Trafalgar Products responsible for England and Scotland. The Chairman has asked you to write a sales report since the Board of Directors will be discussing the company's performance in England and Scotland at their next meeting.

The Chairman wishes the report to contain the following information:

1 a summary of Trafalgar Products' sales performance in England and Scotland over the last five years plus a sales forecast for the next two years;
2 an analysis of the problems faced by the Sales Department plus a plan for improving sales in England and Scotland. The Board would also like to know the reasons for any of the actions which are proposed.

You may organise the report as you wish. However, you may find the following layout useful:

TITLE	*Choose a suitable title for the report.*
PARAGRAPH 1 (INTRODUCTION)	*Say **who** asked you to write the report; **why** it has been written and **what** it is about.*
PARAGRAPH 2	*Choose a suitable heading. Summarise the sales performance in England and Scotland, indicating significant regional trends and the reasons for these.*
PARAGRAPH 3	*Choose a suitable heading. Summarise the problems facing the Sales Department.*
PARAGRAPH 4	*Choose a suitable heading. Outline your plans for improving sales, bearing in mind points made at your recent sales meeting.*
PARAGRAPH 5	*Summarise the most important points of your report and principal recommendations.*
SIGNATURE	*Sign the report and write your position in the company under your name.*
DATE	*Date the report.*

To: All directors
From: Sales Manager (England and Scotland)

(TITLE)

(INTRODUCTION)

PARAGRAPH 1 ....

....

(HEADING)

PARAGRAPH 2 ....

....

....

(HEADING)

PARAGRAPH 3 ....

....

....

(HEADING)

PARAGRAPH 4 ....

....

....

(CONCLUSION)

PARAGRAPH 5 ....

....

(SIGNATURE)

....

(POSITION IN COMPANY)   (DATE)

....

Understanding the main points

Listen to the following conversation and then decide whether the statements below are true or false.

	True	False
1 Some employees at Trafalgar Products are absent from work more often than they need to be.	☐	☐
2 Kerry Webb suggests that all employees who are absent should be interviewed by the Personnel Department.	☐	☐
3 At Kerry Webb's previous firm, the employees made fun of those people who took too much time off work.	☐	☐
4 In the American scheme described by Frank Collins, absenteeism was reduced by giving cash bonuses to employees who had a 100% attendance record.	☐	☐
5 None of the other executives at the meeting agreed with the scheme which Frank Collins suggested.	☐	☐

Vocabulary focus

Listen again and identify the phrases or expressions in the conversation which mean the same as the following:

1 Actually, Sara, I think Frank's right about this.

' .... '

2 Yes, I agree with you, Don.

' .... '

3 They'd know we were watching them carefully.

' .... '

4 (People) told you to improve your behaviour.

' .... '

5 That's the first point to you, Sara! (as in sport)

' .... !'

6 And hardly anyone took time off work, unless they couldn't avoid it.

' .... '

7 In any case, the unions would be strongly against it (the idea).

' .... '

8 It (the idea) wouldn't be very popular here.

' .... '

9 Performance appraisal

DISCUSSION

Jane Mitchell is Sales Manager of Scorpio, a sports goods firm. Bob is a member of the sales team. One of the area sales managers is about to retire, and Bob is in line for the job. He is the right age, has over ten years' sales experience, and gets on well with his colleagues.

Each year, Jane Mitchell evaluates the performance of her sales staff. When she does these performance appraisals, she studies the work record of the person during the previous twelve months. Jane is especially interested in 'critical incidents'. These are occasions when the salesperson seems to have performed exceptionally well or badly.

Look at these 'critical incidents' concerning Bob. Then decide if he is suitable for the job of Area Sales Manager. Give reasons for your decision.

Date	Incident
February	**Incorrect Filling-in of Call-Sheet**
	Bob had not filled in his call-sheets correctly. He noted down calls to three customers on different days. In fact, he visited all the customers on one day. I asked Bob why he had done this. He explained that his daughter had asked him to attend the first, public exhibition of her paintings. He had needed to have a "free" afternoon to do this. Bob promised me that he would never again fill in his sheet incorrectly.
April	**Sales Promotion**
	Bob persuaded a local tennis club to let us sponsor their competition. Thanks to him, the company received a lot of publicity in local newspapers. There was a front-page photograph in one newspaper of Bob handing out the prizes. According to Bob, the club now recommends to all its members that they use clothing and equipment made by our firm.
June	**Time-keeping**
	On several occasions, Bob has failed to call on his first customer until eleven o'clock in the morning. It is, however, our Department's policy that first calls should be made before 9.30a.m. I asked Bob what the problem was. He said that he had worked late the previous evening. Therefore, he had been too tired to make an early start the next day.
September	**Special Display**
	Bob persuaded a sports shop to set up a special display of our clothing and equipment. He was able to do this because he had become friendly with the shop's manager. It seems that Bob played squash with the manager twice a week at a local club. As a result of the display, sales of our goods to the shop are almost double what they were previously.
November	**Sales Reports**
	Bob's sales report was sent in late — for the third month running. Enclosed with the report was a letter of apology. "Sorry this report is so late," Bob wrote. "But please note, sales for the quarter are up 28% ! ! ! Am I forgiven?"

Most organisations have some form of performance appraisal of their employees. The appraisals are usually carried out once a year. The manager makes an evaluation of the performance of the subordinate. This involves filling out a form or writing a report on the person concerned. After this, there is a meeting at which the two parties discuss the appraisal. A performance appraisal is, then, a judgement on how well a person is doing his/her work.

Why do organisations carry out appraisals? Recently, in the
10   United States, some organisations were asked why they used staff appraisals. Some of the findings of this survey are given below, in Figure 1.

Figure 1

USES OF APPRAISAL			
Uses	Small organisations (%)	Large organisations (%)	All (%)
* Compensation	80.6	62.2	71.3
Performance improvement	49.7	60.6	55.2
Feedback	20.6	37.8	29.3
Promotion	29.1	21.1	25.1
Documentation	11.4	10.0	10.7

*salary

Appraisals help organisations to reward staff properly. They are useful when decisions have to be made about salary increases and bonuses. In addition, they are needed when managers are considering transferring or promoting staff. In these situations, they provide up-to-date information about an individual's performance, skills and career objectives.

An important purpose of appraisals is to give the subordinate
20   feedback on how he/she is performing. The manager can talk to the subordinate about the strengths and weaknesses of his/her performance. He/She can also discuss how the subordinate can learn to work more effectively.

At appraisal interviews, subordinates can not only talk about their future, but also seek guidance from the manager. The interview may help them to think more realistically about their goals. Besides doing this, it gives the subordinate the opportunity to ask the manager for further training.

There are many methods of evaluating a person's performance
30   at work. Some of the better-known methods are described below:

A traditional method has been to give a 'rating'. The subordinate's evaluation is based on traits – qualities – that he/she shows in his/her work. Subordinates are judged on such things as knowledge of the job, reliability, initiative and sense of responsibility. The manager rates the subordinate by marking a letter or figure on a scale. For example, the rating could be A–E, where A indicates outstanding and E unsatisfactory. This type of rating sometimes includes performance factors such as quality of work, productivity and attendance. Figure 2 gives an example of such a rating form.

Figure 2

```
Name _____

Position_____

Department_____          Circle appropriate rating

Factors                                      Rating

                    OUTSTANDING  VERY GOOD   GOOD  SATISFACTORY  UNSATISFACTORY
1 Knowledge of the job   A          B         C        D            E

2 Reliability            A          B         C        D            E

3 Cooperation            A          B         C        D            E

4 Initiative             A          B         C        D            E

5 Quality of work        A          B         C        D            E

6 Sense of responsibilty A          B         C        D            E

7 Productivity           A          B         C        D            E

8 Punctuality            A          B         C        D            E

Reviewed by:_____

Employee's signature and comments_____

_____

Date:_____
```

However, the most popular form of appraisal, in Britain and the United States, is Management by Objectives. This appraisal is based on a person's performance, and how well he/she is achieving his/her goals. The manager and the subordinate agree on a certain number of objectives, which should be achieved in a given period of time. The focus is on results, not personality traits. An example of an MBO evaluation report for sales representatives is given in Figure 3.

Figure 3

OBJECTIVES SET	Period objective	Accomplishments	Variance
1 Number of sales calls	100	104	+4%
2 Number of new customers contacted	20	18	−10%
3 Number of wholesalers stocking new product 117	30	30	0%
4 Sales of product 12	10,000	9,750	−2.5%
5 Sales of product 17	17,000	18,700	+10%
6 Customer complaints/service calls	35	11	−68.6%
7 Number of sales reports in home office within 1 day of end of month	12	10	−17%

Another appraisal method is worth mentioning too. This is the
Critical Incident Method. With this system, the manager keeps
a record of good and unsatisfactory examples (incidents) of a
person's work. (See page 103.) These are kept in a file and
reviewed with the manager when the interview takes place.
An advantage of the system is that the manager has to think
about the subordinate's performance throughout the year.
Furthermore, specific examples of the person's work can be
looked at and discussed at the appraisal interview. Below are
some examples of critical incidents for a factory manager,
recorded by his/her superior, in this case the Production
Director.

Figure 4

```
                    Examples of critical incidents:
                    Factory Manager


     Duties                      Critical Incidents
     Schedule production         The manager ensured that 90% of orders
     for the factory             were delivered on time.

                                 He introduced a new production method
                                 for product APT which has reduced costs.

     Quality control             Rejected goods reduced to 5 per 1,000 units.

     Stock control               Stock costs rose by 7.5%.

                                 Components H2 and H4 over-ordered.


     Maintaining safety standards  Accident rate increased by 10%.
```

In spite of the need for performance appraisals, people do not
like them. Many managers see appraisals as their most
unpleasant duty and those who are appraised rarely have a
good word to say for the system used by their organisation.
One problem is that the manager is expected to criticise the
subordinate and to give guidance at the same time. However,
it is not easy for a manager to combine those roles. Many
people are naturally suspicious of appraisals. They think
managers are trying to find out their weaknesses, so they are
on the defensive. Moreover, managers are often unwilling to
say that a subordinate's performance has been 'outstanding' or
'bad'. So, the individual is described as being 'just above
average'. This means that high fliers in the organisation do not
get a good enough evaluation while the work of poor
performers may be over-valued. Finally, many managers do
not like to criticise, in writing, a subordinate with whom they
are working closely, day-by-day.

Appraisal can be a valuable process. At the interview, the
manager should act as a guide to the subordinate, not as a
judge. The purpose of the interview should be to discuss how
the individual can 'grow' in the organisation, and make an
effective contribution. The situation allows both parties to
review the work of the individual, fix realistic targets, and plan
that person's career development.

Understanding the main points

1 According to the survey conducted in the United States, what is the main purpose of performance appraisals?
2 What is the main difference between the *rating* and the Management by Objectives methods of appraisal?
3 If the critical incident system is used, what does the superior have to do before the performance appraisal interview takes place?
4 Why do some people think that the critical incident system is fairer than the others mentioned?
5 Why do very good employees often complain about their performance appraisals?
6 Which of the three systems of appraisal mentioned in this article do you think is the best for
  a the manager?
  b the employee?

Vocabulary focus

Explain the meaning of the following words and phrases.

1 *skills* (line 18)
2 *career objectives* (line 18)
3 *feedback* (line 20)
4 *reliability* (line 34)
5 *initiative* (line 34)
6 *guidance* (line 66)
7 *on the defensive* (line 70)
8 *high fliers* (line 73)

LANGUAGE STUDY

1 Idiomatic uses of *date*

up-to-date (line 17)

Explain the meaning of the words and phrases in italics in the following sentences.

1 *To date*, we haven't received a single order for our new product.
2 Our advertising is beginning to look very *dated*.
3 We try to use *up-to-date* methods in our Production Department.
4 Our problems *date from* the time we lost that Russian contract.
5 Computer sales people have to constantly *up-date* their knowledge.
6 They are using *out-dated* plant and machinery to manufacture their products.

2 Word building

Complete the following sentences with the correct form of the words in italics.

1 *rely*
  1 He is a very ...**reliable**..... worker.
  2 I am .... informed that he'll be promoted soon.
  3 Her main quality is her ....
  4 My assistant is someone who can be .... on.

2 *criticise*
  1 The report has been received very .... by top management.
  2 The Personnel Director is an outspoken .... of our reorganisation.
  3 I thought her .... were unfair and not based on fact.

3 *skill*

1 The Chairman was .... at avoiding answering awkward questions.
2 The .... workers in the Production Department are well paid.
3 To be a good manager, you need many ....
4 The .... workers in our company are the lowest paid because they need no training for their jobs.

4 *employ*

1 Most .... in an organisation can benefit from training.
2 .... is almost 8% in my country – that's far too high.
3 The .... are entitled to various social security payments.
4 He's fairly old and hasn't had a job for years. I'd say he's virtually ....

5 *sure*

1 Performance appraisals help to .... that promising staff are not overlooked for promotion.
2 At my interview, my boss .... me that I had a bright future in the company.
3 .... you agree she's one of the high fliers in the department.

6 *able*

1 This young trainee has considerable ....
2 Due to our .... to get certain supplies, we lost the order.
3 Because of a production hold-up, we are .... to provide the product.
4 In my work, I am .... assisted by my secretary.

7 *decision*

1 Being a currency dealer in a bank, she has to make quick decisions and be very .... at all times.
2 Because we were .... , we wasted time and lost the contract.
3 I am still .... whether to leave my present job but I must make up my mind soon.

3 Addition and contrast

a *Besides* doing this, it gives the subordinate the opportunity to ask the manager for further training. (lines 27–8)
b *In spite of* the need for performance appraisals, people do not like them. (lines 61–2)

In sentence **a** *besides* introduces the idea of addition: it does this *and also* gives the subordinate the opportunity to ask the manager for further training.
In sentence **b** *in spite of* introduces the idea of contrast: there is a need for performance appraisals *but* people do not like them.

Opposite is a list of words and phrases which express addition and contrast.
Consider how they are used and then do the exercise below.

ADDITION		
besides	not only ... but also	also
as well as	both ... and	too
as well	moreover	
in addition	furthermore	

CONTRAST	
despite	on the other hand
in spite of	while
however	whereas
although	yet

In the table below there are some notes prepared by the Marketing Director of a large company. They concern two members of the Market Research Department, Barbara and Graham. Both these employees have been in the Market Research Department since they joined the company. They have both just applied for the vacant position of Head of Market Research.

Complete the sentences on page 110 using the information in the table below.

e.g. *Both* Barbara *and* Graham are **over thirty** .

In spite of being efficient, Barbara sometimes **works too fast** .

Barbara is single. Graham, *on the other hand*, **is married with three children** .

CANDIDATE	Barbara	Graham
AGE	30	36
STATUS	single	married, with 3 children
YEARS OF SERVICE IN COMPANY	3	8
EDUCATIONAL QUALIFICATIONS	master's degree in marketing; diploma in communications	3 A levels, 6 O levels (no further education.
PREVIOUS WORK EXPERIENCE	2 years in transport department of oil company (B.P.)	2 years as a waiter in Hamburg; 5 years in banking (Lloyds); 3 years in market research firm
SPECIAL SKILLS AND ABILITIES	communicates effectively with staff; articulate; logical mind; sound powers of analysis; fluent French and Italian	writes superb reports; exceptional mathematical ability; highly intelligent
PERSONAL QUALITIES	hard-working; efficient; mobile — will work anywhere in UK; lively, out-going personality; popular with most colleagues	respected because of his knowledge of the job; quiet; reserved; always calm in a crisis
NEGATIVE POINTS	sometimes works too fast and misses important facts; can be too frank and outspoken; one or two colleagues can't stand her; smokes too much; lives on her nerves	considered unsociable by some; speaks rather slowly, and hesitantly; no foreign languages; not mobile — wife has important job at local hospital
INTERESTS	modern jazz dancing; collecting paintings	says he is too busy to have outside interests
HEALTH	had serious illness while at university — studies interrupted for one year	excellent

APPRAISAL

1 *Although* Barbara is popular with most of her colleagues ....
....

2 *Besides* speaking French, ...

3 *Whereas* Barbara could work anywhere in the UK, ...
....

4 Graham has had no further education. Barbara, *on the other hand,*
....

5 Graham is extremely good at writing reports. *Furthermore,* ....
....

6 *Despite* Barbara's ability to communicate well with her
colleagues, some people find her ....
....

7 *As well as* .... ,
Barbara *also* has a diploma in communications.

8 Barbara is fluent in two foreign languages *whereas* Graham ....
....

COMMUNICATION SKILLS

FUNCTION

Talking about statistics

Northern Oil Products Ltd (NOP) recently carried out a survey of their managers' attitudes to their jobs. Questionnaires were sent to 500 middle and senior managers, and completed anonymously.

The responses to some of the questions are summarised in the following table.
First study the table and then do the role play which follows.

NUMBER OF RESPONDENTS: 500			
	YES	NO	DON'T KNOW
Feel that they are satisfied with their jobs.	250	210	40
Feel that their salary reflects the responsibility of their position.	380	75	45
Feel that they could do a better job in another position within the company.	180	255	65
Feel that their abilities and skills have not been fully used by the company.	248	223	29
Feel that their job offers variety and challenge.	272	202	26
Feel that they have been overlooked for promotion.	334	155	11
Feel that the working conditions in the company are satisfactory.	405	85	10
Feel that the company offers sufficient opportunities for staff development.	178	280	42
Feel that they would take a job with another company if they had the opportunity.	23	463	14
Feel that the company shows a caring attitude to its managers.	52	300	148

Role play

Half the managers are satisfied with their job.
Just over 60% think that they've been overlooked for promotion.
The majority of the managers are satisfied with the company's working conditions.
Almost two thirds of the managers feel they have been overlooked for promotion.

Instructions

Work in groups of two or three. First, make comments about the survey's results, as in the examples above. Use the expressions in the table below.

When you have finished making comments about the survey, discuss the following questions.

1 What conclusions can you draw about the company and its management from the results of the survey?
2 What proposals would you make if you were Director of Personnel to improve the attitudes of NOP's managers towards their jobs?

TALKING ABOUT STATISTICS			
(very) few (of) . . . almost none (of) . . . hardly any (of) . . .	quite	a few (of) . . . a (large) number (of) . . . a lot of . . .	
almost (slightly) less than (just) fewer than (a little) under	a quarter (of) . . . a third (of) . . . half (of) . . . three quarters (of) . . .	about roughly approximately	35% (of) . . .
(just) more than (well) over at least	half (of) . . . 50% (of) . . .	the (vast) majority (of) . . . nearly all (of) . . . virtually all (of) . . .	

Case study

The new Assessment Centre

General Plastics Plc is located in the north-east of England – an area of high unemployment. The company is a subsidiary of Northern Oil Products (NOP). Some years ago, General Plastics was in financial difficulties, but things changed when Sir Gerald Harper became Chairman. He introduced a tough, non-nonsense style of management. Some people, such as union officials, didn't like it, but it paid off. The company is now profitable again.

Gina Marsden is Director of Personnel at General Plastics. About a year ago, she got the results of a survey into managers' attitudes to their jobs, conducted by head office. The results confirmed what she had been thinking for some time. The company had to do something about its system of promoting staff. Far too often, managers had complained to her that they had been 'forgotten' when a position became vacant. More than once she had heard it suggested that X had been promoted because he/she was a favourite or protégé of Y.

Linked to this was another problem. Gina Marsden knew, from conversations she had had with staff, that many managers were in the wrong job. They were unhappy because they felt they were 'square pegs in round holes' – unsuited for the work they were doing. They thought they could be more effective in other departments, or even in other subsidiaries within the group.

Setting up the Assessment Centre

Gina was sure that an Assessment Centre would solve these problems. She knew about such centres because she had studied in the United States. Over there, they are common in large companies.

Assessment Centres are set up within the company. They are places where staff can be evaluated. They are used for selecting, developing and promoting staff. Applicants for managerial positions, middle managers and senior managers attend the Centres for a period of time – two or three days, or perhaps even two weeks. At the Centre, they are given psychological and aptitude tests by highly trained psychologists. They take part in group exercises simulating management situations. Their performance is evaluated by colleagues, and by outside observers such as senior managers and members of the Personnel Department. Finally, they are interviewed at length.

At the end of all this, the strengths and weaknesses of each participant are assessed. Talented staff can be identified, a pool of promotable managers can be formed and plans for staff development can be worked out.

Gina put her idea for an Assessment Centre to the Board. It was approved within a matter of weeks. Six months later, the first group of managers came to the Centre.

The case of Dennis Paulson

At the beginning, everything went well. The Board was delighted. It soon became company policy that all managers should attend the centre. All, that is, except the most senior managers like the Financial Controller and the General Manager of the company.

Then, an unexpected problem arose. Dennis Paulson, a senior research worker, refused to attend the Centre – under any circumstances. Dennis Paulson was a scientist in the Research and Development Department. He'd been with General Plastics some ten years, and was now in his late thirties. A brilliant, creative person, he had developed a new range of products which had become known all over the world. At least a hundred employees in the company owed their jobs to his remarkable talents.

When Gina met Dennis Paulson to arrange for his attendance at the Centre, she was amazed at his reaction. 'There's no way I'm going to take any tests, and be spied on by psychologists,' he told her. 'If the company doesn't know my potential by now, it jolly well ought to.'

Gina explained the thinking behind the Assessment Centre, adding, 'In two years' time, the head of your department will be retiring. Surely you want to be considered for the job, Dennis?'

'You can say that again. And I'll be very upset if I don't get it. Mike Westbrook (the department head) has as good as promised me the job when he leaves.'

Gina Marsden looked Dennis Paulson straight in the eyes. 'Would you please think again about attending the Centre? It's company policy that all managers must be assessed there.'

'I'm not going – that's all there is to it. I'm not a "yes-man" like a lot of people round here. If I was, I wouldn't be a top research worker. We've got to have the freedom to do our own thing.'

'We'll see about that,' said Gina Marsden cooly.

'You'll excuse me, Gina,' replied Dennis. 'I'm very busy at the moment. I'm working on the final tests for our new range of heat-resistant plastics. I reckon they've got tremendous sales potential.'

Instructions

A management meeting takes place, chaired by the Director of Personnel. There are two items on the agenda:

1 Progress report on the Assessment Centre; members' views
2 The case of Dennis Paulson

Working in groups, play the roles indicated below. At the meeting, give your reactions to the Director of Personnel's progress report. Then decide what to do about Dennis Paulson.

Note: For smaller groups, roles such as the General Manager and the Senior Executive (Sales) may be omitted.

DIRECTOR OF PERSONNEL

Start by giving a progress report on the Assessment Centre. Be positive. The Centre has been a great success and is popular with executives. It is particularly useful in identifying staff who can fill higher management positions. It has given staff the opportunity to look at their careers, and to plan their future in the company. In your opinion, all executives *must* attend the Centre. If you make exceptions, there is no point in having a Centre. People like Dennis Paulson must learn to follow company rules and policies. This is the attitude you will have at the meeting.

MANAGING DIRECTOR

You are not so happy about the Assessment Centre as you used to be. The reports and paperwork connected with it take up a lot of your time. The Director of Personnel and the Training Manager seem to spend most of their time at the Centre – they never seem to be available when you want them. Some executives have criticised the Centre – privately. They hate doing the psychological tests. You are not sure what to do about Dennis Paulson. Make up your mind during the meeting.

GENERAL MANAGER

You – and Sir Gerald Harper – think that the Assessment Centre is an excellent training facility, although you have never had to attend it personally, for obvious reasons. Try to find the opportunity during the meeting to praise the Director of Personnel for his/her marvellous idea. You admire Dennis Paulson, but feel he should resign from his job if he refuses to attend the Centre.

HEAD OF RESEARCH AND DEVELOPMENT

In your opinion, the company must give people like Dennis Paulson a lot of freedom. Brilliant, creative workers are different from other staff. The company must be flexible and understanding with them. You think that Dennis is the ideal person to take your place when you retire. You like Dennis, and you meet him socially quite often. You don't want him to waste his time attending assessment centres.

TRAINING MANAGER

You are in favour of the Assessment Centre. Since it was introduced, you have had many new ideas for training schemes and have already arranged useful courses for executives. Many members of staff have praised your efforts. Last week, you received a letter from Sir Gerald Harper congratulating you on your fine work! You think that all managers – and even ordinary workers – should attend the Centre. If that happened, you would be a powerful person in the company.

FINANCIAL DIRECTOR

You are against the Assessment Centre. You think it is a waste of company time and money. The old system worked well, on the whole. Now, the company has had to hire two psychologists – at great expense. And the Director of Personnel is continually asking senior executives to act as assessors at the Centre. You think that the Director of Personnel has introduced the Assessment Centre so that he/she and the Training Manager will have more power and influence. Make up your own mind what to do about Dennis Paulson.

SENIOR EXECUTIVE (SALES)

You must attend the Centre next month. You aren't too happy – you hate psychological tests. Members at the meeting may decide to make an exception in Dennis Paulson's case. If they do this, make sure that *you* don't go to the Centre either! Basically, you are sympathetic to Dennis Paulson's point of view.

COMPANY PSYCHOLOGIST

You are in favour of the Assessment Centre. However, you feel that the top management – and especially the Chairman – are far too tough. Sir Gerald acts like a dictator, expecting everyone to obey him without question. It is time for the company to be more flexible with staff and treat them as human beings. The management must show that it cares about each and every employee. Make up your own mind what to do about Dennis Paulson.

WRITING

The management meeting (see **Case study** on page 111) has taken place. The Director of Personnel has given his/her progress report on the Assessment Centre and the case of Dennis Paulson has been fully discussed.

Below is an extract from the minutes of that meeting.
Complete paragraphs 2 and 3 by writing a summary of what was said and agreed at the meeting which you attended.

────General Plastics PLC────

MINUTES OF THE MANAGEMENT COMMITTEE MEETING HELD ON
FRIDAY, 16 APRIL 1988

Present: Director of Personnel (Chairperson), Managing Director,
         General Manager, Head of Research and Development,
         Training Manager, Financial Director, Senior
         Executive (Sales), Company Psychologist

Apologies: Manager, Industrial Relations

1   The minutes of the last meeting, held on March 30 1988, were
    signed and accepted.

2   Assessment Centre Progress Report
    The Director of Personnel informed members that the new
    centre was in full operation. A number of managers had
    attended...
    ....
    ....

3   Dennis Paulson
    The attitude and behaviour of Dennis Paulson were discussed
    at great length. Opinions were divided as to how to deal
    with the situation:
    ....
    ....

Understanding the main points

Listen to the following conversation and complete the candidate report form below.

UNITED AIRWAYS

CANDIDATE REPORT

To: All members of Selection Board
From: Ian Jameson

_____

Vacancy: Operations Manager
Applicant: Derek Schmitt   Age: 36
Present position: Customer Relations Manager

ASSESSMENT OF PERSONAL QUALITIES

Strengths	Weaknesses
	_____
deals with passengers very well	_____
_____	_____
_____	_____

Critical incidents

1 When he was twenty Derek _____
_____ . At first, doctors
thought he was suffering from _____
_____ . He still_____
_____ for this condition.

2 In 1981 _____
_____
_____
_____

Vocabulary focus

1 *Listen again and fill in the gaps in these sentences from the conversation.*

  1 What have you .... him?
  2 Will he .... his .... in a crisis?
  3 Yes, but .... it, it was *serious*.
  4 I'm sorry – I .... that ....
  5 The police .... him in the end.
  6 It's got nothing .... it – his father being a director.
  7 If I .... my .... , he won't go before the Board.
  8 Good. I thought you might .... it my .... – once you knew all the facts.

2 *In pairs, discuss the meaning of the phrases and expressions above.*

10 Centralisation or decentralisation?

DISCUSSION

Read about Sharp and Marsden Ltd and then discuss the questions below.

Sharp and Marsden Ltd. is a group of menswear stores. Its clothes, which are stylish and expensive, are aimed at the fashion-conscious eighteen to thirty-year-old buyer. The group is expanding fast in the UK. It has ten stores at present in large cities, and plans to open many more in the coming years.

The group faces a difficult problem. The directors disagree about how the group should be organised in the future. Some of the directors – Group A – believe that the stores should have a great deal of autonomy. Each store manager should be given considerable independence and responsibility. The other directors – Group B – have other ideas about how the stores should be organised.

Group A want the stores to have responsibility for things like the buying of goods, stock control, warehousing, selection and training of staff, advertising and promotion and payment of salaries and bonuses. The tasks of Head Office would be mainly to set profit targets for the stores and maintain financial controls. Head Office would provide some back-up services, such as market research, information technology, and the keeping of personnel records. Store managers should be allowed to get on with the job of making a profit. As long as they did this, Head Office should not interfere.

Directors in Group B, however, see things differently. They think that Head Office should have more control and more direct involvement in the running of the stores. This group would like Head Office to do the buying of merchandise for all ten stores. Stocks should be held in large regional distribution centres, and supplied to the individual stores when needed. Head Office would carry out such functions as selection and training of staff, salary administration, advertising and promotion etc. In addition, the Finance Department would keep a close check on the performance of each store. Also, Head Office would keep tight control over all aspects of the stores' work. According to Group B directors, the task of the manager should be to run the store under the close guidance of Head Office.

1 What are the advantages and disadvantages of each system of organisation?
2 Which system would be better for Sharp and Marsden Ltd? Why?
3 Give examples, if you can, of businesses which have either type of organisation.

Alfred Sloan (1874–1966) was an outstanding figure in the business world of America. He worked for forty-five years in the General Motors Corporation (GM). From 1923 to 1946, he was Chief Executive of the corporation, and he stayed on as Chairman of the Board until 1956. In 1963, Sloan published an account of his career with the organisation, calling his book *My Years with General Motors*. In it he described some of the management problems he had had, and how he had dealt with them.

10 According to Sloan, every large enterprise has to face one major problem. It must decide how much it wishes to centralise or decentralise its business. What are centralisation and decentralisation? The terms refer to the degree of authority that is given to various levels of management and to the divisions of an organisation. Authority may be defined as the right to make decisions, to direct the work of other people and to give instructions. When we talk about centralised and decentralised businesses, we mean the extent to which authority has been passed down – delegated – to lower levels
20 or divisions of an organisation.

When an organisation is centralised, a limited amount of authority is delegated. If it is decentralised, a greater degree of authority is given to staff and divisions. For example, in a centralised company, Head Office may make most of the decisions concerning recruitment, the purchase of equipment and product lines. It may also be responsible for areas such as advertising, promotion and research and development.

In a decentralised company, the divisions will have wider responsibilities and authority. Divisional managers will, for
30 instance, have authority to purchase expensive equipment and authorise substantial salary increases. In decentralised organisations, more important decisions can be made at lower levels. There are fewer controls from Head Office.

To sum up, a centralised business has a 'tight' structure, whereas a decentralised business has a 'looser' structure.

No enterprise chooses complete centralisation or decentralisation. In practice, it tries to find a balance between the two forms. The problem for organisations is to decide how much decentralisation they want, and what kind?

40 When Alfred Sloan took over the running of General Motors, he inherited a corporation which was already decentralised. The previous Chief Executive, William Durant, had founded the company. Durant brought many businesses into General Motors and gave their managements a lot of independence. Alfred Sloan believed in decentralisation and practised it in the corporation. He made sure his division managers (e.g. those in charge of Cadillac, Buick and Chevrolet) had self-contained divisions. Each handled its own manufacturing, marketing, staff recruitment etc. However, Sloan did not give
50 the divisions complete freedom. He wanted Head Office to coordinate action and keep a measure of control over the units. Therefore, he decided that certain functions would be controlled centrally.

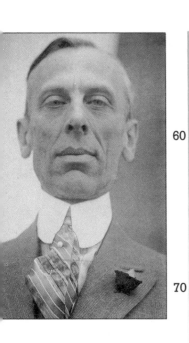

Very early on, he realised that Head Office would have to control finance more tightly. When he arrived, each division controlled its own cash, having its own accounts and paying its own bills. This meant the corporation was getting little direct income. When it had to pay things like taxes and dividends, the treasurer used to ask the divisions for cash. Sometimes, he had to go to a division, first talk about general business matters, and then later on bring up the subject of cash. The division's staff would often show surprise at the amount asked for, and delay handing it over! Clearly, with that system, cash was never available where and when it was needed in the corporation.

Alfred Sloan set up a new, centralised cash system. Cash accounts were controlled by the financial staff at Head Office. Cash receipts were made to them. And they authorised payments made from the corporation's accounts. With this system, money could be quickly transferred to units needing it. The central staff also decided how much would be kept in local accounts, to be used by the divisions.

As time went on, Alfred Sloan and his top managers worked out a balance between central control and delegated authority. Head Office controlled things like cash, capital expenditure and stock control. In addition, it controlled the profitability of divisions by developing measures of efficiency. But the divisions had a great deal of autonomy, being responsible for designing, making and marketing the cars.

Nowadays, decentralisation is the fashion, the 'buzz' word. Believers in decentralisation argue along these lines: they say that it helps to 'develop people' because staff get more responsibility, make more decisions, and so gain experience for later managerial positions. If an organisation is too centralised, people become robots – which is demotivating. Decentralisation allows top managers to delegate jobs, so these managers will have more time to work on setting goals, planning corporate strategy and working out policies. The strongest argument for decentralisation is that, in competitive conditions, the 'looser' companies will be more flexible, better able to make quick decisions and to adapt to change.

In a famous book on management, *In Search of Excellence*, the writers argue that America's best-run companies know how to balance control and delegation. Excellent companies, say the authors of the book, have 'loose-tight' characteristics. On the one hand, they have a simple structure, generally based on product divisions which also have great autonomy. These divisions have control over functions like product development, purchasing, finance, personnel etc. On the other hand, the centre of these excellent companies – top management – provides 'firm central direction'. It continually stresses the 'core values' of the organisation, e.g. quality, need for innovation, service, informal communications and so on. These central values provide the context within which staff can be creative, take risks – even fail.

It is normal for people to like independence, to dislike control. The more educated staff are, the more they will want to make decisions, to have authority. However, it is not easy to have more decentralisation if the right staff are not available. For example, if you own a chain of stores, it may be difficult to give more authority to employees. The employees may be used to following rules, so they may not be able to take decisions, to show initiative. As Charles Handy, the expert on organisation says, 'It is one thing to prescribe diversity, decentralisation and differentiation. It is another to manage it.'

110

Understanding the main points

1 *Decide whether the following statements are true or false.*

	True	False
1 Alfred Sloan's book was mainly about the organisational problems of General Motors.	☐	☐
2 In a decentralised company most key functions are the responsibility of the head office.	☐	☐
3 The majority of companies have either a totally centralised or decentralised structure.	☐	☐
4 William Durant and Alfred Sloan had a completely different approach to running General Motors.	☐	☐
5 Alfred Sloan believed in what could be called 'coordinated decentralisation'.	☐	☐
6 When Alfred Sloan joined General Motors he established a new system which gave Head Office more control of the corporation's finances.	☐	☐

2 *Note down the benefits which a company can gain by decentralising.*

1 ....
2 ....
3 ....
4 ....

3 *Explain what Charles Handy meant when he said, 'It is one thing to prescribe diversity, decentralisation and differentiation. It is another to manage it.'*

LANGUAGE STUDY

1 Word hunting
Working in groups of three or four, find the words or phrases in the text which have the same meaning as the following definitions. The first team to complete the exercise successfully are the winners.

DEFINITIONS	LOCATION IN TEXT	WORD OR PHRASE
1 the right to make decisions or give instructions	lines 10–20	....
2 the employment of new staff	lines 20–27	....
3 became responsible for	lines 40–53	....
4 started, established	lines 40–53	....
5 complete in itself	lines 40–53	....
6 raise or introduce a subject (for discussion)	lines 54–65	

7 move or act slowly (often on purpose)	lines 54–65	....
8 transferring or giving	lines 54–65	....
9 gave official permission	lines 66–72	....
10 freedom to act independently	lines 73–79	....
11 something everybody is talking about	lines 80–91	....
12 removing somebody's incentive or desire to do well	lines 80–91	....
13 fixing objectives	lines 80–91	....
14 adaptable	lines 80–91	....
15 adopt a middle position between	lines 92–105	....
16 emphasises	lines 92–105	....
17 things a company believes in and considers very important	lines 92–105	....
18 ability to assess a situation and decide on what action to take independently	lines 106–115	....

2 *First, check the meaning of the following words and phrases in your dictionary. Then use them in your own sentences to show their meaning clearly.*

a initiative
b to take the initiative
c on one's own initiative
d to show initiative

3 *Complete the following sentences with suitable forms of the words in the box below.*

authorise	authority	control	function	autonomy
innovate	innovative	delegate	delegation	initiative

1 In many department store groups, buying and finance are two .... which are handled by Head Office.
2 Managers who like power find it difficult to .... responsibility.
3 To stay competitive, high technology firms must constantly .... , or else their products become out of date.
4 When you delegate authority in a business, you lose a degree of .... over certain functions.
5 In some multinational organisations, subsidiaries are given a great deal of .... – they rarely have to consult Head Office.
6 .... firms often make the mistake of not concentrating enough on marketing.
7 In our factory, the General Manager is .... to spend up to £1,000 a month on repairs and maintenance.
8 I like my staff to make decisions for themselves, but they seem afraid to show any ....

4 Phrasal verbs with *bring*

bring up (line 61)

A *Match the following verbs with the correct definitions.*

1 bring up	**a** reduce (a price)
2 bring out	**b** persuade someone to change his/her
3 bring about	opinion
4 bring round to	**c** raise, mention a matter
5 bring down	**d** cause to happen
	e put on the market

B *Complete the following passage with suitable verbs from the list above.*

At our management meeting, the Marketing Manager
.... (1) the subject of our new lawnmower, the PX2
model. He mentioned that sales had been disappointing. The
Production Manager said that problems with the PX2 had been
.... (2) by bad timing. We had put the mower on the
market at the wrong time of the year. However, he also thought
the mower was too expensive. We should .... (3) its
price, he thought. He presented his arguments well and, in the
end, ... almost everyone .... (4) to his
point of view. Finally, the Chairman gave his opinion. He advised
us to forget about the PX2. In his view, it was a lemon! He thought
we should .... (5) an entirely new model – something
that would be a real breakthrough, technologically speaking.

Which words in the above passage mean

a not as good as expected?
b to introduce a new product?
c a failure (slang)?
d an important development or discovery?

COMMUNICATION SKILLS

FUNCTIONS

Plans and intentions
Possibility and probability

Winner Electrical Products is an electrical goods group, with its
head office in Minnesota, USA. It has subsidiary companies in
several European countries.

Dialogue

*Listen to the following conversation, in which a marketing manager
of a subsidiary talks to her Board of Directors about an idea for a
new product.*

MARKETING MANAGER	We intend to produce a hair-drier that'll have many distinctive features. It'll be extremely light, but at the same time strong, and not at all cheap-looking. We're planning to have it designed by an independent organisation – we already have a firm in mind.
BOARD MEMBER	Surely that'll add to its development costs, won't it?
MARKETING MANAGER	Yes, indeed. But we've allowed for the extra cost in our pricing.
BOARD MEMBER	I see.

MARKETING MANAGER	As I say, it's going to be light-weight, independently designed, and ... er ... very efficient at drying hair.
BOARD MEMBER	Why's that exactly?
MARKETING MANAGER	Young girls today – they're our target consumer – are always in a hurry, rushing to get to work or go out in the evening. So, the drier's got to be efficient – it's got to dry their hair quickly, I mean.
BOARD MEMBER	But there'll be a number of speed settings, I trust.
MARKETING MANAGER	Of course. Now, I should tell you, we're aiming to keep the noise level extremely low. It's going to be almost silent – all you'll hear is a low humming sound.
BOARD MEMBER	What about pricing? And sales potential?
MARKETING MANAGER	It'll be priced at the upper end of the market, say £25–£30. As for sales potential, it's possible that we'd sell 30,000 units in the first year. We might even sell 40,000, if we were lucky. After three years, there's a good chance we'd be selling 70,000 units. In fact, it's highly likely we'd be selling a lot more than that.
BOARD MEMBER	What's the break-even point?
MARKETING MANAGER	50,000 units. We'll probably reach that after two years – if it does well.
CHAIRMAN	It seems to me that this drier could well be a 'winner', ha, ha, provided we don't run up against technical problems.

PLANS AND INTENTIONS

We plan/We're planning
We intend/We're intending
We aim/We're aiming
} {
to bring it out in June.
to produce a revolutionary hair-drier.
to sell 30,000 units in the first year.

POSSIBILITY

It's possible (that) we'll have the prototype ready by Christmas.

We {
may be able to
might be able to
could
} launch it next autumn.

There's
We have
} a good chance {
(that) it'll be ready next month.
of becoming the leaders in this field.

PROBABILITY

It's (highly) {
likely (that)
probable (that)
} we'll sell 15,000 next year.

We're {
certain
bound
} to break even.

It's {
obvious (that)
clear (that)
} we'd need to do some more market research first.

Role play

Instructions

The class should divide into four groups. The groups represent marketing teams of the European subsidiaries of Winner Electrical Products. Each group is given one of the following products:

an electric toaster
an electric kettle
an electric coffee-maker
an electric food-processor

The four groups should take turns telling the Board of Directors about their plans for the product, describe its special features and give details of its pricing and sales potential.

While each group presents its product, the other groups should play the roles of Board members. Use the words and phrases in the table on page 123 to help you prepare your presentation.

Finally, the whole class discuss together – as objectively as possible – which products, if any, are worth putting on the market.

Case study

Which way for Henry Winner?

Henry Winner Junior, grandson of the founder of Winner Electrical Products Group, likes to tell people that he runs a decentralised organisation. Only recently he was saying to a Japanese visitor, 'At Head Office, we're in charge of finance, and that's about it. We let the subsidiaries get on with the business of making money. And we only interfere if things start going wrong. We've got a hands-off policy here at Minnesota.'

However, things did go wrong from time to time. Like last January, for example, at their Belgian subsidiary. Henry found out that the marketing people there had plans to bring out a range of micro-wave ovens. He quickly put a stop to that idea, even though a good deal of work had been done on developing the ovens. 'Let's stick to what we know best,' he told the subsidiary's Chief Executive, Olivier Andrieu. 'Leave micro-waves to the Japanese – they've got the market sewn up.' Andrieu protested weakly for a while, then gave in. The plans for producing the ovens were cancelled. And a month or so later, the Marketing Manager of the company handed in his resignation and left.

It was not the first time that Head Office had taken such an action. About two years before that, they had appointed a Communications Manager. The manager had greatly improved communications between Head Office and the European subsidiaries. Because of this, a huge amount of data from the subsidiaries was flowing into Head Office daily. This made it much easier for Head Office executives to control the subsidiaries, if they wished to do so. And sometimes they did.

The question was, did the group need more central control? It was the newly-appointed Vice-President, Tony Benedetti, who put the idea into Henry's head:

'It's all very well giving the subsidiaries complete freedom. Letting them compete against each other and against other firms. Allowing them to sell what they like, where they like ...' Tony paused. 'But what's the result of it all?'

'I'm not with you,' said Henry, puzzled.

'Look, we've five European subsidiaries, and they're all producing their own brand of coffee-maker. If you walk into a store in Paris, say, all five brands will be on sale there. What's the point of that?'

'They're all making profits, presumably, or they wouldn't be there,' replied Henry.

'Maybe, but all our European companies are spending a fortune on advertising their products. Wouldn't it be better if they produced just one or two top-selling coffee-makers? And invested the rest of the money in other, more profitable products?'

'Hm, possibly.' Henry was listening carefully by now.

'And that food-processor that is selling so well in Italy. Think of the money we'd be making if *all* the subsidiaries were selling it.'

'You've got a point there,' Henry admitted.

Tony gave some other examples of group products which were competing against each other on the store shelves.

'So what are you trying to tell me?' asked Henry.

'What I'm saying is that our decentralisation has gone too far. We need a Product Planning Department here at Head Office. We must standardise our products more. It's us who should be telling the subsidiaries what to sell. And we should be developing new products here in Minnesota. We could do the job more efficiently and economically.'

'You reckon?' Henry looked thoughtful.

'Another thing,' went on Tony Benedetti. 'Why do we need manufacturing facilities in five European countries? I say we should have a manufacturing plant in, say, France or West Germany, and sales facilities in the other countries. Then we'd have a streamlined European operation. And we could have an *integrated* approach to marketing our products throughout Europe.'

'But that would mean a centralised organisation,' Henry pointed out, 'a complete change of policy for us.'

Tony Benedetti smiled briefly. 'Would it be such a big change?'

There was a knock at the door. Cathy Baker, Henry's Personal Assistant appeared.

'Bad news, I'm afraid, Henry.'

'Oh?'

'I've just had a call from Eric Wise.' Wise was Deputy Chief Executive at the German subsidiary. He used to be a Head Office executive, but Henry had transferred him to Germany about a year ago when the subsidiary's profits began to fall.

'It seems that Heinz Muller is going to resign.' Muller was the Chief Executive of the German subsidiary.

'Do we know why?' Henry asked his Personal Assistant.

'Apparently, he couldn't get on with Eric Wise. A personality clash – or something like that.'

Henry sighed. Then he leant back in his chair and turned to Tony. 'Running this business used to be fun,' he said. 'Now, I'm not so sure. The market's becoming more and more competitive. And our European operation isn't making the profits it used to. Maybe we should move into new fields. Buy up a few businesses. Perhaps that would put some fizz back into this organisation?'

Instructions

First, work in groups of two or three.
Analyse the problems facing the Winner Electrical Products Group, and make recommendations which will improve its efficiency and long-term profits. To help you in your analysis consider the following questions.

1 What type of organisation is the Winner group? It is centralised or decentralised?
2 What does the incident with the Belgian subsidiary tell us about Henry Winner's style of management?
3 How did the appointment of the Communications Manager affect the running of the Group?
4 What is Tony Benedetti's point of view? Explain it in detail.
5 Do you think Tony Benedetti is right?
6 Is Muller's resignation significant in any way?
7 Is it time for the Winner Group to diversify? Or are there other solutions to its problems? If so, what are they?

Finally, the whole class should discuss what the organisation could do to improve its efficiency and long-term profits. One of you should chair the meeting, playing the role of Henry Winner.

WRITING

Winner Electrical Products has a Customer Relations Department. One of the main duties of staff in this department is to deal with complaints from customers about the company's products. Last week, the Customer Relations Manager received the following letter from a customer.

Read the letter, then write a suitable reply.

Basil Heathcott-Jones
51 Dudley Road, Wembley, Middlesex HA5 6DM

15 October, 1988

The Manager
Customer Relations Department
Winner Electrical Products
Tor Leigh
Wessex

Dear Sir,

About a week ago, I bought your new coffee-percolator intending to keep it in my office so that I could offer fresh coffee to my visitors.

Last Wednesday, I received an important Chinese businessman and, naturally, I offered him a cup of coffee. He accepted my invitation. I placed a filter in the machine, filled it with ground coffee, and turned on the machine. I'm quite sure I followed to the letter the instructions for operating the percolator.

While we were discussing the finer points of a draft contract, I heard the coffee-percolator making a strange noise. I can only describe it as a bubbling, gurgling sound. Not wishing to appear rude to my Chinesé guest, I ignored it. He also, by the way, gave no sign that he had heard anything unusual.

About five minutes later, a tremendous noise came from the machine. It seemed to explode! Coffee shot out from it and sprayed all over the carpet. Some of it fell on the trousers and coat of my guest. And it also splashed over documents I had on my desk. The carpet was soaked, the mess <u>unbelievable.</u>

I don't need to tell you how embarrassed I was. My guest was extremely polite, but we did no further work on the contract. I haven't seen him since. And I'm beginning to think I never will.

Of course I expect financial compensation from your firm for the loss I have suffered because of your faulty product. Perhaps you'd let me know how much you're prepared to offer me. Let me say now, the sum must be substantial. If not, I shall place the matter in the hands of my lawyer.

Yours faithfully,

Basil Heathcott-Jones.

B. Heathcott-Jones

Understanding the main points

As you listen to the following conversation note down the arguments in favour of each of the two proposed sites for Jolawear's new manufacturing plant.

ADVANTAGES OF THE TWO SITES PROPOSED	
WAKEFIELD	HONG KONG

Vocabulary focus

1 *Listen again and fill in the gaps in these sentences from the conversation.*

1 We'll try to work out what sort of .... we'll get on our .... in each case.
2 Yes, we've still got a lot of .... to do and feasibility studies to .... before we can .... a decision.
3 We'll have to take .... investment grants and tax concessions.
4 I say the arguments are .... for having a plant there.
5 And, I might say, our staffing .... and .... were too high.
6 They were pushing us to .... more modern machinery.
7 We also had very tight financial .... all our manufacturing plants.
8 If we have a plant in Hong Kong, it's going to be more difficult for us to .... control .... it.
9 Do we have the management .... for it?
10 I might as well tell you, you'll have to make .... a pretty strong .... for Hong Kong.
11 We're not going to .... sales for ever in the EEC.
12 There are lots of .... for us in the Far East.
13 It would be a big .... into unknown ....

2 *In pairs, discuss the meaning of the phrases and expressions above.*

11 *Communications*

DISCUSSION

Listen to the following conversation and then discuss the questions below.

David Johnston, General Manager of Northern Textiles Ltd, visits the Supplies Department to talk to Valerie Harper. Valerie has been working in the department for about a year.

JOHNSTON   Hello Valerie. Just dropped by to check that those spare parts have arrived – the ones for the cutting machines.

HARPER   The spare parts? Oh, yes. Look, I'm sorry . . .

JOHNSTON   What? Don't tell me . . . Oh no!

HARPER   I'm really sorry. I called Jack Peters at Humber Engineering, but there's been some sort of go-slow at the factory – some dispute over overtime pay – and they just can't meet all their orders.

JOHNSTON   Come on, Valerie, you can do better than that. It's your job to make sure spare parts get here on time.

HARPER   Yes, but surely . . .

JOHNSTON   No 'Yes, but's. You're a university graduate, aren't you? I thought you people knew how to solve problems – anyway, that's what you told me at your interview.

HARPER   I tried one or two other firms. The trouble is, these machines are really old. No one seems to be making spare parts for them any more.

JOHNSTON   Nonsense, try some more firms. And, if you have to, lean hard on Jack Peters. We're one of his best customers.

HARPER   All right. But to be honest . . .

JOHNSTON   That's more like it. You can go far in this company if you have the right attitude, Valerie. Now, you will have those parts here by Monday, won't you?

HARPER   Er . . . yes, Mr Johnston.

JOHNSTON   Great. How's the boyfriend these days? The one I met at the office party.

HARPER   Oh Tom? He's fine, thanks.

JOHNSTON   Glad to hear it. OK, Valerie, don't let me keep you from your work.

HARPER   OK, Mr Johnston, fine.

1 Are David Johnston and Valerie Harper communicating effectively?
2 If not, how could they improve communications between them?

'Now, you <u>will</u> have those parts here by Monday, won't you?'

In recent years, few books on management have been more acclaimed than *In Search of Excellence.* Written by two business consultants, Thomas Peters and Robert Waterman, the book identified factors which have accounted for the success of some of America's best-run companies. Forty-three top companies were studied. Many examples of the experiences of these organisations are given in the book. These provide useful lessons for all managers.

10 One of the points made by the writers is that communications in excellent companies are different from those in other companies. Excellent companies have a 'vast network of informal, open communications'. People working in them keep in contact with each other regularly. They meet often, and have many unscheduled meetings. In the best-run businesses, few barriers exist to prevent people talking to each other. The companies do everything possible to ensure that staff meet easily and frequently.

The authors give many examples to back up their view. For instance, one day, they visited the Minnesota Mining and 20 Manufacturing Company (3M). They soon noticed that there were a lot of casual meetings going on with 'salespeople, marketing people, manufacturing people – even accounting people – sitting around, chattering about new product problems . . . It went on all day – people meeting in a seemingly random way to get things done.' One of the 3M executives told the authors, 'We just plain talk to each other a lot without a lot of paper or formal rigmarole.'

The book is full of examples of companies who believe in 'keeping in touch': firms like IBM where the Chairman personally 30 answers any complaint which is addressed by members of staff; other companies where managers are encouraged to get out of the office and walk around and some which make a point of informality, like Walt Disney Productions, where everyone wears a name-tag with his/her first name on it.

Figure 1

EXTENT TO WHICH SUBORDINATES FEEL FREE TO DISCUSS IMPORTANT THINGS ABOUT THE JOB WITH SUPERIORS – AS SEEN BY SUPERIORS AND SUBORDINATES				
	Top Staff Says About Supervisors	*Supervisors Say About Themselves*	*Supervisors Say About Employees*	*Employees Say About Themselves*
Feel very free to discuss important things about the job with my superior	90%	67%	85%	51%
Feel fairly free	10	23	15	29
Not very free	. . .	10	. . .	14
Not at all free	. . .	. . .	. . .	6

Source: Rensis Likert, *New Patterns of Management*, p. 47. New York: McGraw-Hill Book Company, 1961

One problem with communication is that people think they have got their message across when in fact they have not. We do not, in fact, communicate as effectively as we think we do. Several studies have shown this. In 1954, a study was made of a production department in a British company. The department
40 manager believed he had given 'instruction or decisions in 165 out of 236 episodes, but his subordinates considered they had received instruction on only 84 occasions.' Research done by Rensis Likert in 1961 (see Figure 1) showed that 85% of the supervisors thought their subordinates felt free to discuss important things with them. However, only 51% of the employees agreed with this opinion!

This finding is important for managers. It suggests that, when giving instructions, managers must make sure that those instructions have been understood and interpreted correctly.

50 A breakdown in communication is quite likely to happen if there is some kind of 'social distance' between people. In organisations, people may have difficulty communicating if they are different in status, or if one person has a much higher position than the other. For example, a couple of production workers will probably speak frankly to each other about things that are going wrong in their department. But if the Chief Executive of the company passes by and asks how things are going, they'll probably say, 'Just fine, thank you.' It is risky to tell the truth to someone higher up in the hierarchy – they may
60 not like what they hear and hold it against you.

For this reason, staff often 'filter' information. They deliberately alter the facts, telling the boss what he/she wants to hear. They do not want to give bad news, so they give their superior too good an impression of the situation. 'The project's coming along fine,' they say, when in fact it is a month behind schedule! There's nothing new about all this. One thinks of Cleopatra and the problem she had in her military campaigns. She used to give gold to messengers bringing good news, but executed those bringing bad news. It is not surprising, therefore, that the
70 information she received was unreliable!

One way of reducing social distance – and improving communications – is to cut down on status symbols. It is possible, for example, to have a common dining-room for all staff. It is worth noting, too, that in Japanese companies, it is common for all the staff to wear uniforms.

Physical surroundings and physical distance limit or encourage communication. Studies show that the further away a person is, the less he/she communicates. At the Massachusetts Institute of Technology (MIT), Thomas Allen studied the effect of location on communication in engineering and research departments. He showed that if people were more than ten metres apart, the probability of communicating at least once a week was about 8%. When they were five metres apart, the probability was 25%.

The physical layout of an office must be carefully planned. Open-plan offices are designed to make communication easier and quicker. However, it is interesting to note that employees in such offices will often move furniture and other objects to create mini-offices.

Excellent companies use space to create good communications. The Corning Glass Company in the United States installed escalators, rather than lifts, in their new engineering building because they wanted to increase the chances of employees meeting face-to-face.

Another important barrier to communication is selective perception. Put simply, this means that people perceive things in different ways. The world of the sender is not the same as the world of the receiver. Because their knowledge and experience is different, sender and receiver are always on slightly different wavelengths. Therefore, a manager will say something, but the employee will interpret his meaning incorrectly. The message becomes distorted. An example of this is given in Figure 2.

Figure 2

HOW COMMUNICATIONS BREAK DOWN		
What the manager said	What the manager meant	What the subordinate heard
I'll look into hiring another person for your department as soon as I complete my budget review.	We'll start interviewing for that job in about three weeks.	I'm tied up with more important things. Let's forget about hiring for the indefinite future.
Your performance was below par last quarter. I really expected more out of you.	You're going to have to try harder, but I know you can do it.	If you screw up one more time, you're out.
I'd like that report as soon as you can get to it.	I need that report within the week.	Drop that rush order you're working on and fill out that report today.
I talked to the boss but at the present time, due to budget problems, we'll be unable to fully match your competitive salary offer.	We can give you 95 percent of that offer, and I know we'll be able to do even more for you next year.	If I were you, I'd take that competitive offer. We're certainly not going to pay that kind of salary to a person with your credentials.
We have a job opening in Los Angeles that we think would be just your cup of tea. We'd like you to go out there and look it over.	If you'd like that job, it's yours. If not, of course, you can stay here in Denver. You be the judge.	You don't have to go out to L.A. if you don't want to. However, if you don't, you can kiss good-bye to your career with this firm.
Your people seem to be having some problems getting their work out on time. I want you to look into this situation and straighten it out.	Talk to your people and find out what the problem is. Then get with them and jointly solve it.	I don't care how many heads you bust, just get me that output. I've got enough problems around here without you screwing things up too.

SOURCE: Richard M. Hodgetts and Steven Altman, <u>Organizational Behaviors</u> (New York: Holt, Rinehart, & Winston, 1979). p. 305. With permission.

Communication problems will arise, from time to time, in the best-run companies. However, to minimise such problems, managers must remember one thing. Communication should be a two-way process. Managers should encourage staff to ask questions and to react to what the managers are saying. Feedback is essential. The most useful question a manager can ask is 'Did you understand that?'.

Understanding the main points

1 *Number the following ideas 1–8, depending on the order in which they appear in the text.*

a In *In Search of Excellence* the authors give many examples of the ways in which organisations try to break down the barriers between management and employees. ☐

b Subordinates are often reluctant to tell their superiors when things are not going well. ☐

c In the most successfully managed organisations communications are extremely good because staff meet to discuss things openly and informally. ☐

d Communication problems sometimes occur when employees misinterpret what their managers tell them. ☐

e Better communications between managers and employees can be achieved by trying to reduce the social divisions between them within the company. ☐

f The purpose of the book was to illustrate the good management techniques which are used in top American companies. ☐

g One of the problems faced by managers is that their staff do not always feel that they are able to come and discuss important matters freely with them. ☐

h Staff communications are much easier if work places are designed in such a way that people frequently come into contact with each other. ☐

2 What are the advantages and disadvantages of having open-plan offices?

3 Why are the manager and subordinate in Figure 2 not communicating properly?

4 Supposing you were Communications Manager in a large organisation, what advice would you give managers to avoid communications problems?
Note down a few of the suggestions you would make.

1 ....

2 ....

3 ....

4 ....

5 ....

Vocabulary focus

1 *Find words in Figure 2 'How Communications Break Down' which mean the same as the following:*

  1 examine, investigate, consider (a matter)
  2 very busy
  3 not as good as usual
  4 make a mistake (US slang)
  5 you're fired
  6 goods required in a hurry
  7 offer as much as, equal
  8 qualifications
  9 exactly what you want, very suitable for you
  10 inspect, examine
  11 solve a problem, deal with a difficult situation
  12 together

LANGUAGE STUDY

1 Idiomatic uses of *point*

make a point of (line 32)

come to/get to/reach the point	give the important part of what one is trying to say
keep to the point	limit oneself to what is relevant to the subject being discussed
get away from/off the point	say something irrelevant
point out	draw attention to something
make a point	express your opinion, offer an argument, e.g. He made several valuable points at our last production meeting.
make a point of	make a special effort to, e.g. I shall make a point of visiting our agent when I go to Madrid next week.
on the point of	about to do something, e.g. I was on the point of leaving my office when I got a telex from Japan.
up to a point	not completely
point-blank	in a forceful, direct manner

Complete the following sentences, using suitable verbs, phrases and expressions from the table above.

1 Our Chairman likes to know everyone in the firm. When he visits our factory he .... chatting with all the staff he meets.
2 Harry is boring at meetings. He talks for hours and never ....
3 Pamela is very good at chairing meetings. She makes sure that speakers ....
4 I thought John .... at the meeting about our need to improve our distribution system.
5 I don't entirely accept your analysis of the situation, but I agree ....

6 I've heard a rumour that there will be quite a few redundancies when we're taken over. There's only one way to find out. I'll have to ask the Personnel Director ....

7 Peter seems to be really fed up with his job at the moment. I'd say he is .... leaving the company.

8 The Financial Director .... that the loan would have to be repaid within ten years.

2 Idiomatic uses of *back*

back up their view (line 18)

put your back into it	work very hard (usually physical work)
back out	withdraw (from an agreement, a contract etc.)
back down	admit that you are wrong
back up	support someone (in a discussion or argument)
back-date (v.)	make effective from an earlier date e.g. My salary increase was back-dated to January.
break the back of	finish the most difficult/main part of a job/task
have your back against the wall	be in a difficult situation
background	a person's social class, education, training or experience
backing	support (moral or financial)
backhander (informal)	bribe
backlog	accumulation of uncompleted work, unfulfilled orders etc. e.g. When I returned to work from my holiday, there was an enormous backlog of correspondence to deal with.
back-breaking	very hard, tiring physical work

Answer the following questions using suitable verbs, phrases and expressions from the table above.

1 If you are not happy when negotiating a contract, what's the best thing to do?

2 What sort of person would you select to run a major car manufacturing company?

3 Suppose you are a creative person and you have just invented a revolutionary electric razor but do not have enough money to develop it yourself. What would you try to do?

4 In some countries, goods can be delayed at customs for a long time. How might some dishonest people speed up clearance of the goods?

5 Some workers have to spend all day lifting heavy cases on and off trucks. How would you describe that sort of work?

6 How does the owner of a firm feel when he/she is faced with a desperate situation such as a huge tax bill or bankruptcy?

7 It is September. After several months of hard negotiations between your union and management you learn that you are to receive a pay increase. What do you hope management have agreed to?

8 You have been working all morning on a difficult task. Now you feel fairly happy. Why?

*Use the remaining verbs, phrases and expressions with **back** in your own sentences.*

COMMUNICATION SKILLS

FUNCTIONS

Complaining
Threatening
Calming people down

Superservice is a chain of US-owned supermarkets. Highly profitable and expanding, it is presently setting up new stores throughout the UK. One of the new supermarkets will be in Oldchester, a small, market town of 20,000 inhabitants with a steadily growing population.

Superservice have already bought a site in the centre of town. As they prepare to build the store, they become aware that there is a good deal of opposition to it from townspeople. In order to avoid bad publicity, the Managing Director plus some senior managers from Superservice agree to meet individuals or groups to hear their objections.

Dialogue

Listen to the following conversation, between a local café owner and the Public Relations Manager of Superservice.

CAFE OWNER	Let me tell you, I'm really annoyed about this supermarket idea, right in the middle of our town. What makes you think we want one?
P.R. MANAGER	We've carried out an opinion survey. Most people think it's an excellent idea.
CAFE OWNER	Yeah, and how much did you pay them?
P.R. MANAGER	How dare you!
CAFE OWNER	Look, I'm really upset about this, especially about the fast-food take-away you'll have in it. I'll lose all my customers.
P.R. MANAGER	Oh, I don't know. It shouldn't make too much difference to your trade.
CAFE OWNER	That's what you think. I warn you, I'll do everything I can to stop you building that store. You Americans think you can come to our town and do exactly what you like. Well, you're wrong.
P.R. MANAGER	Oh, come on, now. I'm sure we can understand each other.
CAFE OWNER	Don't try that with me. I wasn't born yesterday. Listen to me now. You try to build that supermarket here and there'll be trouble – you'll see.
P.R. MANAGER	Don't worry. It's not as bad as you think.

OH, COME ON, NOW. I'M SURE WE CAN UNDERSTAND EACH OTHER.

SUPERSERVICE THE STORE YOU CAN TRUST!

Role play

Instructions

The class should divide into two equal groups, members of the Superservice management team and opponents of the proposed Superservice supermarket. Each member of the group should take one of the roles described below. If more roles are required, use your imagination and invent further roles for each side.

1 Each member of Superservice's management should meet one of the supermarket opponents.

SUPERMARKET OPPONENT
Read the notes for your role and then note down some additional reasons why you are opposed to the new supermarket. Explain your objections clearly to the Superservice manager. Check that he/she has understood your point of view. Use the words and phrases in the table below to help you.

SUPERSERVICE MANAGER
Listen carefully to what the supermarket opponent has to say. Note down the main points of his/her argument. Ask for further clarification where necessary. Use the words and phrases in the table below to help you.

COMPLAINING

I'm not happy (about) ...
I'm really annoyed/upset (about) ...
I object to ...
I'd like to complain (about) ...

THREATENING

If you ..., I'll ...
Unless you ..., I'll ...
I warn you.   ⎫
                   ⎬ I'll ...
I'm warning you.   ⎭
You'd better not ... or else ...

CALMING PEOPLE DOWN

Oh, come on now.
Don't worry. It's not as bad as you think.

Supermarket opponents

PRESIDENT – THE OLDCHESTER PRESERVATION SOCIETY

Your society protects the town's old buildings and historical character. The supermarket site is right next to a row of two-hundred-year-old shops. If the supermarket is built, it will look out-of-place with its surroundings. One of the old shops is on part of the site itself, so it would probably need to be pulled down if a supermarket was built there. Oldchester is famous for its historical buildings and character. Will people want to live in the town if it loses its olde-worlde charm? Put this view to the Public Relations Manager.

OWNERS OF SMALL BUSINESSES (two roles)

Your businesses are on the other side of the street opposite the site and you have been trading there for years. You know that if the supermarket comes there will be fierce competition in the form of price cutting and special offers and that in the end you will both be forced to close down your businesses. After this the supermarket will start putting up its prices. You feel that the town doesn't need a supermarket, and certainly not one with a take-away fast-food outlet in it. Just imagine the litter that will be thrown onto the street. One of you should put your point of view to the Managing Director, the other to the Communications Manager. Threaten to write to the newspapers for support. There are much larger towns near Oldchester. Why can't the supermarket be built in one of them?

MEMBER OF THE PUBLIC

You object strongly to the proposed supermarket. The town has many historic old buildings and shop fronts. The supermarket will spoil the town's character. And what about the traffic jams caused by all the delivery vans coming and going at peak travelling times, just when you are in a hurry to get to work? As for the take-away fast-food outlet, you think it would be a stupid idea. Think of the litter – the paper bags, the boxes dropped onto the streets. Talk to the Community Relations Manager and explain your point of view. Threaten to get your local member of parliament to raise the matter with the Minister of the Environment.

HEAD TEACHER – OLDCHESTER PRIMARY SCHOOL

Your school is close to the proposed supermarket. Children attending the school are aged 5–12. You are worried about the increase in traffic which is bound to occur. Children have to cross the road near the supermarket site to get to school. There are certain to be accidents even if there is a traffic controller there. Oldchester has always been a safe, peaceful town, with its old shops and sleepy atmosphere. The supermarket would ruin the picturesque appearance and the character of the town. Speak to the New Projects Manager and explain your objections.

LOCAL RESIDENT

You live in a small block of flats at the side of the site. If the supermarket is built, the view from your front windows will be ruined. All you'll see is the tall brick wall – the side of the building – and you think that this will affect the value of your flat. Also there will be a lot of noise as customers push their trolleys – full of goods – past your flats to the car-park at the back. Talk to the Financial Director. Ask for £20,000 compensation. Threaten to take Superservice to court and sue them if they don't agree to give you the money.

Superservice managers

MANAGING DIRECTOR

You are going to meet the owner of a small business opposite the proposed supermarket site.

FINANCIAL DIRECTOR

You are going to meet a local resident from the small block of flats at the side of the proposed supermarket site.

NEW PROJECTS MANAGER

You are going to meet the head teacher of a local primary school near to the site of the proposed supermarket.

PUBLIC RELATIONS MANAGER

You are going to meet the President of the Oldchester Preservation Society.

COMMUNITY RELATIONS MANAGER

You are going to meet a member of the public who objects strongly to the proposed supermarket.

COMMUNICATIONS MANAGER

You are going to meet the owner of a small business opposite the proposed supermarket site.

2 The management of Superservice invite all the opponents of the proposed supermarket to attend a public meeting, chaired by the Managing Director of the supermarket chain.
Read the following notes before you begin the meeting.

SUPERSERVICE MANAGERS

Before the public meeting begins each manager should tell the others about the objections he/she was given at his/her individual meeting with an opponent of the supermarket. Discuss how you are going to deal with the arguments of your opponents. Work out your strategy carefully! You are determined to set up a supermarket in Oldchester. You also intend to have a take-away fast-food outlet in it, which you feel would be very profitable.

SUPERMARKET OPPONENTS

Before the public meeting begins discuss your individual objections to the building of the supermarket with the other opponents. Decide which are the strongest arguments against the proposed new store and also what action you could take if the Superservice managers refuse to cancel their plans. At the meeting listen to what the Superservice team have to say but don't be taken in by their pleasant manner and promises! You are in an angry mood and are determined to persuade them to locate the store in another town.

WRITING

You are a reporter for the Oldchester Evening News.
*Write an article about the meeting. Choose an appropriate, eye-catching headline for your article. Bear in mind that the newspaper has always been **against** developments which could threaten Oldchester's historical character.*

LISTENING

Understanding the main points

Listen to the following conversation and complete Gina's notes opposite about the job offer.

JOB WITH COMPUTEX IN PARIS
Position?
Duties?   selling computer systems to Parisian companies;
Salary?   Bonuses?
Perks?
ADVANTAGES?   DISADVANTAGES?
much higher salary;   might not be as interesting
as present job;

Vocabulary focus

1 *Listen again and fill in the gaps in these sentences from the conversation.*

1 People .... a lot.
2 It .... a business services outlet.
3 The sort of thing we're doing, in fact – .... a complete .... to firms . . .
4 But I thought you were happy here, Gina. .... me if I'm ....
5 It's flattering, isn't it, ... ?
6 You're a seasoned representative. Now the other companies are ready to ....
7 If we had to, we'd pay over the ....
8 He works .... – he's his own boss.
9 He could do the same sort of thing in Paris, after he'd .... his French a bit.
10 Why move then? And .... and your family?

2 *In pairs, discuss the meaning of the phrases and expressions above.*

12 Leadership

DISCUSSION

Work in groups of three or four. Each member of the group should choose a famous leader, either living or dead.

First, members should say briefly

(i) what the leader achieved
(ii) what qualities and abilities the leader has (or had)
(iii) whether group members think the person they chose was an *effective* leader

Then, the group should discuss the following questions.

1 Do the leaders you have described have any common characteristics, e.g. similar qualities, abilities, skills etc.
2 Are leaders born or made?

READING

Leadership is needed at all levels in an organisation. It is likely, however, that the leadership qualities required by a supervisor or manager are not the same as those required by the chief executive of a company. It is, therefore, difficult to define leadership satisfactorily.

A typical definition is that the leader 'provides direction and influences others to achieve common goals.' This is true in the case of supervisors and managers, but is it a good definition of the leader of an organisation? A chief executive
10 must indeed give 'direction' but he must do much more than that. He has to create 'a sense of excitement' in the organisation, and convince staff that he knows where the business is going. In addition he must be a focus for their aspirations. As Peter Drucker, the American writer, says, 'Leadership is the lifting of a man's vision to higher sights, the raising of a man's performance to a higher standard, the building of a man's personality beyond its normal limitations.'

When psychologists and other researchers first studied
20 leadership, they tried to find out if leaders had special
personal qualities or skills. They asked the question: Were
there specific *traits* which made leaders different from other
people? The results of their research were disappointing. In
time, it became clear that there was not a set of qualities
distinguishing leaders from non-leaders. Some studies had
suggested, for example, that leaders were more intelligent,
more self-confident, had better judgement etc. than other
people. But, it was pointed out, many people with these traits
do not become leaders. And many leaders do not have such
30 traits!

In 1974, a researcher, Ralph Stogdill, reviewed a large number
of projects on leadership. In Chart 1, you can see the personal
qualities which were considered important for success as a
leader.

Chart 1

CHARACTERISTICS OF A LEADER	
	Number of Studies
Fluency of speech	28
Ascendance, dominance	42
Knowledge	23
Emotional balance, control	25
Originality, creativity	20
Self confidence	45
Achievement drive, desire to excel	28
Drive for responsibility	29
Task orientation (interest in work)	19
Sociability, interpersonal skills	49
Participation in social exchange	29

Source: R. Stogdill. *Handbook of Leadership*. Macmillan, 1974.

However, as early as the 1950s, the *trait* approach to
leadership had become discredited. It is generally agreed
now that you cannot say a person is a leader because he/she
possesses a special combination of traits. All you can say is that
some qualities, like above-average intelligence and
40 decisiveness, are often associated with leaders.

An important analysis of leadership has been made by Fred
Fiedler, Professor of Psychology and Management at the
University of Washington. For over twenty years, he has
carried out research into effective leadership in a number of
organisations – businesses, government agencies and
voluntary associations. Fiedler observed how leaders
behaved, and he has identified two basic leadership styles:

Task-motivated leaders 'tell people what to do and how to
do it.' Such leaders get their satisfaction from completing the
50 task and knowing they have done it well. They run a 'tight
ship', give clear orders and expect clear directives from

their superiors. This does not mean that they show no concern for other people. But their priority is getting the job done.

Relationship-motivated leaders are more people-oriented. They get their satisfaction from having a good relationship with other workers. They want to be admired and liked by their subordinates. Such leaders will share responsibility with group members by encouraging subordinates to participate in decisions and make suggestions.

60

One of Fiedler's most original ideas was to offer a method for measuring a person's leadership style. In a questionnaire, he asked leaders to think of all the people they had worked with. From this group, the leaders had to choose the person with whom they could work the least well. The leader then had to rate this person – the least-preferred co-worker (LPC) – on a number of scales, as in the chart below.

Chart 2

People-Oriented versus Task-Oriented Leadership Styles

Least Preferred Co-Worker (LPC) Scale

Think of the person *with whom you can work least well.* He or she may be someone you work with now, or may be someone you knew in the past. He or she does not have to be the person you like least well, but should be the person *with whom you had the most difficulty in getting a job done.* Describe this person as he or she appears to you.

Scoring

Pleasant	8 7 6 5 4 3 2 1	Unpleasant	_____
Friendly	8 7 6 5 4 3 2 1	Unfriendly	_____
Rejecting	1 2 3 4 5 6 7 8	Accepting	_____
Tense	1 2 3 4 5 6 7 8	Relaxed	_____
Distant	1 2 3 4 5 6 7 8	Close	_____
Cold	1 2 3 4 5 6 7 8	Warm	_____
Supportive	8 7 6 5 4 3 2 1	Hostile	_____
Boring	1 2 3 4 5 6 7 8	Interesting	_____
Quarrelsome	1 2 3 4 5 6 7 8	Harmonious	_____

A person who described his least-preferred co-worker favourably tended to be 'human-relations oriented and considerate of the feelings of his men.' He was a *relationship-motivated leader.* On the other hand, someone who described his least-preferred co-worker unfavourably, giving him/her a low LPC rating, tended to be 'managing, task-controlling, and less concerned with the human relations aspects of the job.' This person was a *task-motivated leader.*

Throughout his work, Fred Fiedler emphasised that both styles of leadership could be effective in appropriate situations. There was no best style for all situations. Effective leadership depended on matching the leader to the task and the situation.

In a book called *The Winning Streak*, the authors studied leadership in some top British companies. The managers of those companies believed that effective leadership was a crucial factor in their organisations' success.

The authors were able to identify some characteristics of the chairmen and chief executives of the companies, which made them good leaders: firstly, the leaders were 'visible'. They did not hide away in some ivory tower at Head Office. Instead, they made regular visits to plants and sites, toured round their companies and talked to employees. Leaders made their presence felt. There are some fascinating examples of this practice. Sir Hector Laing, Chairman of United Biscuits, travels around his company with a jug of orange juice. He uses this to show employees how the company profits are divided up between employees, re-investment, dividends, tax etc. Lord Sieff, Chairman of Marks and Spencer until 1984, kept close contact with his staff. Once, when there had been heavy snowfalls, he drove from London to Chatham – a long way – just to thank sales assistants for turning up in spite of the weather. Lord Sieff had the habit of making telephone calls every Saturday, at about 5 p.m. to a few stores, chosen at random. He wanted to know how the day's trading had gone. No doubt, by doing this, he kept the staff on their toes. And he showed them that the Chairman had not forgotten them!

Another example of being 'visible' is provided by Brian Nelson, Group Managing Director of Bulmer, the cider-making firm. Every six months, he goes out in a lorry which delivers cider, and works as the lorry driver's mate. This gives him the opportunity to learn about the delivery service, and to talk frankly to employees about their problems.

Besides being visible, the leaders of these top companies provided a 'clear mission'. In other words, they knew where the organisation was going and persuaded staff to follow them. Sometimes, they spelled out the mission in a written statement. For example, Saatchi and Saatchi, the advertising group, include a statement of their principles in all annual reports. The statement says that Saatchi and Saatchi must be 'sharp in the definition of their long-term objectives.' And the documents also cover matters like employees, clients, creativity, market position and profitability.

Finally, successful organisations have clear values. And it is the job of the leader to show what they are. As Douglas Strachan, Managing Director of Allied Lyons Beer Division, says, 'You have to keep telling people your values. If you repeat it often enough, it does go down the line.' Thus, the leader is not only someone who 'lifts a man's vision'. He/She must also protect and promote the organisation's values.

Understanding the main points

1 *Complete the following sentences, using your own words.*

1 The main problem with the *trait* approach to leadership was that ....

2 According to Fiedler the most important aim of a task-motivated leader is ....

3 On the other hand, a relationship-motivated leader's main concern is ....

4 By asking managers to complete a questionnaire about their least preferred co-worker, Fiedler was able to ....
....

5 Fiedler does not think that one style of leadership is necessarily better then the other because ....
....

2 The authors of *The Winning Streak* have identified the main characteristics of the leadership styles of effective company chairmen and chief executives.
Note down the three characteristics described in the text.

1 ....
2 ....
3 ....

Vocabulary focus

Explain the meaning of the following words and phrases.

1 *where the business is going* (lines 12–13)
2 *focus for their aspirations* (lines 13–14)
3 *disappointing* (line 23)
4 *discredited* (line 36)
5 *directives* (line 51)
6 *priority* (line 53)
7 *getting the job done* (lines 53–4)
8 *people-oriented* (line 55)
9 *rate* (line 66)
10 *tended to* (line 69)
11 *considerate* (line 70)
12 *crucial* (line 84)
13 *kept the staff on their toes* (line 104)
14 *it goes down the line* (line 127)

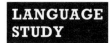

1 *self*-confident (line 27)
self-confidence

Below are some adjectives and nouns with *self.*
Study them and, if necessary, check their meanings in a
dictionary. Then use them to complete the following sentences.

ADJECTIVES	NOUNS
self-confident	self-control
self-addressed	self-discipline
self-educated	self-satisfaction
self-made	self-confidence
self-appointed	
self-important	
self-explanatory	
self-evident	
self-employed	
self-reliant	

1 The instructions on this package are simple to follow. They're really ....
2 He got to the top in business by his own efforts in spite of having little education or training. He's entirely a .... man.
3 We need salespeople who can work on their own initiative. They must be ....
4 It's not easy to start work at six o'clock every morning. You need plenty of .... to get to work on time.
5 Bill has no official position but he's very influential with the shop-floor workers. He's their .... leader.
6 I get a sense of .... when I think that I entered this company as an office boy and I'm now its chairman.
7 .... businessmen generally like the feeling of independence.
8 It is .... that a bank manager won't lend you money to start a company if you don't have some kind of business plan.
9 She's confident she'll be the best Office Manager we've ever had. Her .... is remarkable.
10 It's easy to lose your temper if an employee makes a silly mistake. However, a good manager learns to show ....
11 If you need more information, please write to us including a .... envelope.
12 A leader needs to be .... because if he doubts his own judgement, others will do so too.
13 Despite her culture and knowledge, she is in fact largely .... since she left school at fifteen.

2 *market* position (line 122)

What expressions do you know with the word *market*? Below is a quick quiz.

1 What does a firm usually carry out before it introduces a product onto the market?
2 What expression means 'the proportion of the market held by one manufacturer or brand'?
3 What do we call the place where shares are bought and sold in large quantities?

4 When you develop a product, you hope people will eventually buy it. You hope the product will be ....
5 Sony are continually putting new products ....
6 What does a firm do when it goes 'up-market' and 'down-market'?
7 If you buy currency or goods illegally, you buy them on the ....
8 What is a 'seller's market' and a 'buyer's market'? Can you give an example of each from the world of business?
9 What do we mean when we say that a market is 'saturated'?
10 An interesting property has just come .... the market.
11 We have no idea what the present market .... of our buildings is.

3 Phrasal verbs and nouns with *turn*

turn up (line 100)

A *Match the following verbs and nouns with the correct definitions.*

1	turn up	a	do something in an agreed order
2	turn down	b	the amount of sales in a certain period of time
3	turn over		
4	turn round	c	do business or sell goods worth a certain amount
5	turn out		
6	turn against	d	make a business profitable again after it has had losses
7	take turns		
8	turning point	e	a point in time when an important change takes place
9	turnover		
10	turnover	f	the number of workers employed to replace those who have left
		g	produce
		h	refuse, reject
		i	change one's attitude and become hostile
		j	arrive, appear

B *Complete the following passages with words from the list above.*

1 I work for a kitchen appliance manufacturer. We're a fairly large organisation. Our .... (1) is over £20m annually, and I'd say we .... (2) roughly 2,000 units a month. We're profitable now but we had a difficult time in the early 1980s. We almost went bankrupt. The .... (3) was when we got a new Chief Executive. Within two years, he completely .... (4) the company. Now we're doing well. Our only problem is that our labour .... (5) is rather high – well above average for the industry.

2 I'm meant to start work at 8.30 a.m. but I often .... (1) late. On Fridays, someone in the office has to work until 10 p.m. We usually .... (2) – it's fairer that way. I quite like my job and I don't want any more responsibility. In fact, I've already .... (3) two offers of promotion, much to my boss's annoyance. I hope he doesn't .... (4) me because I've refused opportunities for promotion. By the way, my firm .... (5) about £200,000 a month.

FUNCTIONS

Persuading
Giving way in arguments
Interrupting
Considering possibilities

Dialogue

Listen to the following conversation, in which two executives discuss the risks involved in signing a contract with an American company.

KEN   What about this contract with the Americans, Ian? Don't you think it's great news?

IAN   You seem to be forgetting, we haven't even started negotiating it yet.

KEN   That's true. But surely you'd agree it's a great opportunity for us.

IAN   That may be so Ken, but what if we can't supply them with everything they want?

KEN   How do you mean?

IAN   Supposing we got the contract and . . . let's say we tied ourselves down to delivery dates. Right? Are you with me?

KEN   Uh huh.

IAN   Well, if we had a strike here, like last year . . .

KEN   You've got a point there. We'd never be able to meet the orders coming in from the States.

IAN   Exactly. If that happened, we'd be in trouble. It's no use signing a contract if . . .

KEN   Hold on a second, Ian. Surely the American deal could be very profitable for us. We shouldn't miss it just because we *might* have labour problems.

IAN   Hm . . . I don't know.

PERSUADING

Don't you } { agree (that) . . .
Wouldn't you } { accept (that) . . .
              { think (that) . . .

I'm sure you'd }
Surely you'd } agree (that) . . .

Isn't it a fact that . . .

GIVING WAY IN ARGUMENTS

That's true.
That may be true.
You've got a point there.
I can see that but . . .

INTERRUPTING

Now, hold on a second.
Wait a minute.
Could I just make a quick point, please? } { (polite, usually used
I'd like to come in here, if I may.   } { in group discussions)

CONSIDERING POSSIBILITIES

What if we can't supply them with everything they want?
Supposing we had labour problems like last year.
Let's say } we failed to meet the delivery date.
Let's imagine }
If that happened, we'd be in trouble.

Role play

Situation

Textafabrik is a clothing manufacturer, based in Northern England. Recently, a large American company, the Forbes Corporation, has shown interest in distributing Textafabrik's merchandise throughout the United States. This is an important deal for Textafabrik. If the negotiations are successful, the company's future will be secure for years to come. However, the deal will not be easy to finalise. There are many problems concerning the contract that will have to be resolved. The negotiations, clearly, are going to be long and tiring.

Textafabrik are aware, too, that a rival company – Pretport – are waiting to jump in if Textafabrik's deal falls through.

The negotiations are due to start in Chicago in two weeks' time. Who is going to go there and negotiate the contract? Four people at Textafabrik are being considered for the assignment, but only *one* person – for reasons of time and money – will go. The four persons, with details about each, are listed below.

Instructions

*Work in groups of four. Each of you is one of the persons described below. Study your own role card and also read carefully the role cards of the other executives. When you are all ready, each of you must try to persuade the others that **you** are the most suitable person to negotiate the contract in Chicago.*

MANAGING DIRECTOR

You made the first contact with the Forbes Corporation and the Chairman of Forbes has now become almost a personal friend. Therefore, you are the obvious choice to conduct these vitally important negotiations. However, you are not used to negotiating this kind of contract. Normally you leave contract negotiations to your Overseas Sales Manager or the Financial Director. You spend most of your time on organisation and labour relations. But you do have a degree in company law, however, which you obtained many years ago. Unfortunately, at the moment you have a problem in your personal life. Your husband/wife has just left you and is asking for a divorce, so you are very upset.

OVERSEAS SALES MANAGER

You usually negotiate contracts with overseas agents and distributors. However, in a few days' time, you are due to start a six-week European sales trip, which you do at this time every year. This trip helps you to keep in touch with the firm's important customers, and you generally come back with some large orders. You feel that, because of your experience, you are the ideal person to handle the negotiations with Forbes. Besides, you are not confident that any of the others could do the job properly. Unfortunately, you are rather worried at the moment about your daughter, who is having difficulties at school. In fact, the headmaster has suggested that she ought to be seen by a psychologist.

FINANCIAL DIRECTOR

You have always accompanied the Overseas Sales Manager when he/she negotiates contracts with agents and distributors. Therefore, you know a great deal about this kind of work. However, you have a reputation for being slow at negotiating, and are known to worry too much about small details. Also, some people in the firm consider you too frank, and lacking in tact. If you could negotiate a good contract with the Americans, you would gain a lot of respect from your colleagues. At the moment your wife is suffering from bad health. She gets upset when you are away, which makes it difficult for you to concentrate on the job. This means that you spend a lot of time phoning her when you are away on foreign trips.

GENERAL MANAGER

You think you are a sharp, shrewd negotiator – most of your colleagues would agree with you. You are used to negotiating because you deal with the unions a lot. Also, you are an honest person, with a strong personality, and everyone in the company respects you. You know the United States well because you spent three years there after university. You are a qualified engineer and have a master's degree in Business Administration. You have not been overseas for the company very often because you have to spend most of your time at the factory. You are a very busy man – you have not had a real holiday for five years. Recently you have been feeling under stress. 'Take it easy,' advised the company doctor.

Case study

The big deal

In the end, it was Brian Young, Textafabrik's Managing Director, who went to Chicago to negotiate the deal with the Forbes Corporation. Young was accompanied by the Deputy Managing Director, James Palmer. Palmer, a competent but rather colourless person, went along mainly to give moral support to Young and to back him up if negotiations became difficult.

The other executives got on with their jobs. Overseas Sales Manager, Shirley Drake, went on her sales trip to Europe. Kenneth Rossiter, Financial Director, continued his work on the departmental budgets. And the General Manager, Ron Wilde, continued to dream of having a holiday!

For the next three weeks, there was little news from the negotiators. Just two telexes from Brian Young saying that all was going well. In the middle of the fourth week, Kenneth Rossiter received a call from James Palmer – a very worrying call indeed:

'I don't know what's going on here, Kenneth,' said Palmer. 'Brian's behaving in the most extraordinary manner. Believe it or not, he's agreed to supply Forbes with 200,000 shirts and 20,000 suits a month. Starting next month. Now what do you think of that?'

Kenneth Rossiter gasped. 'He must be out of his mind. We can't supply half that number. At least, not unless we cut supplies to our European customers. And they wouldn't put up with that, would they?'

'Exactly,' said Palmer. 'But I'll tell you another thing. It's going to cost us a lot of money if we don't deliver the merchandise on time. Brian's agreed to a penalty clause – a really stiff one – for non-delivery.'

'Why on earth did you let him do it, James? Couldn't you have stopped him?'

'Not a chance. I tried to, but he didn't want to know. I can't get through to him. Ever since he got that call from his wife a few days ago, he's been acting very strangely.'

'How do you mean?'

'Well, er ...' Palmer hesitated, searching for words. 'He's ... drinking a lot and ... er ... I'd say he's very depressed. Right on the edge, if you know what I mean. The Americans don't know what to make of it. But the negotiations are going well for them – I guess they don't care too much.'

Crisis point

That evening, Ken Rossiter called Shirley Drake in Zurich. 'Come back right away, Shirley, we've got big trouble,' he told her. She arrived at the plant just before lunch the following day. 'Do you think I should go over there?' she asked Rossiter.

'Let's call James and see what he thinks,' was his answer.

It wasn't easy to get hold of Palmer, but eventually they reached him at his hotel.

BUT PAULINE, I LOVE YOU...

'Thank goodness you've called!' he said. 'All hell has broken loose here. I've just picked up Brian from the jail. Yes, that's what I said, the J.A.I.L. He spent the night there. Over the speed limit. Drunk in charge of a vehicle. Abusing a police officer.'

'I can't believe what I'm hearing, James,' said Rossiter.

'That's the way it is. I should have known something like this would happen. All last evening, he was talking about Pauline (his wife). He sounded extremely depressed – as if he was on the verge of a breakdown. Then he said he was going for a drive. "To clear the cobwebs out of my mind," was how he put it. I tried to stop him – he wouldn't listen. What do we do now, Kenneth?'

'Where's Brian now?'

'Sleeping it off in his room. He looks in bad shape. I cancelled today's session with the Americans. They weren't pleased, I can tell you.'

'Let me talk to Shirley and Ronald. I'll call you back in about an hour,' said Kenneth. 'We'll work something out.'

Instructions

Working as one group, consider the following questions and then discuss them.

1 Why are the management of Textafabrik facing these difficult problems? What factors, in other words, led to the crisis?
2 Is there any chance of signing a contract with the Americans, which will be satisfactory for both sides? If so, what actions should be taken? And by whom?

3 Brian Young is known to be a strong-minded person. Supposing he refuses to cooperate with the other executives. What should they do in that situation?

4 How can Textafabrik avoid similar problems in the future?

WRITING

Telex

The advantage of the telex is that it is a fast and economical means of communication. Telex messages are less expensive than telegrams. However, long messages are expensive, so the sender of a telex should be as concise as possible. Abbreviations are often used in telexes. But the sender should not use so many abbreviations that the message becomes unclear.

Below are some common abbreviations found in telexes.
Study them and then use some of them in the following writing exercise.

Attn	attention	pls	please
adv	advise	poss	possible
b	be	qty	quantity
cld/wld	could/would	r	are
conf	confirm	recv	received
fr	for	req	required
msg	message	tlx	telex
nxt	next	rgds	regards
o	our	asap	as soon as possible
yr/y	your	telcon	telephone conversation
U	you	foll/flwg	following

Kenneth Rossiter (see **Case study**) talks to his colleagues about the situation in Chicago. They try to phone James Palmer, but the international lines are busy. Therefore, they decide to send Palmer an overnight telex advising him what to do.

Below, you can read Kenneth Rossiter's notes, indicating what he wants to include in the telex.
Write the telex which Rossiter sends to Chicago. Use the framework on page 154 to help you.

Kenneth Rossiter's notes

- Tell Palmer that he must take over the negotiations for the contract;
- One of us will fly out this weekend to support him;
- Palmer must persuade Brian Young that he's not fit enough to take part in further negotiations;
- If Young is difficult, Palmer must tell Young that we will organise an emergency board meeting and take steps to replace Young as Managing Director;
- Palmer must tell the Americans as soon as possible that the clause concerning the shirts and suits must be re-negotiated. We suggest offering: 100,000 shirts, 5,000 suits per month. Explain to the Americans that Young has had a nervous breakdown;

LEADERSHIP

– *Palmer must get Young a good lawyer. We'll talk to his wife,*
Pauline – she may be able to help;
– *Ask Palmer to confirm that this message has been*
received and understood.

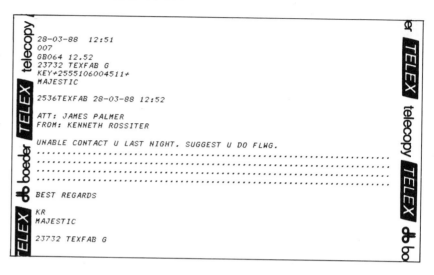

```
28-03-88   12:51
007
GB064 12.52
23732 TEXFAB G
KEY*2555106004511*
MAJESTIC

2536TEXFAB 28-03-88 12:52

ATT: JAMES PALMER
FROM: KENNETH ROSSITER

UNABLE CONTACT U LAST NIGHT. SUGGEST U DO FLWG.
.....................................................
.....................................................
.....................................................

BEST REGARDS

KR
MAJESTIC

23732 TEXFAB G
```

LISTENING

Understanding the main points

1 *Read the article below, which appeared in the monthly newsletter
of the Porchester Chamber of Commerce.* You will notice that parts
of the article are missing.

HOW TO BE A WINNER

On 30 April the Porchester Chamber of Commerce was
addressed by Frank Evans, the manager of Porchester
United Football Club, who are the current leaders of the First
Division. Introducing Mr Evans, our Chairman, Robert
Higginbotham, reminded the audience of the manager's
remarkable record. In the previous five years . . . .
. . . .

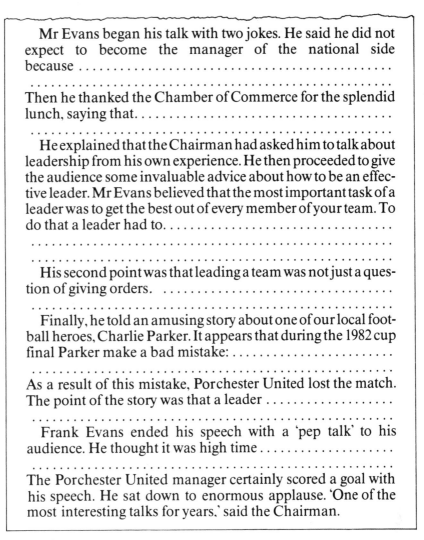

Mr Evans began his talk with two jokes. He said he did not expect to become the manager of the national side because . . . .

Then he thanked the Chamber of Commerce for the splendid lunch, saying that. . . . .

He explained that the Chairman had asked him to talk about leadership from his own experience. He then proceeded to give the audience some invaluable advice about how to be an effective leader. Mr Evans believed that the most important task of a leader was to get the best out of every member of your team. To do that a leader had to. . . . .

His second point was that leading a team was not just a question of giving orders. . . . .

Finally, he told an amusing story about one of our local football heroes, Charlie Parker. It appears that during the 1982 cup final Parker make a bad mistake: . . . .

As a result of this mistake, Porchester United lost the match. The point of the story was that a leader . . . .

Frank Evans ended his speech with a 'pep talk' to his audience. He thought it was high time . . . .

The Porchester United manager certainly scored a goal with his speech. He sat down to enormous applause. 'One of the most interesting talks for years,' said the Chairman.

2 *As you listen to the passage, note down the information which is missing from the article and then complete it.*

13 Management in multinationals

DISCUSSION

Study the following examples of mistakes that foreign business people have made when doing business abroad and then answer the questions below each one. When you have finished, compare your answers with those given in the key.

A An American airline company operating in Brazil advertised proudly that it had luxurious 'rendezvous lounges' on its jets. The advertisement upset many people in Brazil. Can you suggest why?

B Some time ago an American company in Spain decided to have a company picnic – such picnics had been successful at their headquarters in the US. At the picnic in their Spanish branch, the US executives dressed up as chefs and served food to the Spanish workers in the company. The idea was to promote friendly relations between executives and workers. The atmosphere at the picnic was not good, and the picnic was not very successful. Can you guess why?

C This advertisement appeared in magazines and other media in Quebec, Canada. A woman, dressed in shorts, could be seen playing golf with her husband. The caption said that housewives could have an enjoyable day on the golf course and still quickly prepare a delicious evening meal by serving the advertised canned fish. The advertisement was totally inappropriate for the Quebec market. Do you have any idea why?

D A manufacturer of cosmetics wanted to break into the French market. It decided to use chain stores to distribute its goods because (**i**) marketing and distribution costs would be decreased and (**ii**) its goods would be given plenty of shelf space. This approach was disastrous for the company. Why do you think this was?

E A foreign buyer negotiated with a Japanese businessman. During the negotiations, the Japanese man sat back in his chair several times, maintaining complete silence. When the foreign buyer got back to his hotel, he realised he had paid too much for the goods supplied by the Japanese man. Why did this happen?

(Examples A–D taken from:
International Business Blunders
Ricks, Fu and Arpan, Grid Inc. 1974
Columbus, Ohio 43214
Examples E and F use ideas from the same book.)

F A foreign businessman had been negotiating a deal in England. When he got back to the hotel, his boss phoned him. 'How did it go?' asked the boss.

'Just great,' replied the foreign businessman. 'I made several proposals to the Englishman and he kept shaking his head up and down – he obviously agreed with everything I said.' What mistake has the foreign businessman made? And why?

READING

Management in multinationals

If asked to define a multinational, most people would say that it is a company doing business in more than one country. Many experts, however, would not be satisfied with this definition. They believe that it does not indicate the size and scale of the multinational's activities. To be a 'true' multinational, they say, an organisation should operate in at least six countries and have no less than 20% of its sales or assets in those countries. In addition, it should 'think internationally'. That is to say, the management should have a 'global perspective'. It should see

10 the world as inter-related and inter-dependent.

An example of this global approach is provided by the Massey Ferguson company. Its tractors are assembled from parts made in several countries. As one of their executives says, 'We combine French-made transmissions, British-made engines, Mexican-made axles and United States-made sheet metal parts to produce in Detroit a tractor for sale in Canada.'

The size and international organisation of some multinationals is impressive. The larger enterprises, like IBM, British Petroleum and Mobil Oil, have subsidiaries in sixty to eighty

20 countries. Some, like Heinz, Singer and Exxon, get more than half their profits from overseas business. Details of the top fifteen multinationals are given in Figure 1.

Figure 1

The Top 15 Multinational Companies			
Country	Company	Foreign Sales As Percentage of Total	Number of Countries in which Subsidiaries Are Located
USA	General Motors	19	21
USA	Exxon	50	25
USA	Ford	26	30
Netherlands	Royal Dutch/Shell	79	43
USA	General Electric	16	32
USA	IBM	39	80
USA	Mobil Oil	45	62
USA	Chrysler	24	26
USA	Texaco	40	30
Britain	Unilever	42	40
USA	ITT	42	40
USA	Gulf Oil	45	61
Britain	British Petroleum	88	52
Netherlands	Philips Gloeilampenfabrieken	n.a.	29
USA	Standard Oil of California	45	26

Source: United Nations data.

Some economists have estimated that, by the year 2000, about 200 to 300 multinationals will be providing half of the world's total goods and services.

Because of their global approach, multinationals often make decisions which are against the interests of their host countries. They may decide, for example, to close down their plant in Country A because they wish to concentrate production in Country B. Obviously, this will be an unpopular decision in Country A. The government of that country will probably put pressure on the multinational to change its mind. Multinationals are criticised by foreign governments for other reasons. Sometimes, a subsidiary in one country will supply another subsidiary with cheap – or below-cost – products. This happens when a subsidiary has just started up in a country. The other subsidiary will help it to get on its feet. Difficulties often arise when a multinational wishes to transfer its earnings back to Head Office. The host country may feel that the transfer will have a bad effect on the exchange rate of its currency. Or, it may want the multinational to re-invest profits in the business. The interests of multinationals and foreign governments frequently clash. This can lead to friction between the two sides, and even bitterness.

The list of complaints against multinationals is a long one. As a result, many countries have tried to restrict their operations. Some, such as Nigeria and India, have said that a certain percentage of the equity of the foreign company must be owned by local investors. Other countries insist that a percentage of the managers of the multinational must be local staff.

Multinational managers will spend much of their time working overseas. They will, therefore, be living and working in a strange environment. They will have to deal with people who have a different language, customs, religion and business practices. They will find that they cannot do things the way they did at home.

In a book entitled *International Business Blunders*, the authors give some examples of what happens when managers do not take foreign conditions into account. They describe, for example, how an American company sent sewing-machines to a developing country. Unfortunately, the machines became rusty because the natives drank the lubricating oil. They believed it to be a fertility potion! In another example the authors describe how an American manager in Japan offended a very important Japanese executive because he did not show the executive enough respect. The two men had met first in the Japanese man's office. This was small and had little furniture in it, so the American assumed the other man was a low-level executive. He did not realise that, in Japan, a top executive does not necessarily have a plush office.

Managers working abroad need various skills. Clearly, it is a great advantage if they know the language of the country they are working in. But this is not the most important requirement. A recent study has shown that they need, above all, these qualities: human relations skills, an understanding of the other culture and the ability to adapt.

Human relations skills are vital because, to be effective, the manager must persuade local staff to cooperate with him. In the study mentioned above, some Asian executives described how they felt about American managers, after working with them for some time. The executives were from Taiwan, the Philippines and India. They suggested that the American managers sometimes had an attitude of intellectual and cultural superiority. They seemed to be 'know-it-alls'. And they tried to impose their way of life on local workers. The Americans needed to lose those attitudes. They had to be more willing to learn from their fellow workers, and to treat them as 'partners'.

Differences in culture are important when a manager is negotiating in a foreign country. For instance, many Europeans and Americans like to get to the point quickly when negotiating. This is not so in some countries, like Brazil, where people prefer to beat around the bush more. They take their time, trying to create a relationship of trust. In such countries, the European or American manager must be patient, or else he will come away from a deal empty-handed. In Japan, there are often long silences during negotiations – especially if things are not going smoothly. European and American executives tend to react in the wrong way when this happens. They make a concession or talk in an over-eager way, so that they lose ground in the discussions.

Finally, those working abroad must remember that a deal is not always a deal. In some countries, a person may say 'yes' to a proposal simply to be polite, or agreeable. Even written contracts, in some areas, may not be worth much.

Understanding the main points

1 In the opinion of experts, what are the two factors indicating that a company is truly a multinational?
2 Which of the top fifteen multinationals in Figure 1 depends most heavily on earnings from foreign trade?
3 Why might a foreign government object if a subsidiary of a multinational in one country supplies a subsidiary in another country with below-cost products?
4 What must a multinational do if it wishes to have a subsidiary in Nigeria?
5 What do you think the aim of the book *International Business Blunders* is?
6 Why did the Asian executives criticise their American managers?
7 How might an unfamiliarity with Japanese culture put European businessmen at a disadvantage in Japan?

Vocabulary focus

Explain the meaning of the following words and phrases.

1 *assets* (line 7)
2 *close down* (line 28)
3 *put pressure on* (line 32)
4 *started up* (line 36)
5 *get on its feet* (line 37)
6 *earnings* (line 38)

7 *friction* (line 43)
8 *equity* (line 48)
9 *offended* (line 65)
10 *get to the point* (line 92)
11 *beat around the bush* (line 94)
12 *empty-handed* (line 97)

1 The Zanek Pharmaceutical Group, known simply as ZNK, set up its first factory in Manchester, which is the administrative centre of the group. ZNK is a small multinational organisation. Information about it is given in the chart below.

Notes

Companies 1, 2 and 3	ZNK holds 100% of the companies' equity capital (shares giving the right of ownership)
Companies 4 and 5	ZNK has 51% of the companies' equity capital
Companies 6 and 7	ZNK has 30% and 20% respectively of each company's equity capital

Study the following definitions. Then, using words and phrases from the list on the left, make statements about the ZNK group.

holding/parent company	a company which controls a number of others, which are known as subsidiaries
subsidiary	a company which is controlled by another one. The controlling company (holding/parent company) owns over 50% – and sometimes 100% – of the ordinary shares of the subsidiary
associated company	A company of which at least 20% and not more than 50% of the ordinary shares is held by another company

have a stake/shareholding in	have money invested in another company, e.g. That large newspaper group has a stake in two television production companies.
partly/wholly owned subsidiary	less than 50% of the equity/*all* the equity of the subsidiary is owned by another company
head office	the controlling centre of an organisation
be based/located in	be situated in
diversify	move into a new field, vary one's range of products in order to spread the risk

2 *Complete the following passage, using suitable words from the box below.*

agreement	equity	stalemate ⎫
compromise (verb)	inflexible	deadlock ⎭
concession	investment	withdraw ⎫
counter-proposal(s)	negotiate	pull out ⎭
deal	shareholding	

Many countries, such as Nigeria and India, are trying to get more control over their economies. They welcome foreign .... (1) but insist that their own nationals own a percentage of the foreign company's .... (2). The size of the .... (3) varies, ranging from 20% to 60%, though it can be higher or lower.

When governments try to increase their nationals' equity shareholding, foreign companies are not pleased. Generally, they try to .... (4) with the government to keep the percentage as low as possible. They argue and haggle, make proposals and .... (5), to persuade the government to give way and make some kind of .... (6). If the foreign company employs many local people, or earns a lot of foreign currency, the government may be willing to .... (7).

Some governments are very .... (8) and will make no concessions. In this case, the negotiations end in a .... (9), with neither side giving way. The foreign company ends up by .... (10) from the country. This usually leads to feelings of great bitterness on both sides. No company wants to leave a country. In general, the foreign firm will make every effort to reach .... (11) or make some sort of .... (12) with the host government.

3 Idiomatic uses of *foot/feet*

get on its feet (line 37)

Study the following list of expressions. If necessary, check their meaning in a dictionary.

get back on one's feet (again)
get a foot in the door
fall on one's feet
have/get cold feet
put one's foot down
put one's foot in it
have a foothold in

Rewrite the following sentences, replacing the words in italics with the correct forms of the expressions above.

1 The management *has acted firmly* concerning smoking in the factory.
2 We don't have a contract with them but we've *taken the first steps towards getting one*.
3 I was laid off in January but I *was really lucky* because I found an even better job a month later.
4 I *made a bad mistake* when I told our Marketing Director that the new product would fail.
5 For some time, we were planning to enter the US market. Then, at the last moment, we *lost our nerve and decided not to*.
6 The group of department stores made losses for three years running. However, now it *has recovered*.
7 It took three years' hard work, but at last we've *got a secure position* in the Japanese market.

4 Idiomatic uses of *mind*

change its mind (line 32)

A *Complete the following sentences with suitable words.*

1 Companies sometimes have difficulty .... up their minds which market to enter.
2 We are in .... minds whether to set up a subsidiary in West Germany. We're not sure if sales will be large enough.
3 Our agent's results have been disappointing but we must .... in mind that he's only been handling our goods for eighteen months.
4 .... my mind, overseas postings upset one's family life.
5 Our Chairman's a bore. He goes on and on about exports. I reckon he's got a .... -track mind!
6 When you work in a foreign country, you've got to be .... -minded and respect the opinions of the people living there, even if you think those people are rather intolerant and .... -minded.
7 I'm not really happy working in the Personnel Department. I've a .... mind to ask for a transfer.
8 When my boss was sent to Hong Kong, it never .... my mind that I would be asked to replace him.

B *Working in groups of two or three, discuss the meaning of the words in italics in the following sentences.*

1 We've had little success in the Saudi Arabian market. *Mind you*, it's a tough one to break into.
2 I've forgotten to send off those letters. *Never mind!* I'll post them first thing tomorrow morning.
3 Efficient secretaries are rarely *absent-minded*.
4 This is the third time this week Jean has been late for work. I'm really going to *give her a piece of my mind*.
5 That sales presentation I've got to give – you know, it's *been on my mind* all week.

5 Multinationals are *criticised* by foreign governments *for* other reasons. (lines 33–4)
And they tried to *impose* their way of life *on* local workers. (lines 85–6)

The words or phrases listed below can be followed by *of, to, for* or *on*.
Working in pairs, decide which preposition follows each one.
(v. = verb, n. = noun, sb. = somebody)

criticise (sb.)	...*for*......	gamble (v.)	....
focus (v.)	....	succeed	....
responsible	....	approve	....
agree	....	accuse (sb.)	....
praise (sb.)	....	chance (n.)	....
congratulate (sb.)	....	in favour	....
famous	....	object (v.)	....
set one's heart	....	think	....

Rewrite the following sentences without changing their meaning. Use the words and phrases above and make any other necessary changes.

e.g. Susan's job is to order supplies.
    responsible
    Susan is responsible **for** ordering supplies.

1 Some people have said that multinationals do not train enough local staff.
    criticised
2 'Today, we shall pay special attention to the problems of multinationals,' said the television presenter.
    focus
3 Their proposal was unacceptable to us.
    agree
4 IBM make high-quality products and give good service, as everyone knows.
    famous
5 Because of his actions, several local firms have gone bankrupt.
    responsible
6 I'm absolutely determined to work in our Los Angeles plant for a year or two.
    set one's heart
7 Is it at all possible for you to be transferred abroad?
    chance
8 We are taking a chance, hoping that the host government will make concessions.
    gamble

9 Some governments cannot accept the fact that multinationals dominate key industrial sectors.
object

10 They were able to persuade the government to offer more favourable conditions.
succeed

Finally, make your own sentences using the following words or phrases followed by the correct prepositions.

praise   congratulate   approve   accuse   in favour
think

COMMUNICATION SKILLS

FUNCTIONS
Giving tentative opinions and advice
Giving warnings

Dialogue

A German executive is about to be transferred to a subsidiary company in England.
Listen to the following conversation, in which an English colleague tells him what to expect when he gets there.

DAVID   I suppose I'd better tell you something about the English now. I'd say you'll find your English colleagues fairly easy to get on with and pretty tolerant. Oh, by the way, don't expect to start work too early. Quite honestly, it's usually 9.15 a.m. before much happens in an English office.

KARL   I'm glad you told me that. As you know, we start a lot earlier here.

DAVID   Right, so I thought I'd better warn you. Don't get to the office too early on your first day – you probably won't even find the building open!

KARL   OK. You were telling me about the people...

DAVID   Oh yes. You may well find them, er, a bit reserved at first. They may not be too friendly to begin with. And they sometimes seem to be a bit ... er ... cool towards foreigners.

KARL   I see. Then I mustn't expect to be invited to dinner during the first week.

DAVID   And I wouldn't bank on an invitation in the first month, either!

KARL   Really?

DAVID   Yes, I'm afraid so. But, mind you, once they do get to know

'The flowers are for you, and the Schnapps is for your wife.'

you, English people are very hospitable. They really put themselves out for you.

KARL   And when I go to their home, should I take a gift? A bottle of schnapps, perhaps?

DAVID   No, I wouldn't do that if I were you. Flowers would be safer. You never know, your host might not drink alcohol. Then you'd start the evening off on the wrong foot.

KARL   Yes, I certainly wouldn't want to . . . how do you say . . . put my foot in it. Ha, ha!

GIVING OPINIONS AND ADVICE

Take flowers if you are invited to dinner.
Don't get to the office too early on your first day.

Make sure you $\begin{cases} \text{wear a white shirt.} \\ \text{don't get to the office too early on your first day.} \end{cases}$

Be careful about what you wear to the office.
Be careful not to smoke without first asking permission.
You ought to/should always wear a tie at the office.
You oughtn't to/shouldn't take alcohol for your host.
If I were you, I'd/I wouldn't take his wife a box of chocolates.

It might be $\begin{cases} \text{wise} \\ \text{a good thing} \\ \text{advisable} \end{cases}$ to call people by their first names.

Role play

Situation

You work at the head office of a multinational which has subsidiaries or sales offices in over sixty countries. Your organisation has recently created an Overseas Briefing Department, whose purpose is to prepare staff for overseas postings and to give them information about the countries they are going to.

When several executives are about to be transferred to an overseas subsidiary, the head of the department tries to find someone at Head Office who has special knowledge to hold a briefing session on the country concerned. The head of the department says to the person:

'Just tell them the sort of things they ought to know, which will make life easier for them when they first arrive in the country. You know, things such as what kind of people they'll be meeting, what to do if their boss invites them to dinner, tips about suitable clothes to wear at the office. Anything that'll help them adjust or stop them from making fools of themselves – you know what I mean.'

The head of the department ends by reminding the person giving the briefing that most employees at overseas subsidiaries are local nationals.

Instructions

Work either individually or in small groups.

First, prepare notes on your own country or a country that you know well. (If necessary, use your imagination!)

The other members of the class should play the roles of the executives going to the overseas subsidiary. They should ask questions both during and after the talk.

MULTINATIONALS

Case study

The executive who came in from the cold

Nancy Freeman, Brand Manager for a coffee manufacturer, came back to Head Office in England after a five-year spell in the company's Montreal subsidiary. Within months of her return, her relationship with her boss, Harry Coates, Divisional Marketing Manager, had become extremely difficult. So much so that both Nancy and Harry felt they could no longer work together. At this point, Derek Allot, Personnel Director, stepped in. He had several talks with the two of them to find out what the problems were. Here is a summary, in each person's words, of what they had to say.

Nancy's story

'You know, I would never have stayed in Montreal for five years by choice. When I went there, I understood I'd have a couple of years there – at most. The whole idea, I thought, was for me to get a better understanding of our overseas operations. After that, I'd come back to something really interesting at Head Office. Like Marketing Manager of one of the divisions. I mean, that's where I should be, with my experience and work record.

Sure, I was disappointed when I was asked to stay on in Montreal. Those winters are no joke, I can tell you. Then I thought, what the hell, if the company wants me to do it, I'll play ball. It'll pay off for me in the end. OK, but what happened when I got back to England? I got put in charge of one of our new brands. Exactly the sort of work I was doing before I left. And which I can do in my sleep now.

All right, I thought, at least I'll show people here that I picked up a thing or two in Montreal. North Americans are way ahead of us in marketing, in my opinion. So, I started on the deliveries of my brand. I really got on to the sales staff. Bullied them to get my brand to customers on time. It's funny, the reps seemed to resent what I was doing. They seemed to think there's something wrong with doing a job properly. And the Sales Manager wasn't much help either – I had quite a few arguments with him.

I had trouble with Harry Coates from the start. He was obviously jealous of me because I had some new and exciting ideas. Maybe he thought I was after his job or something. Though, I must admit, I do think he ought to be moved on now – where he can't do any harm. Anyway, what really annoyed me with Harry was that he was so damned negative about everything. I made lots of suggestions to improve sales of my brand, like having stands at railway stations and airports, and giving travellers free cups of coffee; tasting sessions at big companies; banners from aeroplanes, which would fly over London during the Royal Wedding when the city's packed – and a dozen other ideas. Huh! Harry didn't want to know. He was so sarcastic, too, about my ideas. I felt . . . really bad, sort of humiliated.

The last straw came when he criticised me for being late for work. That was unfair. In Montreal, my boss never complained if I came in sometimes at 9.30 in the morning. He knew that I often stayed late in the office, till nine or ten at night. Like I do here.

I reckon I'll give the company another year. And if things don't improve, I'll go elsewhere. Pity! I thought I'd be here for life.'

Harry's story

'I've seen this sort of thing happen before. Staff come back from overseas postings and they think they're the cat's whiskers. Like we owe them something. They don't realise how lucky they are to go abroad. Travelling at the company's expense. Getting top salaries, and terrific experience. And being treated like princes, what's more. But you see, then they get back to England, and they've got to come back to earth. And sometimes they don't make a very good landing. Like Nancy.

Frankly, Nancy's been a damn nuisance – ever since she got back. She's brought back her North American ideas and thoroughly upset everyone. I do wish she'd calm down a little. I had our Sales Manager on the phone the other day. Absolutely furious. "What on earth is Nancy playing at? Can't you get her off my back?" Apparently, she was calling them at all hours of the day, wanting to know what was happening about this delivery and that one. I believe two or three of the staff just won't have anything more to do with her.

She's a pest. Yes, a pest. And I have to put up with her far-fetched ideas for promoting her brand of coffee. Let me explain. We're trying to create a special image for that brand. Our message is, it's the brand of coffee you drink when life becomes tough. You know, when the taxman's after you, your wife's just left you, and your daughter's come home with a fellow with purple hair and gold earrings. Well, then you sit down, and you have your cup of coffee – Nancy's brand. Are you with me? Nancy's ideas just weren't appropriate. We're not using the hard sell approach. In fact, we *never* do – for any of our brands.

'... *so take some time out for TIVOLI – Italian coffee at its best.*'

Look, Nancy's got to go. Or at least be transferred to another department. Why don't we give her a sinecure job? Something quiet in Public Relations. Information Officer, or something like that. Or let her study for a year. Maybe after that, she'd be ready to do a *real* job for this company.'

Instructions

Working in groups of two or three, discuss the following questions.

1 What did Nancy gain and lose by spending five years in Montreal?
2 Who is to blame for the uneasy relationship between Nancy and Harry? Is it Nancy, or Harry, or both of them?
3 How do you think the problem should be resolved?

When you have finished, compare your ideas with those of the other groups.

Just after Derek Allot, Personnel Director (see **Case study**) had finished talking to Nancy Freeman and Harry Coates, he received this memorandum from Don Black, Managing Director of the company.

MEMORANDUM

To: Derek Allot

From: Don Black

Subject: Ms N Freeman   Date: July 5 1988

I happened to sit next to Ms Freeman at lunch today. She mentioned to me that she was rather unhappy in her present position of Product Manager.

I am dismayed to hear this. A few years ago, she was considered to be one of our 'high fliers' and was, I understand, sent to Montreal to broaden her experience. It is disturbing that we could now lose the services of this promising executive.

From what Ms Freeman told me, it appears that she has had a difficult working relationship with the head of her department, Harry Coates.

Would you please put me in the picture concerning this member of staff and explain what the problem is. Perhaps you'd also like to tell me what we might do to remedy this situation.

Imagine that you are the Personnel Director. Write a reply, in memo form, to this message from the Managing Director.

LISTENING

Understanding the main points

Listen to the following conversation and then answer the questions below.

1 According to the caller, what has happened to Carlos Hernandez?
2 Why is it difficult for the government to attack the National Freedom Movement?
3 How does the government generally deal with the demands of terrorists?
4 How does the company feel about the terrorists' ransom demand?
5 What does the Minister instruct Goodman to do?
6 What happened to the company director who was kidnapped two years ago? Why?

Vocabulary focus

Listen again and identify the phrases or expressions in the conversation which mean the same as the following:

1 They want to gain control of the country.

   ' .... '

2 They'll do whatever is necessary.

   ' .... '

3 It's very hard to make them come out of their hiding-places.

   ' .... '

4 They know the jungle extremely well.

   ' .... '

5 We will never agree to what they want.

   ' .... '

6 Make the negotiations last a long time, you mean?

   ' .... '

7 They won't really mean it.

   ' .... '

8 . . . when a man's life is at risk.

   ' .... '

9 Don't do anything without telling us about it.

   ' .... '

10 I promise.

   ' .... '

14 Social responsibility

Study the following situation and then answer the questions below.

Let us suppose you are a top executive for a multinational organisation. You are sent out to run a subsidiary in a small African country. The subsidiary, a chemical manufacturing plant, has had poor results recently. Your job is to make it profitable again.

Shortly after you take up your appointment, you realise that the plant is causing a lot of pollution. Fumes are pouring out of the old-fashioned chimneys and the wind blows them towards the nearby towns. In addition, chemical waste is finding its way into rivers and streams. To reduce all this pollution, you will need to spend a great deal of time and money.

This may not, however, be necessary. Some of your managers, who are nationals of the country, tell you not to worry. They can 'pull strings' with government officials, so that the government will turn a blind eye to the pollution. Other foreign companies, say the managers, look after their pollution problem in this manner.

1 If you were the executive in this situation, what would do you?
2 What do you think most companies would do if faced by the same problem?

Social responsibility of business

What is the purpose of a business? Is it just to make as much profit as possible for its shareholders? Or does a business have a wider responsibility to help solve society's problems? This is the controversial topic we shall now examine.

Thirty or so years ago, discussions of social responsibility were of three types. Firstly, there was a lot of talk about how business people should behave in their work. Should they have the same ethical standards – the same principles – as they had in their private life? A question which was often discussed was: should an executive offer a bribe to secure a contract, when he knew that his competitors were likely to do so? Secondly, people discussed the social responsibility of business towards its employees. They were interested in how organisations could improve the working conditions of their employees. Finally, social responsibility included the idea that business people should contribute to cultural activities. They should support activities like music festivals and art exhibitions. Executives were also expected to serve on educational committees, hospital boards, and so on. In other words, they had to take an active part in the life of their community.

These days, there is a new approach to social responsibility. Many people say that a business should try to meet the needs and interests of society. It has an obligation to help solve the problems of society. Because of this new concept, society expects more from its business organisations. For example, pressure is put on businesses to provide a safer environment. A chemical company, therefore, is not only expected to meet government standards regarding pollution. It must take steps to reduce pollution to as low a level as possible – even if this means reduced profits.

These days, businesses are expected to show social responsibility in all kinds of ways. They are urged to provide safer products; to protect and respect the environment; to hire more people from minority groups; to offer work opportunities to unemployed youngsters; to oppose racial discrimination and at all times to behave with integrity. The list is endless.

An example of the new approach can be found in banking. Some well-known British banks have had pressure put on them to stop doing business in South Africa. This is because many of their customers are opposed to South Africa's policy of Apartheid. For example, in 1986 Barclays Bank withdrew its business from South Africa. Similarly, a few years ago, some Swedish companies were criticised for taking part in an electrical power project in Africa. The project was located in a country which was then a Portuguese colony. Some Swedish newspapers accused the companies of 'supporting imperialism'.

The new concept of social responsibility means that businesses and business people must have integrity. They must deal honestly with their employees, and with the outside world. As Sir John Clark of the Plessey company says, 'I attach more importance to integrity than to ability'.

Successful companies are very sensitive if their integrity is attacked. They usually respond sharply. Some time ago, an English health inspector found fault with the standards of hygiene in a Trusthouse Forte hotel. Lord Forte was most upset by the inspector's accusations. Making no attempt to plead guilty and by so doing avoid publicity, the Trusthouse Forte Group fought the case in the courts. It also advertised in several national newspapers to give its side of the case.

The integrity of the shoe-making firm, Clark's, was recently questioned. To make its shoes, Clark's were using leather cured by sperm-whale oil. Conservation groups heard about this and put pressure on the company to stop using such leather. They even talked of boycotting the company's shoes. At first, Clark's said that it had no control over leather provided by its suppliers. However, a little later, the Chairman Daniel Clark gave a direct order that the company should only buy leather cured without sperm whale oil. He also invested in testing equipment to ensure that supplies of leather were free from this type of oil.

A lot of business people agree with the 'wider' concept of social responsibility. They accept that businesses should help to solve social problems – even if their businesses did not create them. And even if the social actions do not bring profits.

There are, nevertheless, some famous people who are against the new approach. One of these is Milton Friedman, an American economist who won the Nobel Prize for Economics in 1976. Milton Friedman believes that business has only one social responsibility. That is 'to use its resources and energy in activities designed to increase its profits as long as it stays within the rules of the game ... and engages in open and free competition, without deception and fraud.' Friedman says that a business's social responsibility is 'to make as much money for its shareholders as possible'. Another famous person makes a similar point. Ian MacGregor has been chief executive of large organisations like British Steel and the National Coal Board. He says that a business's first priority is to create wealth. Many companies, he believes, have a concept of social responsibility which distracts them from this task.

It is certainly true that social actions cost money. And businesses have to bear that cost often by raising prices, lowering wages or having less profit. Someone has to pay for the social actions in the end – it may be the customer, the employee or the shareholder.

Of course, by showing social responsibility, the company may well benefit in the long run. A spokesman for the Rank-Xerox company spoke recently of the wide range of social projects Rank-Xerox were engaged in: grants of equipment to universities; information technology projects and seminars;

Prakash Parmar, prize-winner in the National Selected Painting and Sculpture Competition, sponsored by Rank Xerox.

110 training programmes in universities and schools; career seminars; sponsorship of art competitions etc. The spokesman said that the social projects were 'an integral part of the company's business strategy'. They were not some sort of charity work which would get a brief mention in the company's annual report. Being a large organisation, Rank-Xerox had many contacts with government departments and other groups in society. And, since it was a knowledge-based company, it needed to hire highly skilled people. Its social programmes were 'critical to its success'. There was no doubt that, in the long run, these activities were profitable to the organisation.

Understanding the main points

Decide whether the following statements are true or false.

	True	False
1 Nowadays business organisations are expected to have more social responsibilities than they used to.	☐	☐
2 It is accepted that a company should not lose profits in order to become socially responsible.	☐	☐
3 Some Swedish companies were criticised because they expressed unpopular political opinions.	☐	☐
4 Trusthouse Forte took legal action in order to protect the reputation of its hotels.	☐	☐
5 Milton Friedman suggests that a company does not need to show integrity, provided that it competes freely.	☐	☐
6 Ian MacGregor says that some organisations do not make as much profit as they could because they have wrong ideas about social responsibility.	☐	☐
7 Rank-Xerox has a large programme of social projects because it believes that these will improve its image and reputation with the public.	☐	☐
8 It is probably in the long-term interests of a business to show a strong sense of social responsibility.	☐	☐

Vocabulary focus

Find words or phrases in the text which mean the same as the following:

1 standards of moral behaviour (paragraph 2)
2 something offered or given to persuade somebody, usually to do something wrong (paragraph 2)
3 the natural conditions (air, water and land) in which we live (paragraph 3)
4 strongly against (paragraph 5)
5 refusing to buy or persuading people not to buy (paragraph 8)
6 dishonesty or trickery (paragraph 10)
7 criminal deception (paragraph 10)
8 make people well-off, prosperous (paragraph 10)
9 in the end, ultimately (paragraph 12)
10 vital (paragraph 12)

1 *Match the following verbs with the correct nouns.*

e.g. **7–f**

VERBS	NOUNS
1 offer	**a** the cost
2 pull	**b** a contract
3 solve	**c** strings
4 bear	**d** a point
5 secure	**e** a problem
6 take	**f** a blind eye to
7 turn	**g** a need
8 put	**h** pressure on
9 meet	**i** a bribe
10 make	**j** steps to

*Now choose four of the above phrases and make your own
sentences to show their meaning.*

e.g. The government turned a blind eye to the pollution of the
river caused by the factory.

2 *Complete the following sentences with suitable prepositions.*

1 The company were accused .... (1) polluting the
environment and were criticised .... (2) doing so.
Naturally, they were upset .... (3) the charge and
denied responsibility.

2 The government has brought .... (1) a new law to
protect minority groups. The aim of the law is to prevent
employers .... (2) discriminating .... (3)
such groups.

3 We are engaged .... (1) many programmes which
help the community. For example, schoolchildren benefit
.... (2) the training programmes we run, and from
the equipment we have provided them .... (3).

4 Our management is strongly opposed .... (1)
expenditure on social programmes and objects
.... (2) people putting pressure .... (3) the
company to contribute more .... (4) society.

5 We pay lip service to the idea of social responsibility but really
we are only interested .... (1) making a profit.
Nothing must distract us .... (2) that purpose.

3 Idiomatic uses of *run*

in the long run (line 98)

A *Rewrite the following sentences without changing their
meaning. Replace the words in italics with verbs from the list and
make any other necessary changes.*

run up	run down	run out of
run up against	run through	run out

1 We won't meet that urgent order unless we speed up
production. We *have little time left*.
2 Can we *review* the plan for the sales campaign, please?
3 We won't be able to launch the product in February. The
Design Department have *met* some technical problems.

4 Our firm is gradually *reducing* its marketing operation in the Far East.
5 This contract *comes to an end* next month, then we'll have to renew it.
6 They have *incurred* so many debts that they'll have to close down soon.

B *Match the following expressions with the correct definitions.*

1 run-of-the-mill (adj.)	**a** period leading up to
2 run-down (adj.)	**b** in second place in a competition
3 runner-up	**c** very busy
4 in running order	**d** after a good deal of time has passed
5 run off one's feet	**e** ordinary, not special
6 in the long run	**f** having a chance of winning
7 in the running for	**g** in poor condition, not very profitable
8 run-up (n.)	**h** working properly

Now, complete the following conversations with expressions from the list above.

1 – Is the machine worth buying?
 – Certainly. It's old but in perfect ....
2 – Who'll be our next department head?
 – No idea. I gather several people are ....
3 – You look tired out.
 – It's not surprising. We're preparing the annual accounts at the moment and everybody in our department is ....
4 – Why is that hairdressing salon going so cheap? They're selling it for under £10,000.
 – I understand the business is very .... – the owner has neglected it badly.
5 – I hear you didn't get the prize for best salesman this month.
 – That's right, but I was .... and our Sales Manager gave me a couple of free tickets for the theatre.
6 – Why was the AZ 502 launch delayed by three months?
 – In the .... to the launch our engineers discovered some technical faults.

COMMUNICATION SKILLS	FUNCTION Reporting what has been said

Dialogue

Listen to the following conversation, between Tony, the general manager of a construction company, and Rex, the owner of an electrical contracting company.

REX   Hello, Tony, Rex here.
TONY   Hello Rex, how are things?
REX   Fine, thanks. Look, It's about that South American job – the electrical fittings for the apartment buildings.
TONY   Oh yes?
REX   I'm really sorry, Tony, but I'm afraid we can't do it.
TONY   Oh no. What's the problem?
REX   We're just too busy at the moment. We're in the middle of a big job in Saudi Arabia – we're doing the fittings for an airport lounge. Trouble is, we've come up against some

problems. So we've had to send some more people out there. So, you see, we couldn't guarantee to complete the work you've offered on time. Certainly not by 1 November.

TONY   Now you tell me. I was banking on you to do the work. It's really a bit late to get someone else.

REX   Sorry about that. But, you know us Tony. We don't take on a job unless we can finish it on time.

Oral report

Tony received the call in the morning. Later that afternoon, he reported the conversation to his Purchasing Manager, Fred Roundtree. Below is what Tony said. (Note that Fred's comments have been left out.)

'Rex called this morning. It was about the South American job. He said they couldn't do it. Apparently, they're working on a big job in Saudi Arabia, airport fittings. They've had some problems, so they had to send out more staff. According to him, they couldn't guarantee to do our job by 1 November. I told him I'd been depending on them, and that it was too late to get another firm. He apologised, and said they never took on jobs unless they could finish them.'

Note that when you report this kind of conversation, you summarise the main facts. Note also the changes to the tenses of the verbs in reported speech:

DIRECT SPEECH	REPORTED SPEECH
'It is about ...'	It was about ...
'I'm afraid we can't do it.'	He said they couldn't do it.
'I was banking on you...'	I told him I'd been depending on them ...
'Sorry about that ... We don't take on ...'	He apologised, and said they never took on ...

Work in pairs. One of you studies Conversation 1, the other studies Conversation 2. Imagine you are Tony and report the conversation to your partner.

Conversation 1

IAN   Hello, Tony. This is Ian here.

TONY   Hi, Ian. How's everything going?

IAN   Oh ... up and down. You know what this business is like.

TONY   I sure do. Now what about the South American job – can you do it for us?

IAN   Maybe, with a bit of luck. But you haven't given us much time to get organised, have you? And you're not allowing us much profit margin. There's nothing in it for us, is there?

TONY   That's true, Ian. But we're not making much out of it either. Our costs have been shooting up, it's unbelievable. I reckon we'll make a loss on the contract.

IAN   That's your problem. Look, we may be able to do the job. But only as a favour to you, you understand. If we work for you again, we'll want a lot more from the deal.

TONY   You will, I promise you.

IAN   OK. Well, the big problem for us is, where on earth do we get 5,000 wall sockets, light fittings and all that wiring in a hurry? And at the right price, so we make something on this work. It won't be easy.

TONY   I appreciate that.

IAN   There is one possibility ... an East European firm we've heard about. They're offering electrical fittings – at give-away prices. Maybe they're the answer to our prayers.

TONY   OK Ian, do your best. And thanks. We owe you one.

Conversation 2

MR KAPLIN   Hello, This is Mr Kaplin here.

TONY   Oh yes. Tony Bridges here.

MR KAPLIN   I'm calling about your letter asking us to quote for a job in South America – electrical fittings for some apartment buildings, you remember.

TONY   Oh yes, of course. I hope you can help us.

MR KAPLIN   Well, I'm sorry we can't. I must say, I'm surprised you asked us. At such short notice, I mean. How on earth could any firm do the work by 1 November? Electrical fittings for three apartment buildings, 500 apartments in all! It's a tremendously big job.

TONY   Yes, I know. But our usual contractor has let us down.

MR KAPLIN   I'm not surprised. You're only allowing a 5% profit margin over costs. That's ridiculous. We always work on a 25% margin.

TONY   I'm sorry. You see, we're not making anything on the deal either. In fact, we could end up making a loss.

MR KAPLIN   I tell you this, I'll be amazed if you can find a reputable firm to do the work at such short notice. No one would take it on.

TONY   Oh come now, Mr Kaplin. At this time of the year, firms are always glad to pick up business ...

MR KAPLIN   Nonsense! Those sort of firms won't do the job properly. They'll cut corners, especially on safety. And you can't rush electrical jobs. Everything's got to be done according to the book.

TONY   I think you'd better let *us* worry about safety precautions, Mr Kaplin.

MR KAPLIN   Oh well, if that's your attitude, there's nothing more to be said. Perhaps next time you'll get in touch with us a little earlier and maybe we'll be able to help you. Goodbye.

Case study

Let us now go to the South American country where the three apartment buildings have been built. In two days' time, the buildings will be officially opened by the mayor of the city. The painters are putting the finishing touches to the signs in front of the buildings, and the gardeners are planting the last few rose bushes in the freshly dug earth.

Everyone connected with the planning and construction of the buildings is delighted. The mayor of the city is sure to stay in his job after the coming elections because 2,500 poor people – but voters nevertheless – will at last have a decent place to live in. The management of the construction company haven't made any money from this contract. However, a minister of state has promised that they will be allowed to build the country's new national football stadium, a magnificent project, which will make the construction company a household name in the area. It is also a lucrative project.

'You'll make millions from it,' the minister told the company's managing director. Most pleased of all, however, is the electrical contracting company responsible for doing the wiring of the buildings, and for installing all the wall sockets and light fittings in each apartment. Let us call the company Livewire Ltd, though that is not its real name.

The story began a few days ago. James Farlow, one of Livewire's most experienced electricians, was having a drink in a local bar. With him was Charles Pemberton, an engineer working for the construction company. James and Charles had become good friends during the last two months. The other member of the group was Georgia Watson, a supplies officer for the construction company.

All three had been drinking together, celebrating the completion of the building project. As the evening wore on, Charles and Georgia noticed that James wasn't really enjoying himself much. He would laugh, then suddenly appear distracted or thoughtful. 'What on earth's the matter?' Georgia asked him. 'I thought you wanted to let your hair down tonight. But you're not yourself at all.'

James laughed, a little falsely. 'It's nothing.'

'Come on, James, out with it. We're your friends, aren't we?' said Charles.

James was silent for a moment. 'All right, I'll tell you what's bothering me. But this is confidential, OK? I don't want it to go any further. Promise?'

'We promise.' Charles and Georgia looked serious. The air in the bar seemed to become colder, all of a sudden.

'It's the job I've just done on some of the apartments. I'm not happy about the wiring – or the fittings, for that matter.'

'In what way?' asked Charles.

'The wire they gave me, it's ... well, the plastic covering didn't seem thick enough. The bare wire was showing through in one or two places. I had to patch it up. I don't think the stuff's good enough for the job. It may last for a few years, I suppose, but who knows?'

'What about the fittings?' asked Georgia.

'Most of them were all right. But I had to throw away two wall sockets. They were faulty. Lucky I checked them – I don't normally.'

'Do you think the other electricians checked the wiring and the fittings?' asked Charles.

'Good Heavens, no. Most of them wouldn't bother to.'

'Who was the supplier, James?' asked Georgia.

James mentioned the name of the East European manufacturer. Georgia could not hide her surprise:

'But their products have been banned in Britain and the USA, haven't they?'

'Oh, have they? I didn't know that.'

'Well, I'm sure I'm right,' said Georgia.

'Oh.' James looked very worried.

They left the bar a little later. As they were waiting for a taxi James said to the other two, 'Remember, not a word of this to anyone. It would create an enormous scandal if this came out into the open.'

Instructions

1 *Work in pairs. One of you should imagine that you are Charles, the other Georgia. Discuss what you should do now, if anything.*

2 *When you have finished, compare your ideas with those of the other groups. Try to agree on what Charles and Georgia should do now.*

3 Suppose that the managing director of the construction company is told about the faulty fittings but refuses to take any action. Should Charles and Georgia 'blow the whistle' on the company? That is to say, should they tell the newspapers, or other groups such as the government, opposition political parties etc. about the faulty fittings?

   If they do that, what do you think would happen to
   (i) Charles and Georgia?
   (ii) the construction company?
   (iii) the electrical contracting company?

WRITING

The day before the official opening of the apartment buildings (see **Case study**), a rumour goes round the city that the buildings are unsafe to live in because of faulty electrical installations.

There are two daily newspapers in the city. One is owned by the brother of the mayor. This newspaper always supports the mayor and his political party. The other newspaper belongs to a politician from the opposition party. This newspaper usually criticises any actions connected with the mayor and his party.

A reporter from each newspaper is asked to write an article about the apartment buildings, and to deal with the rumour of the faulty electrical fittings.

On the day of the opening ceremony, the articles appear in the two newspapers. One article is full of praise for the buildings, saying that they are perfectly safe. The other article suggests that they are 'death traps'. It severely criticises the mayor for allowing people to live in the buildings.

Imagine that you are one of the reporters. After inventing an eye-catching headline, write an appropriate article about the apartment buildings.

Understanding the main points

Listen to the following conversation and complete the sentences below.

1 Jock Smith was unhappy because ....

2 Alexandra feels that Margaret has not been paying enough attention to her work because ....

3 As a result of Margaret's involvement with the Education Committee...

4 The company has also benefited from Margaret's work on the Community Businesses Project because ....

5 Margaret enjoys doing community work so much because ....

6 Margaret might accept the offer to manage the charity if ....

Vocabulary focus

1 *Listen again and fill in the gaps in these sentences from the conversation.*

1 I've got a lot .... my .... at the moment.
2 ... you know, helping immigrants to ....
.... their own firm.
3 After all, it's .... for our ....
4 It's fascinating, and it's .... for us, too.
5 Your outside work has been useful, I .... you.
5 Maybe you're .... it a bit, Margaret.
7 We're your .... and .... , don't forget.
8 You turned it .... , I hope.
9 I can't do ....
10 Let me see how I can cut .... the outside activities.

2 *In pairs, discuss the meaning of the phrases and expressions above.*

TAPESCRIPT AND KEY

1 The manager's role

Tapescript

Mervyn is supervisor in the Supply Department of an oil company. The workers in this department plan the routes of the oil tankers owned by the company. Brian Smith is head of the department. In the following conversation Brian and Mervyn are talking about a new member of staff, Peter Martin.

Section 1

BRIAN   Right, let's talk about Martin now. He's been here almost three months, so his probationary period's almost over. How's he making out, Mervyn?

MERVYN   Mm, I'm not too happy about him. I wonder if we made the right choice.

BRIAN   What? After all the interviews and tests, I can't believe it. What's the problem?

MERVYN   I can't really put my finger on it. Somehow, he doesn't seem to be enjoying the job. That's probably why he's making mistakes. Not big ones – but mistakes nevertheless.

BRIAN   Like what?

MERVYN   Well ... a couple of weeks ago, he was slow telexing instructions to a tanker, in Lagos. The ship hung around port two days longer than it should have.

BRIAN   Hm, careless.

MERVYN   Yes, he's done that kind of thing quite a few times. Got the dates wrong on his schedules. We spotted them in time. But if we hadn't ...

BRIAN   It would've been expensive for us, uh?

MERVYN   Right.

BRIAN   I don't understand it. Martin's got a brilliant academic record. First-class degree in mathematics. He should be able to cope. It should be a piece of cake for him.

MERVYN   I know. Brian, I'm as baffled as you. I've no idea what the problem is.

BRIAN   Have you talked to Peter?

MERVYN   Of course. I just don't seem to get anywhere, though. Peter's very reserved. Not someone who bares his heart to you. It's not easy.

BRIAN   I tell you what, why don't *I* have a word with him? We've got to get to the bottom of this. We don't want people in the department performing below their best.

MERVYN   OK, when do you want to see him then?

BRIAN   Hold on, let me look in my diary. Mm ... Wednesday morning's free ...

Section 2

Brian meets Peter Martin and, during their conversation together, he talks about Peter's relations with the other workers in the office.

BRIAN   Now, how are you settling in, Peter? Made any friends?

Who do you have lunch with usually?

PETER   Er . . . no one really. I . . . eat on my own.

BRIAN   By yourself. Mm.

PETER   Yes, I go to the restaurant. Across the street.

BRIAN   The others eat in the canteen, don't they?

PETER   Yes. I believe they do.

BRIAN   How do you find them? Friendly? Have they made you feel at home? Helped you to settle in?

PETER   Oh . . . er . . . Yes . . . I suppose so.

BRIAN   Anything you'd like to tell me, Peter? I'm here to help, you know. You can be frank – it won't go outside this office.

PETER   To tell the truth, I don't get on very well with the others. I don't fit in. I don't feel one of them. And I can't do anything about it.

BRIAN   They are a close group, I admit. You find it difficult to be accepted, do you?

PETER   Yes, they don't talk to me much. Never ask me to have lunch with them. I feel an outsider, as if I don't belong, somehow.

BRIAN   Yes?

PETER   You know, they do things together. Even at weekends, they're together. Most of them play for our football team. They're always talking about matches they've played. I can't join in – I don't . . . like football that much.

BRIAN   I see.

PETER   I should love the job. The work's interesting. Right up my street, really. I spend hours reading magazines about the oil industry. It's just . . . I feel uncomfortable in the office.

BRIAN   You think the others . . . well, they're a clique. They stick together too much, right?

PETER   Yes, that's it. They have their 'in' jokes – I don't know what they're talking about half the time.

BRIAN   Mm. I think I'm getting the picture, Peter. I must say, what you're telling me is rather . . . disturbing – to say the least.

Section 3

Some days later, Brian telephones the Chief Personnel Officer of the company.

BRIAN   Jack, Brian here. I thought I'd better tell you this. Unofficially, first.

JACK   Yes?

BRIAN   It's about Peter Martin. Remember? I've just received his letter of resignation. He's accepted a job with an airline company. In their planning department. What? No, there's nothing we can do about it. Nothing at all. He's made up his mind. He wants to make a fresh start. Somewhere else.

JACK   Oh, well. You can't win them all.

Key

READING

Understanding the main points

1 To use the resources of their organisation effectively and economically to achieve its objectives.

2 Because they think that a manager should motivate or direct and lead instead of commanding.

3 A company director is more involved in planning, policy-making and company strategy whereas a middle manager is more involved in the day-to-day decisions affecting the daily operation of the organisation.

4 A manager should be keen to improve people's lives, interested in other people, able to give clear orders, honest, admired by others and able to examine carefully and make judgements.

Vocabulary focus
1   1 economically
    2 diversify
    3 run
    4 sorting out
    5 spelled out
2   An objective is a purpose, target or goal.

1   1 middle managers   7 colleagues
    2 Directors   8 supervisor
    3 junior executive   9 superior
    4 work-force   10 subordinates
    5 staff/employees   11 staff
    6 Senior executives/Middle managers   12 managing director

2   Word building
    1 b products   c Productivity   d productive   e produce
    2 a competitor   b competitive   c competition
    3 a planned   b planning   c plan
    4 a analytical   b analysis   c analytically

3   1a   2c   3d   4a   5a   6d   7b

4   1 turn(s) out   6 make out
    2 sort out   7 carry out
    3 sell out   8 pulled out
    4 spell out   9 buying, out
    5 brought out   10 sounded out

Understanding the main points
1 . . . he has made some mistakes.
2 . . . he has a first-class degree in mathematics.
3 . . . he doesn't get on very well with his colleagues.
4 . . . tell him that Peter Martin has resigned.

Vocabulary focus
1   1 probationary period   5 settling in
    2 put, finger   6 get on
    3 piece, cake   7 up, street
    4 get, bottom   8 made up, mind

2 Frederick W. Taylor: Scientific Management

Tapescript

Lily Jacobavitz is Chief Executive of a fashion house in New York. She is having lunch with the firm's Production Manager, Sydney Gorman, and its Personnel Director, Gloria David. During their conversation Gloria David mentions the subject of flexitime.

DAVID	I was talking to Don Harper the other day. He's Personnel Manager at IC Electronics. He was telling me about their flexitime scheme – they introduced it a year or so ago. Apparently, it's pretty popular.
JACOBAVITZ	Flexitime ... mm ... that's when staff come and go as they please, isn't it?
GORMAN	Yes. And the supervisors never know where anyone is!
DAVID	It's not like that at all, Sydney. At least, not as far as I understand it.
GORMAN	Huh!
JACOBAVITZ	Go on, Gloria. Tell us all about it. How does it work at Don's place?
DAVID	First of all, at the moment, they've got flexitime for their office staff only. But I believe they're thinking of having it for their factory workers as well.
JACOBAVITZ	Good Heavens!
GORMAN	You must be kidding!
DAVID	I was surprised to hear that too, I must say.
JACOBAVITZ	Anyway, how does the scheme work, Gloria? The one they've got now.
DAVID	Something like this. I can't remember all the details, mind you. You see, the office staff have to work a certain number of hours a week – thirty-five, thirty-eight – one or the other anyway, and they've also got to be at their desks at certain hours of the day. They call that the 'core' period.
JACOBAVITZ	Uh, huh. When is that exactly?
DAVID	If my memory serves me well, it was twelve to four o'clock.
JACOBAVITZ	And what about the other hours?
DAVID	Well, they're flexible. From seven to twelve, and from four to seven in the evening, the staff can start and finish when they want. It's up to them.
GORMAN	Tell me, what happens if they work more than the hours they're meant to. I mean, suppose they have to work thirty-five hours a week, and they work forty-five hours. What happens then?
DAVID	No problem. They carry over their credit hours, as they're called, to the next month. So then they can take a couple of mornings off, or leave work early one week.
JACOBAVITZ	That's quite useful, from the firm's point of view, I mean. Because if you're really busy one month, the office staff will work extra hours. And when things are quieter, they can be compensated by having time off.
GORMAN	Yeah, that's certainly an advantage – for staff and management. Did Don mention any benefits they'd got from flexitime, Gloria?
DAVID	Oh yes. He told me there'd been less absenteeism since the scheme was introduced and that staff turnover had gone down.
GORMAN	Any effect on productivity?
DAVID	Mm. The staff have been getting through a lot more work, and the quality's been higher too.
GORMAN	Astonishing.
JACOBAVITZ	Is it so surprising, Sydney? They're probably a lot happier now that they have flexible hours.
DAVID	That's it. It seems they feel more responsible. They feel

that the management's treating them as mature people.

JACOBAVITZ   That's reasonable.

DAVID   Also, don't forget, they can come to work later now. They miss the rush hour. The hustle and bustle, the traffic jams ... They're not tired and bad-tempered when they get to work.

JACOBAVITZ   Right. And they don't get a talking-to from the supervisor if they're late. Well, with flexitime, they can't be late, can they?

DAVID   Precisely.

GORMAN   That must improve relations between employees and supervisors, Gloria.

JACOBAVITZ   Yes, I would have thought so too.

DAVID   It does. The staff at Don's place really like the system. They feel they're organising their lives better. They're in control.

JACOBAVITZ   Do you know, you've put an idea in my head. Maybe ... well, it might just be worthwhile trying flexitime here. With the office staff, that is.

DAVID   I was waiting for you to say that. Actually, that's why I brought up the subject – I was sounding you out.

JACOBAVITZ   I had a feeling you might be. I wasn't born yesterday, you know.

Key

READING

Understanding the main points

1   1 ... it meant that the best way of doing a job would be worked out scientifically, not by guesswork.

   2 ... the productivity of its workers would increase.

   3 ... they would earn higher wages.

   4 ... they could increase their daily output.

   5 ... had halved the handling costs of materials, which led to annual savings of $80,000.

2   ADVANTAGES

   1 The efficiency of workers is improved.

   2 Productivity is increased.

   3 Workers' output increases, and so, therefore, do their wages.

   DISADVANTAGES

   1 It focuses on the system of work, rather than on the worker – leading to the worker becoming a tool in the hands of management.

   2 It leads to the de-skilling of workers – causing frustration and dissatisfaction.

   3 Doing and planning are separated – workers may be more productive if they are involved in planning, decision-making, controlling and organising.

Vocabulary focus

1   1 guesswork   5 load

   2 work out   6 shift

   3 output   7 insight

   4 set up

2   the place where ordinary workers do their work (usually in a factory)

1

PERSON	NOUN	VERB	ADJECTIVE
critic	criticism	(criticise)	critical
(performer)	performance	perform	—
scientist	(science)	—	scientific
trainer/trainee	(training)	train	—
analyst	analysis	analyse	(analytical)
industrialist	(industry)	industrialise	industrial/industrious
observer	observation	(observe)	observant
engineer	engineering	engineer	(engineering)
revolutionary	revolution	revolutionise	(revolutionary)
consultant	consultation	(consult)	consultative

2 A   1–b   2–d   3–f   4–c   5–e   6–h   7–g   8–i
       9–a   10–j

   B   1 set out   6 set up
       2 set back   7 set about
       3 set in   8 set aside
       4 set-up   9 set-back
       5 set, against   10 set down

3 1 components   8 quality control
    2 bonus   9 layout
    3 overtime   10 capacity
    4 incentive   11 laid off
    5 shifts   12 redundant
    6 foreman   13 assembly line
    7 schedule   14 robots

Understanding the main points
1 ... introduce a flexitime scheme.
2 ... the staff have to be in the office.
3 ... carry over their credit hours to the following month and take some time off work then.

THE ADVANTAGES OF FLEXITIME
BENEFITS TO STAFF
 (i) can start and finish when they want
 (ii) if they work overtime one month they can take some time off work the next month
 (iv) feel happier because they feel more responsible, more in control of their lives
BENEFITS TO COMPANY
 (i) staff will be prepared to work extra hours during busy periods
 (ii) less absenteeism
 (iii) staff turnover reduced
 (v) better relations between staff and management

Vocabulary focus
1 1 be kidding   6 getting through
   2 serves, well   7 treating, as
   3 up to   8 worthwhile
   4 take, off   9 brought up
   5 point, view   10 sounding, out

3 The Quality of Working Life

Tapescript

Don Aiken, Managing Director of ELM Electronics, has a meeting with some of his company's senior executives to discuss staff morale. He feels that many of the employees are not happy in their work, and that this is affecting their efficiency. At the meeting are Patricia White, Personnel Manager, Jonathan Laidlaw, Production Manager and William Cooper, General Manager. Listen to their conversation.

AIKEN　OK, we'll get started then, shall we? You've all received my memo, so you know I want to discuss the question of staff morale. What I want to know is, are our employees satisfied, on the whole, with their jobs? And if they aren't, what can we do about it? Please be frank with me. Right, Patricia, perhaps you'd give us your opinion first.

WHITE　Very well. I think my opinion will be the same as everyone else's in this room. On the whole, I'd say morale's very low at the moment. It's hard to find anyone who has a good word to say about the company. But it's not surprising is it, really, when you think about it?

AIKEN　What? You mean, the fact that we've just laid off two hundred or so workers? Everyone's afraid they'll be the next to go?

WHITE　That's part of it. No one feels his job's safe. People are anxious, worrying about when the next round of redundancies will come.

AIKEN　I hope it won't. Making people redundant is not the most pleasant of jobs, I can tell you. But what else can you do when your profits are falling? How about you, Jonathan, do you agree with Pat?

LAIDLAW　A hundred per cent. People are unhappy, they do fear the future. But I'm not sure morale's low just because we've had redundancies. I mean, lots of firms have had to get rid of workers. But the people who remain are loyal and enjoy their jobs.

AIKEN　What are you getting at, Jonathan?

LAIDLAW　What I'm saying is, even if times are difficult, we seem to be having a lot of problems here. More than our fair share, perhaps.

AIKEN　Like what, for example?

LAIDLAW　Well, look at our labour turnover. 16% for the company as a whole. And wasn't it over 20% in my department, Production? That's far too high. And what about our graduate trainees – a third had left by the end of the year.

AIKEN　Mm ... that's food for thought, I must admit. And absenteeism was high too, wasn't it? I believe we lost more working hours last year than ever before. Bill, how do you feel about all this?

COOPER　Jonathan's right. I don't think the recession's causing all our problems. I can tell you this, though, I've never had a year like last year. Two strikes by the machine shop workers, people complaining to me about this, that and the other. We even had a fight on the shop floor. A couple of workers had a go at one of the foremen. Something to do with allocating overtime hours. It never used to be like that in my department.

AIKEN   I think I'm getting the picture now, and it's not a very pretty one. Thank you for being so frank with me.

WHITE   May I make a suggestion, Don?

AIKEN   By all means, Patricia.

WHITE   I've been thinking about this problem of staff morale for some time now. And you know, I may have come up with the answer. At least, I have a positive suggestion to offer.

AIKEN   Uh huh.

WHITE   Why don't we carry out an opinion survey? Let's find out what our staff really think about us. We could ask them all sorts of questions, like: Are they satisfied with their jobs and working conditions? What do they think of their superior? Do they have enough responsibility in their work? Enough variety? . . . that sort of thing. A survey could tell us what's going wrong in this firm.

AIKEN   An interesting idea, Pat. Very interesting indeed. Of course, we've never done anything like it before. Maybe now's the time to start. Any comments, anyone?

COOPER   I like the idea too, Don. If we had a survey, it would show staff that we care how they feel. They would understand that we're interested in solving their problems. That might be a first step towards improving their morale.

LAIDLAW   A survey's a good idea, I think, as long as the information is treated as confidential. Everybody must feel free to speak the truth, or else the data won't be of any use to us.

AIKEN   A good point, Jonathan. We must bear that in mind when we prepare our opinion survey.

Key

READING

Understanding the main points

1   1 True   2 True   3 False   4 False   5 True

2   Originally, the Hawthorne experiments focused on the factors influencing productivity. Later, they concentrated on people's social relationships at work.

3   The productivity of the workers increased whether conditions were made better or worse.

4   Because they had developed a high morale during the experiment and had been motivated to work hard.

5   The feeling of belonging to a group and the workers' status within that group.

6   Because they challenged the theory of Scientific Management put forward by Frederick W. Taylor.

Vocabulary focus

1 desire or incentive to do something

2 factory workers who each have a particular job to do in the production of a vehicle, machine etc.

3 arrangement of workers and machines in a factory whereby each worker is responsible for one stage of assembly, and the article being assembled is passed from one worker to the other (usually on a moving conveyor belt)

4 interesting, difficult, stimulating

5 conducted, held

6 assess, study

7 state of mind

8 asked (them) to come and help

9 causing them to operate
10 at their own speed
11 position in relation to others
12 questioned

1 1c   2c   3a   4a   5b   6b   7c   8c   9c   10c

2 A 1 ... we'd better put back   6 put forward
        the meeting a week.   7 ... I put it down to ineffective
    2 put up   leadership.
    3 put off   8 ... I just can't put my finger
    4 put up with   on it.
    5 ... put across her ideas
      to the rest of us.

   B 1 put paid   5 put, on
     2 put, through   6 put my foot in
     3 putting, out   7 put in a good word
     4 put, out

Understanding the main points
Minutes of senior management meeting – 2/4/88 – 11.30.
Subject: *Staff morale*
Present: Don Aiken, Patricia White, Jonathan Laidlaw, William
Cooper

D.A. wanted to know if the staff were happy; and if not, what could
    be done about it?
P.W. thought that morale was very low at present. Some people
    were worried that *they might be made redundant/they might lose
    their jobs.*
J.L. pointed out another problem affecting morale – *the company's
    labour turnover was very high last year – 16%.*
D.A. added that last year the company lost *more working hours
    than ever before* because of *absenteeism.*
W.C. reminded us that in his department *there had been two strikes
    by the machine-shop workers, a lot of complaints about working
    conditions and a fight on the shop floor.*
P.W. suggested *carrying out an opinion survey to find out what the
    staff think about management,* with questions such as: *Are you
    satisfied with your job and working conditions? What do you think
    of your superior? Do you have enough responsibility in your
    work?*
W.C. agreed with P.W. He said it would show that management
    were concerned about staff feelings and problems – so it would
    be good for morale.
J.L. also liked P.W.'s idea, but stressed that *the answers to the
    survey should be confidential.* If not, *people wouldn't feel free to
    speak the truth, and the data wouldn't be of any use.*
D.A. noted J.L.'s point and said that we must bear it in mind when
    the survey is prepared.

Vocabulary focus
1 1 On, whole   5 getting, picture
    2 mean, fact   6 come up with
    3 getting at   7 going wrong
    4 food, thought   8 of any use

4 Decision-making

Tapescript

LISTENING

Listen to the following news broadcast about the opening of a new micro-wave oven factory in Plymouth, Devon.

NEWSREADER   And now, industrial affairs. To give you the latest on commercial and industrial developments in the area, here's Peter O'Driscoll.

O'DRISCOLL   Good evening, everybody. Well, the big story today is the opening of the Japanese conglomerate Toshiba's micro-wave oven factory at Plymouth. The company has invested roughly £3.6 million in this development, which is the first micro-wave oven plant ever to be set up in Great Britain. The factory, which should provide a great number of jobs for young people in the area, will eventually service the whole of the European market. Toshiba estimate that production in the first year will reach 90,000 units, and after that they expect to turn out about 20,000 ovens a month.

Of course, Toshiba already has a television and video factory in Plymouth, at Ernesettle. Productivity at Ernesettle has been truly remarkable, with output trebling in the last five years. Undoubtedly, it was the success of the TV and video plant which influenced Toshiba's decision to locate their micro-wave factory here in Devon.

Today's opening ceremony was attended by the Managing Director of Toshiba UK, Mr Toshihide Yasui. Also present were the Managing Director of Toshiba Consumer Products, Desmond Thomson, and local Member of Parliament, Dr David Owen. All three men made speeches, whose main theme was that good industrial relations between the union and management had been the key to Toshiba's success.

NEWSREADER   After the ceremony, Mr Eric Hammond, leader of the Electrical, Electronic, Telecommunication and Plumbing Union, talked to our reporter on the spot, Dick Kerslake.

KERSLAKE   Now tell me, Mr Hammond, what sort of agreement did you work out with the Toshiba management when the company first set up a factory in this area?

HAMMOND   We agreed on one principle, right from the start. That was, that there would be no strikes in the factory. It's unthinkable that we would settle a problem, a dispute, by means of a strike. We rely on negotiation, and compromise.

KERSLAKE   I see. No strikes under any circumstances.

HAMMOND   Exactly.

KERSLAKE   What about relations between staff and management? What ideas did you have about that?

HAMMOND   On both sides – management and union – we felt that the employees should have a say in the running of the company. That's why there's a Company Advisory Board at Toshiba. Workers from all levels of the company are members. They attend meetings of the Advisory Board where they discuss things like sales figures, profit-and-loss accounts, production targets, quality control, that sort of thing. They see confidential documents and can give their opinion about decisions affecting the company's future.

KERSLAKE   How interesting. Finally, Mr Hammond, can you tell me something about Toshiba's performance in Britain? How's the company been doing?

HAMMOND   It's got a very good track record here, I can tell you. The company as a whole has a turnover of £200 million and ... let me see ... it's growth rate is about 30% a year.

KERSLAKE   Remarkable.

HAMMOND   Yes, very impressive, indeed. There've been no strikes in its factories, of course. Absenteeism is low too. But the important thing is, Toshiba's creating jobs in the area. That's what we need here, isn't it. Plenty of job opportunities, especially for young people.

Key

READING

Understanding the main points

1 False	2 False	3 False	4 True	5 False
6 True	7 True	8 True		

Vocabulary focus

1 key
2 on the spot
3 arises
4 locate
5 weigh up
6 take into account
7 secure
8 options
9 stepped out
10 compromise

LANGUAGE STUDY

1 1 bear/keep
   2 take, making/taking/reading
   3 come to/reached/arrived at
   4 gave/expressed, come
   5 made/put forward/came up with
   6 run
   7 put
   8 made
   9 reached/drawn
   10 given
   11 reached
   12 take

2 A 1–e 2–i 3–a 4–j 5–b 6–g 7–c 8–f
      9–d 10–h
   B 1 in a spot
      2 in the spotlight
      3 spot on
      4 spot cash
      5 on the spot
      6 putting, on the spot
      7 spot check
      8 high spot
      9 weak spot
      10 knock spots off

3 1 arisen 2 rose 3 raise 4 rise 5 raising
   6 rise

4 1 drawing up
   2 step up
   3 take up
   4 bring up
   5 take it up
   6 weigh up
   7 take up
   8 picked up

LISTENING

3 The following mistakes were made in the article:
   (i) The new factory cost £3.6 *million*, not just under £3 million.

(ii) In its second year it will be producing 20,000 ovens *per month*, not per year.

(iii) Growth at the TV and video factory has been extremely high since the factory was set up – output has *trebled* in the last five years. So 'steady growth' is incorrect.

(iv) There were *three* speeches at the opening ceremony, not just one.

(v) Strikes were *unthinkable* and would not happen under any circumstances. However, the newspaper article says that strikes would be allowed in exceptional circumstances, which is wrong.

(vi) *All* members of the Company Advisory Board have access to important documents, not just senior managers.

(vii) The figure of £200 million refers to Toshiba's turnover, not to its profits.

(viii) Toshiba *already* has a growth rate of 30% per year.

5 Top management – planning and strategy

Tapescript

LISTENING

The following conversation takes place in the office of Philip Masters, a company executive. When one of Philip's colleagues, Jane Lake, comes to visit him, she finds him in a happy mood.

PHILIP Ah Jane, come in and sit down.

JANE You're very cheerful this morning, Philip. How come?

PHILIP I've just had some very good news. My stockbroker phoned. Apparently, one of the shares I bought has really shot up. I've made a real killing.

JANE Good for you! If you don't mind me asking, what company was it?

PHILIP Futura Technics.

JANE Well, you lucky devil! They've just announced their annual results, haven't they? What was their profit? Fifty million, or something like that.

PHILIP Not far off. Fifty-five million, actually. And to think the year before it was just under twenty. So their profits have almost trebled.

JANE Incredible. How come they did so well? Oh hold on, they brought out a new word-processor, didn't they? It must have sold well.

PHILIP Yes, it did. The word-processor made all the difference. It's called the WPX 25, by the way. I don't think many people realised how well it was selling, though. It's only in the last three months or so that the shares began to shoot up.

JANE What's so special about the WP ... whatever you call it?

PHILIP It's cheap – only £259 – so its undercutting all the competition.

JANE Uh huh.

PHILIP And its compact. You get the computer, screen and printer all in one package. That's an advantage. You don't have to buy different bits of equipment, then connect them together.

JANE   I see. It's – what do you say – user-friendly.

PHILIP   Exactly. A child could set it up. Well almost.

JANE   Sounds just right for me!

PHILIP   Come on, Jane, I know perfectly well you went on that computer course last month.

JANE   Ah ha! My secret's out then.

PHILIP   Another thing about Futura's word-processor, it's got a superb printer. So you get high-quality lettering, and you can do very good graphics on it.

JANE   Mm. What's the price of the shares now?

PHILIP   600 pence. When I bought my shares, they were only 400 – that was six months ago. And just a year ago, you could get them for just 150 pence.

JANE   If only I'd bought some then! I'd have made a fortune. Tell me, what made you put your money in them? Just a hunch, was it, or did you have inside information?

PHILIP   Bit of both really. A fellow at the stock exchange told me Futura were an up-and-coming firm. They had the knack of producing the right products, he said.

JANE   Ah, so you were tipped off, then.

PHILIP   Yes, but I still hung back . . .

JANE   Mm.

PHILIP   Till I noticed that the word-processor was on display in all the business machine shops. That decided me. It must be doing well, I thought.

JANE   It's lucky you backed your hunch. Do you think the company will do well this year? It's pretty competitive, the computer business, isn't it?

PHILIP   I'm certain Futura will go on doing well. They're bringing out new products all the time. And the management's very good. Small but efficient.

JANE   Ah, so they keep their overheads low.

PHILIP   Mm. And also they're a very liquid company.

JANE   Plenty of cash reserves for future development, eh?

PHILIP   Right. They don't have to run to the shareholders for more money. They're self-financing. That's the kind of company I like.

JANE   You know, I think I'll put a few pounds in Futura. I reckon their shares could go even higher.

PHILIP   You may well be right. Even at this price, they're probably a bargain.

Key

READING

Understanding the main points

1   1–b   2–h   3–a   4–e   5–d   6–g   7–c   8–f

Vocabulary focus

A *strategy* is a particular plan which management might decide to adopt in order to achieve its aims or *objectives*.

LANGUAGE STUDY

1   1 growth rate   5 product range
2 product-line   6 sales revenue
3 resources   7 production capacity
4 productivity   8 market share/sales revenue

2 1 It often has to pull out of the market.
  2 You work out a strategy which will enable you to improve your performance in the market.
  3 You usually draw up a contract with the agents.
  4 You can carry out a market survey/market study to find out if potential customers will buy the product.
  5 You can try to break into an overseas market.

3
1 set up	6 finance	11 delegate
2 innovative	7 planning	12 rights
3 expertise	8 personnel	13 venture
4 strategies	9 segment	14 skills
5 trust	10 drawback	

4 1 We make a point of giving good service to our customers.
  2 The Chairman congratulated our Advertising Manager on keeping within his budget.
  3 The Managing Director insisted on the new product being launched/that the new product should be launched by January.
  4 Marks and Spencer are concentrating on selling fashionable clothes for young people.
  5 We take pleasure in satisfying our customers.
  6 The owner isn't interested in selling the business at the moment.
  7 I think our Chief Executive is wrong to say/in saying we should expand the range of our products.
  8 We are thinking of breaking into new markets.
  9 He is depending on the bank lending him the money for future development.
  10 Marks and Spencer have always succeeded in forecasting accurately what their customers want.

LISTENING

Understanding the main points
COMPANY PROFILE

NAME OF COMPANY: *Futura Technics*
INDUSTRY: Business machines

PROFITS:
MOST RECENT YEAR	PREVIOUS YEAR
£55 million	*£20 million*

SHARE VALUE:
PRESENT	−6 MONTHS	−12 MONTHS
600 pence	*400* pence	*150* pence

REASONS FOR CURRENT SUCCESS:
  1 *very liquid company – self-financing*
  2 launching high number of new products
  3 *very good, **small** management team – low overheads*

LATEST PRODUCT: TYPE: *word-processor*
  BRAND NAME: *WPX 25*
  PRICE: *£259*
  COMPONENTS: computer, *screen and printer*
  STRENGTHS: cheaper than competition, *compact (all in one package), user-friendly, superb printer*

---

1 'I've made a real killing.'
2 'Good for you!'
3 'It's user-friendly.'
4 '...Futura were an up-and-coming firm.'
5 '...they're probably a bargain.'

6 Goal-setting

Tapescript

LISTENING

Vanessa McIntyre is Marketing Manager of the Candymix Company Limited, a manufacturer of confectionary products. She receives a phone call from Ralph Harris, Head of Research and Development. Ralph has some bad news about a new product his department are developing. It's a biscuit, consisting of a wafer covered with chocolate, whose brand name will be Krackle. Listen to their conversation.

McINTYRE	Hello, Vanessa McIntyre speaking.
HARRIS	Hello Vanessa. Ralph here.
McINTYRE	Hello Ralph.
HARRIS	How's everything going?
McINTYRE	Fine. And you?
HARRIS	Not too good, I'm afraid.
McINTYRE	Oh? What's the trouble?
HARRIS	It's the Krackle biscuit. It won't be ready for test marketing by January. I'm sorry. We've run up against some problems, I'm afraid. We're going to need more time.
McINTYRE	Oh no. Everything was going fine, I thought. What are the problems, then?
HARRIS	They're technical. We can't seem to get the right type of wafer yet. It's not crisp enough. After we coat it with chocolate, it seems to go soft for some reason. Because of that, it doesn't make the right crackling sound.
McINTYRE	I don't understand. I tasted some of the Krackle biscuits last week. I thought they were just fine.
HARRIS	But you're not a teenager, Vanessa – they know what they want.
McINTYRE	Mm.
HARRIS	Look, our brief – and it came from the Board, don't forget – was to develop a new biscuit for young people.
McINTYRE	True.
HARRIS	It had to look different, and taste different, from everything else on the market. Right?
McINTYRE	Yes.
HARRIS	It had to have a crackling sound when you ate it. And it had to be nutritious – the sort of biscuit children would take to school and eat at lunch-time. Uh?
McINTYRE	OK, OK. But you've done that, surely? Or come pretty close.
HARRIS	That's not good enough. Everyone in our department's

	tried Krackle. And they've taken it home and tried it out on their children. None of us think we've got it right yet.
McINTYRE	Mm . . . all I can say is, it's damned annoying. When will it be ready by?
HARRIS	Mm . . . with a bit of luck – by the end of March, or thereabouts.
McINTYRE	The end of March. Good Heavens! That means we'll never get it on the market by June. No way!
HARRIS	I'm sorry. Things don't always go as you plan, Vanessa.
McINTYRE	It's really disappointing. It means I won't meet one of my main objectives for next year.
HARRIS	Oh?
McINTYRE	Yes, I agreed with George Holbrook that Krackle would be on the market by the beginning of June. Huh, it's not on, is it?
HARRIS	No, it isn't. And I won't be meeting my objective either, for that matter. I said to George we'd have Krackle ready for test marketing by January. Our Managing Director's certainly not going to like it, is he?
McINTYRE	Not at all. He doesn't accept excuses when you don't meet your objectives. He's so . . . rigid. Trouble is, my salary increase and bonus depend on meeting objectives.
HARRIS	Mine too. Even so, I'm not going to cut corners, Vanessa. They'll get the product they asked for, or none at all.
McINTYRE	That's fair enough, I suppose.
HARRIS	There is one thing we could do.
McINTYRE	Yes?
HARRIS	Maybe we could talk to George. Tell him he's got to be more flexible, if this MBO programme is going to work properly. We could ask him to change the objective for Krackle. Substitute September for June.
McINTYRE	It's certainly worth a try. But are you sure it'll be ready for test marketing in March?
HARRIS	Positive. We'll have solved the technical problems by then.
McINTYRE	OK. I'll fix up a meeting with George. He might bend if we're persuasive enough – you never know!
HARRIS	Good. We'll get round this one, don't worry. Ha! I don't know what you think about the MBO programme, but I reckon things were a lot simpler in the old days when no one had ever heard of Management by Objectives.
McINTYRE	Mm . . . maybe you're right. Let me think about that one.

Key

READING

Understanding the main points

1 The manager evaluates the subordinate's performance in relation to how well or badly he/she has achieved the goals or objectives set by both the manager and the subordinate together.

2 Stage 1 The subordinate's job is defined.
   Stage 2 His/Her current performance is evaluated.
   Stage 3 The subordinate and the manager develop new objectives together.
   Stage 4 The programme is put into action.
   Stage 5 The subordinate's performance is reviewed periodically, and his/her progress is checked.

3 THE BENEFITS OF MANAGEMENT BY OBJECTIVES

COMPANY	MANAGER	SUBORDINATE
1 leads to better coordination and communications within a company	1 makes it easier to judge a subordinate's performance objectively	1 helps him/her to see clearly his/her role in the company
2 ensures that all employees understand the company's goals and makes a contribution to them	2 he/she can be sure that the subordinate knows what is expected of him/her	2 makes it clear what tasks he/she must carry out
3 forces the company to pay careful attention to planning-links individual and organisation objectives	3 encourages consultation between the manager and the subordinate when developing objectives	3 he/she has a say in how his/her job is performed and what his/her objectives should be
4 leads to more effective management throughout the company	4 helps the manager to know when the subordinate requires extra training	4 feels more responsible, more motivated and more committed to the company

4 c motivator

Vocabulary focus

1 objectives
2 essential, extremely important
3 connected, joined
4 concentrates
5 re-examinations

6 demanding, difficult
7 reasonable, achievable
8 begins (the task of . . .)
9 loyal, obligated
10 communicate, act together

LANGUAGE STUDY

1

1 performance
2 progress
3 achieving
4 report
5 feedback

6 objectives
7 role
8 stage
9 reach
10 view

2

1 cut out
2 pointed out
3 hold out
4 stood out

5 make out
6 cut out
7 have, out
8 make out

3
1 I suggested that she (should) log/logged my use of time.
2 The Research and Development Manager demanded that the product (should) be taken off the market.
3 The new chairman insisted on reorganising the board of directors./that the board of directors (should) be reorganised.
4 I proposed interviewing the other candidates tomorrow./I proposed that the other candidates (should) be interviewed tomorrow.
5 It's vital that I finish this report by the end of the week.
6 It's time you stopped working now – it's almost midnight.
7 It's essential that the management (should) realise that we are human beings, not machines.
8 He offered to help me write the report.

Understanding the main points

MEMORANDUM
To: George Holbrook
From: Vanessa McIntyre
Subject: *Test marketing and launch of Krackle*

Ralph Harris has just informed me that *the Krackle biscuit will not be ready for test marketing by January.*
Apparently, this regrettable delay has been caused by *technical problems.*
Ralph says that they still haven't managed to develop a biscuit which crackles when you bite into it.
Ralph now estimates that his department will not have solved this problem satisfactorily until *the end of March.* Naturally, this will make it impossible for us to *get it on the market by June.*
In view of these unfortunate circumstances I would suggest that our best course of action would be to postpone the launch *until next September.*
Could we meet to discuss this as soon as possible?

Vocabulary focus

1 1 run up against
   2 tried, out
   3 get, on, No Way
   4 cut corners
   5 fix up, with

7 *The management of time*

Tapescript

Marion and Polyanna work at the head office of Superfare, a group of food stores. Marion's boss, Edward, is Director of Special Projects. Polyanna's boss, Gerald, is Financial Controller of the organisation. While having lunch together, Marion and Polyanna discuss their respective bosses. Listen to their conversation.

MARION   Honestly, Polly, I don't think I'll be working here much longer. Edward's driving me up the wall. He's impossible to work for. Absolutely impossible.

POLYANNA Oh? I've always thought he was rather nice. Mind you, he always seems to be in a rush – never has a minute to talk to you.

MARION   That's it. He's always rushing around in a panic. And he never gets anything done. It's so ... frustrating. I can't stand it much longer.

POLYANNA It's not that bad surely.

MARION   It is. Look what happened last week. We had a report to get ready for Wednesday's board meeting. Right?

POLYANNA Uh huh.

MARION   We'd been given Friday as the deadline for submitting it. So what happens?

POLYANNA You didn't meet the deadline, uh?

MARION	Dead right. And why? Because Edward decided to prepare all the statistics for the appendices himself. I could easily have helped him – I begged him – but he didn't want to know. He's so stubborn – you wouldn't believe it!
POLYANNA	Ah, one of those: wants to do everything himself, then can't understand why he never finishes anything on time.
MARION	Yes. Then blames you when people start complaining. Typical!
POLYANNA	Oh come on . . .
MARION	Anyway, I was telling you about the report. So, Friday came, it still hadn't been finished. Panic! Edward works on it all Saturday morning. And, believe it or not, I have to come in over the weekend. Work *all day Sunday* on the word-processor to get it ready for Monday morning.
POLYANNA	Unbelievable!
MARION	Yes, and no extra payment for it. Just part of the job. That's what happens when you work for the Director of Special Projects!
POLYANNA	Oh well, but at least he's a very nice guy – not like some of the managers round here.
MARION	Yes, I suppose you're right. But I do wish Edward would plan his time better. It'd be so much simpler. You're lucky, Gerald's obviously highly efficient.
POLYANNA	Mm, he certainly knows how to use his time effectively. He's got some useful little tricks, actually.
MARION	Tricks? What do you mean?
POLYANNA	Well, to plan his time. Like, at the end of the day, he makes a list of things he has to do the next day. You know, phone calls he's got to make, meetings to attend, work that's got to be done – that sort of thing.
MARION	Oh, I see.
POLYANNA	Yes. It helps him to get a good start to the day. He always knows what he's got to do.
MARION	Any other things he does? Maybe I can pass on a few tips to Edward? Diplomatically, of course.
POLYANNA	Mm, well . . . I've noticed Gerald always does the important jobs first. He never puts them off, and he works on them until he's finished them. He never gives up on a job.
MARION	Oh, interesting. He must be very patient.
POLYANNA	Mm. Another thing. If he's working on a tough problem, he keeps his door shut. Heaven help anyone who disturbs him then! Once, I even had to ask the Managing Director to come back.
MARION	You didn't, Polly.
POLYANNA	Mm. He was nice about it. He knows what Gerald's like.
MARION	I suppose so. Any other tips to pass on to Edward?
POLYANNA	Let's see . . . Nothing else really. Oh yes, there is one other thing. Gerald makes a lot of phone calls. Hates sending memos. Avoids them like the plague. Saves time, of course – phoning, I mean.
MARION	Oh, it must be great working for him.
POLYANNA	I don't know about that. He does give me a lot of work to do, you know. He's very clever at passing the buck.
MARION	Passing the buck? Oh, I think that's what's known as 'delegating work' round here, isn't it?

POLYANNA   I dare say you're right.
  MARION   Oh well, back to the grindstone, I suppose. And to dear
           Edward.
POLYANNA   Bye, Marion.

Key

Understanding the main points

1   1 ... he/she sometimes finds that he/she does not have enough
      time to devote to the really important jobs.
    2 ... more and more demands are made on their time.
    3 ... can find out exactly how he/she spends his working day or
      week (rather than how he/she thinks he/she spends it).

2   1 They can get rid of unproductive activities – they can learn to
      say 'No' to people demanding their time.
    2 They can delegate tasks to subordinates.
    3 They can re-shape their schedules – by setting aside time for
      certain tasks, e.g. management meetings, production
      scheduling etc., or by working at home one day a week.
    4 They can list the tasks they have to do in order of priority and
      set themselves deadlines for the most important activities.

3   1 Firstly, they log their time to find out how they actually spend
      their time at work – not how they think they spend it.
    2 Then they analyse the time-log to help them re-think and re-
      plan their schedules. They consider whether some of the
      things they do are a waste of time, whether they should spend
      more time on certain activities, whether other people could do
      some of the tasks and whether they sometimes waste their
      colleagues' time.
    3 Finally, they put into practice what they have decided to do in
      order to make a more effective use of their time.

Vocabulary focus

1 trivial   7 rely
2 tackle   8 turning down
3 drops by   9 discriminating
4 demands   10 set aside/earmark
5 precious   11 priority
6 cut out

1   1 a card on which the hours recorded by an employee are
      recorded
    2 the period of time between two closely connected events, or
      between a decision to do something and its accomplishment
    3 the study and analysis of work procedure so that the most
      efficient method of working can be studied
    4 a region in which the same standard time is used. There are
      twenty-four time zones in the world.
    5 a switch that can be set at a certain time to start a machine or
      activity
    6 a period of time within which something must be completed
    7 the handling by a computer of more than one program at the
      same time. Users at different terminals of the computer can
      communicate with it at the same time.
    8 a person or thing which records time
    9 to arrive at the expected or scheduled time
   10 to arrive early or at the appointed time

2 1 in good time 5 before my time
2 in no time at all 6 ahead of its time
3 for the time being 7 At one time
4 are working against time 8 from time to time

3 1a 2d 3a 4d 5c 6d 7d 8b

4 A 1 Hardly had I finished phoning when my boss dropped into my office.
2 Under no circumstances should a manager rely on his/her memory to log time.
3 Not until two years ago did the company begin to make profits.
4 Only after three hours' negotiations did we succeed in reaching agreement on the final contract.
5 Rarely does our company fail to meet its delivery dates.

B 1 Seldom have I been so tired after a meeting.
2 No sooner did I arrive in my office than the telephone rang.
3 Under no circumstances must I be disturbed.
4 Only after a lot of research did they put the project on the market.
5 Rarely does she have any time to relax.
6 Not until 1986 were we able to buy our own factory.
7 Little does he realise that he will soon be made redundant.
8 Hardly had I started the report when my boss dropped by.

LISTENING

Understanding the main points
1 She is unhappy about her boss, Edward's lack of organisation, which makes him 'impossible to work for'.
2 Friday was the deadline for submitting the report for the following Wednesday's board meeting.
3 Marion had to go in to work on Sunday to get the report ready on the word-processor for Monday morning.
4 1 At the end of each day he makes a list of the things he has to do the following day.
2 He always does the important jobs first – he never puts them off.
3 He always works on the important jobs until he's finished them.
4 He shuts himself in his office when he's working on a difficult problem and doesn't let anyone disturb him.
5 He makes a lot of telephone calls, rather than sending memos.

Vocabulary focus
1 'Edward's driving me up the wall!'
2 'He's always rushing around in a panic.'
3 '. . . he didn't want to know.'
4 'Maybe I can pass on a few tips to Edward?'
5 'He never puts them off.'
6 'He never gives up on a job.'
7 'Heaven help anyone who disturbs him then!'
8 'He's very clever at passing the buck.'

8 Motivation

Tapescript

LISTENING

Trafalgar Products, manufacturers of hi-fi equipment, has a problem in its Production Department. Some of the production workers are taking too much time off work. Absenteeism, particularly among part-time workers, is too high. And the number of man hours lost per employee is much higher at Trafalgar Products than at similar firms. Don McCaul, Managing Director, talks about the problem with three other executives: Sara Marshall, Personnel Manager, Kerry Webb, Production Manager and Frank Collins, Financial Director. Listen to their conversation.

Section 1

McCAUL   I must say, I'm worried about this problem. Absenteeism affects our productivity. And the quality of our products. We wouldn't need so many inspections if people spent more time on the job. Don't you agree, Frank?

COLLINS   Absolutely, Don. The trouble is, in my opinion, that we're not hard enough on staff who take too much time off. I mean, some of them take twenty or thirty days off each year. They seem to think it's their *right* to do it. We ought to come down on those people like a ton of bricks.

MARSHALL   That's all very well, Frank, but they are entitled to thirty days paid sick leave a year. It's in their employment contract.

COLLINS   Entitled? Does that mean to say they have to take it? Every year. That's taking advantage of the system, surely?

MARSHALL   All right, but . . .

McCAUL   Look, Sara, Frank's got a point, we are too lenient with staff who take time off. We've got to take a tougher line with them. What do you say, Kerry?

WEBB   Yes, I go along with that, Don. We must do something. Soon.

Section 2

WEBB   I'd like to suggest something – I've been thinking about it for some time.

McCAUL   Uh huh.

WEBB   It might be a good idea to interview staff who take too much time off. We could check attendance records, say, for the last three years. If anyone was absent – on average – for more then twenty days a year, they would have to see someone in Personnel. And Sara could try to find out why they were taking so much time off. What do you think, Sara?

MARSHALL   Mm, it's not a bad idea, that. I might get some useful information from them. If I was sympathetic . . . and didn't appear to be judging them.

COLLINS   Ha! They'd probably say the job was boring. Or they had a sick aunt to look after. You'd never find out the real reason, I bet you.

McCAUL   Maybe you're right, Frank. But at least they'd know we

were keeping an eye on them. And that we value the
work they do for us.

COLLINS Perhaps.

WEBB I'd like to make one other suggestion, if I may.

McCAUL Go ahead, Kerry.

WEBB Well, at my last company, they used to send each person
his or her attendance record, at the end of the year. It
was a good idea . . . you see, we all got them at the same
time, and we used to ask each other how many days off
they had. If you'd had too many days off, people joked
about it. You know, told you to pull your socks up. Quite
effective, really.

McCAUL I like that idea – attendance records. They wouldn't be
too hard to prepare, would they, Sara?

MARSHALL No, I don't think so. Not if I had that new assistant you've
been promising me for months, Don!

McCAUL Ha, Ha! That's one up to you, Sara.

Section 3

COLLINS You know, I heard about a good scheme when I was in
America. A way of reducing absenteeism, and
encouraging people to get to work on time.

McCAUL Tell us about it, Frank.

COLLINS OK then. I forget the name of the firm. Anyway, if any of
their employees had 100% attendance and punctuality record
during the month, the names of the employees were put
on pieces of paper. The pieces of paper were then put
into a box. And a draw was held. The person whose
name was picked out of the box got a prize. Cash – a
hundred or two hundred dollars, something like that.

McCAUL Was the scheme successful, do you know?

COLLINS Oh yes. Attendance improved a great deal at the
company. And not many people had sick leave, if they
could help it.

MARSHALL Ah, that's interesting, Frank. So if you had sick leave,
your name wasn't entered in the draw.

COLLINS That's right. You had to have perfect attendance. No
absences at all. And you couldn't be late for work.

WEBB That doesn't seem very fair to me, Frank. In fact, it's
rather inhuman, isn't it? I don't think our workers would
be motivated by that sort of scheme. Anyway, the unions
wouldn't buy it.

McCAUL I agree with you, Kerry. That sort of thing might work in
America but it wouldn't go down well here.

COLLINS I don't agree. Anyway, there would be no harm trying it.
What have we got to lose? I don't think our workers
would turn their noses up at the chance of earning some
extra cash.

McCAUL You could be right but . . . I doubt it somehow.

Key

Understanding the main points

1 True   2 True   3 False   4 True   5 False   6 True

Vocabulary focus

1 potential   4 status   7 catching on
2 hierarchy   5 conclusive
3 esteemed   6 sense

1 1 dissatisfied   5 disrespectful
    2 inconclusive   6 insecure
    3 Irresponsible   7 unsocial
    4 unpopular   8 inefficient

2 A 1–e   2–g   3–h   4–c   5–a   6–f   7–j   8–b
      9–d   10–i

    B 1 catchy   6 catch-phrase
       2 catch on   7 caught out
       3 caught, eye   8 catching on
       4 catching up   9 caught sight of
       5 catch   10 catch fire

3 A 1 Our Production Department has done some research recently into job enrichment programmes.
      2 The management consultant gave us advice about how to improve labour relations on the shop floor.
      3 We are looking for someone with experience of/in selling IBM computers.
      4 She has extensive knowledge of the hotel industry.
      5 It will be difficult for him to find cheap accommodation in New York.
      6 This is a fascinating piece of research.
      7 This morning my supervisor received some bad news from an important supplier.
      8 That was a piece of invaluable advice.

    B 1 Marlow carried out a great deal of research into motivation.
      2 I asked my boss to give me some advice about my career.
      3 Is it true that travel broadens the mind?
      4 Have you made any progress in overcoming the problem?
      5 I went to a business library to get some information about export practices in Japanese companies.
      6 I looked out of my office window and said, 'What terrible weather!'

Understanding the main points
1 True   2 False   3 True   4 False   5 True

Vocabulary focus
1 'Look, Sara, Frank's got a point . . .'
2 'Yes, I go along with that, Don.'
3 '. . . they'd know we were keeping an eye on them.'
4 '. . . told you to pull your socks up.'
5 'That's one up to you, Sara.'
6 'And not many people had sick leave, if they could help it.'
7 'Anyway, the unions wouldn't buy it.'
8 '. . . it wouldn't go down well here.'

9 Performance appraisal

Tapescript

LISTENING

Derek works for Transam, a large airline in the USA. He has just applied for the job of Operations Manager, an important administrative position in the company, and hopes to go before a selection board shortly. His immediate boss, Robert, supports his application. However, the airline's Personnel Director, Ian, has other ideas. Listen to the following conversation between Robert and Ian.

ROBERT I've come to see you, Ian, because I've heard something that's surprised me. It's about Derek – you probably know that.

IAN Yes, I was expecting to hear from you. You're wondering why I want his name to be taken off the short-list?

ROBERT Yes, I am.

IAN It's simple; he's not the man for the job. If you're going to run our operations at any airport – I don't care whether it's New York, Tokyo or wherever ... you've got to have *all* the right qualities: intelligence, a sense of responsibility, and the ability to keep calm in a crisis. Derek is not our man.

ROBERT Derek, not intelligent? Come on, you're putting me on!

IAN OK, so he's a smart guy, I admit that, but ...

ROBERT But what? What have you got against him? I've worked with him for three years now. He's a really good administrator. He handles passengers superbly. Everyone likes him.

IAN OK, so he's charming and intelligent. But is he reliable? Will he keep his head in a crisis?

ROBERT Yes, he will ... do you know something I don't?

IAN Let's look at some facts. What about his breakdown? It was pretty serious, if you remember.

ROBERT Oh, that's it, is it? Ian, he had that breakdown years ago. He was only twenty then.

IAN Yes, but let's face it, it was *serious*. They thought it was schizophrenia for a while.

ROBERT It wasn't schizophrenia. It was a simple problem. Some sort of chemical imbalance in the brain. He still has to take tablets for it but he's fine now.

IAN You reckon? I'd say he's emotional, moody. Up one minute, down the next.

ROBERT That's crap! Why don't you like the man? Is it something personal?

IAN Now hold on ...

ROBERT I'm sorry – I take that back.

IAN It's not really the breakdown. It's Turkey that bothers me. Remember? Back in '81.

ROBERT Turkey? '81? I was in West Africa then.

IAN Ah, let me tell you about it. Derek had a car accident while he was on holiday there. Crashed into someone else. Driving too fast on a narrow road.

ROBERT Could happen to anyone.

IAN Right. But you see, he panicked. Turned off his lights. And left the scene of the accident. Some of the people in the other car were badly injured.

ROBERT Oh.

IAN The police caught up with him in the end. He spent over two months in jail. I've got a file full of correspondence about the accident. We had a hell of a job getting him out of Turkey.

ROBERT I didn't know about this. I heard he'd had some sort of accident. I didn't realise it was so serious.

IAN Robert, I understand your position. Believe me. I know Derek's done a splendid job for you. And I also know you're very friendly with his father.

ROBERT It's got nothing to do with it – his father being a director.

IAN Of course not. I'm telling you now, my considered opinion is that Derek's not right for the job. If I get my way, he won't go before the board.

ROBERT OK, I understand now. I'm not going to argue Derek's case any longer. Not after what you've just told me.

IAN Good. I thought you might see it my way – once you knew all the facts.

Key

READING

Understanding the main points

1 To help organisations reach decisions about giving salary increases to individuals.
2 The *rating* method of appraisal focuses on the traits that a person shows in his/her work, e.g. knowledge of the job, reliability, initiative and sense of responsibility. The Management by Objectives method, on the other hand, focuses on the results achieved by a person in a given period of time.
3 The superior has to keep a record of good and unsatisfactory incidents of a person's work over a given period of time, usually a year.
4 Because the manager has to think about the subordinate's performance throughout the *whole* year.
5 Because managers are reluctant to describe his/her performance as 'outstanding', which means that the person does not get the evaluation he/she deserves.

Vocabulary focus

1 abilities to do something well
2 work ambitions; the position of power and responsibility at work that an individual would like to reach
3 information about something (here, the subordinate's performance) so that changes can be made or appropriate action can be taken if necessary
4 the extent to which someone can be relied on/depended on/counted on or can be trusted
5 ability to see what needs to be done and then to take the necessary action to achieve it without help
6 help, advice
7 expecting to be attacked or (here) criticised
8 ambitious people who are determined to succeed

LANGUAGE STUDY

1 1 to the present time, up until now
   2 old-fashioned, out of date
   3 modern
   4 began when we . . .
   5 modernise, bring up to date
   6 old-fashioned

2 1 2 reliably   3 reliability   4 relied
   2 1 critically   2 critic   3 criticisms
   3 1 skilful   2 skilled   3 skills
      4 unskilled
   4 1 employees   2 Unemployment   3 unemployed
      4 unemployable
   5 1 ensure   2 assured   3 Surely
   6 1 ability   2 inability   3 unable   4 ably
   7 1 decisive   2 indecisive   3 undecided

3 1 ... one or two of them can't stand her.
   2 ... Barbara speaks fluent Italian.
   3 ... Graham is not mobile because his wife has an important job
        at the local hospital.
   4 ... has a master's degree in marketing and a diploma in
        communications.
   5 ... he has exceptional mathematical ability and is highly
        intelligent.
   6 ... too frank and outspoken.
   7 ... a master's degree in marketing ...
   8 ... does not speak any foreign languages.

LISTENING

Understanding the main points

CANDIDATE REPORT
To: All members of Selection Board
From: Ian Jameson

Vacancy: Operations Manager
Applicant: Derek Schmitt   Age: 36
Present position: Customer Relations Manager

ASSESSMENT OF PERSONAL QUALITIES

Strengths	Weaknesses
intelligent	*unreliable*
deals with passengers very well	*emotional, moody*
good administrator	*irresponsible*
charming	*liable to panic in crises*

Critical incidents
1 When he was twenty Derek *had some sort of nervous breakdown.*
   At first, doctors thought he was suffering from *schizophrenia.* He
   still *has to take tablets* for this condition.
2 In 1981 *Derek was involved in a car accident while he was on
   holiday in Turkey. He panicked and left the scene of the accident
   without reporting it to the police. He was later arrested and spent
   two months in a Turkish jail. The company had great difficulty
   getting him released from Turkey.*

Vocabulary focus
1 1 got against   5 caught up with
   2 keep, head   6 to do with
   3 let's face   7 get, way
   4 take, back   8 see, way

10 Centralisation or decentralisation?

Tapescript

LISTENING

Jolawear Ltd. is a clothing manufacturing company. Its President and Chief Executive is Jolanta Nolan. In the following conversation she is talking to a group of the firm's top executives. Among them is Richard, Head of Production, and Claire, Financial Director. They are discussing the location of a new manufacturing plant.

JOLANTA We've got to choose between Wakefield, in the North of England, and Hong Kong – that's clear. Financial considerations are going to be important. We'll have to compare operating costs at the two sites. And labour and overhead costs. We'll try to work out what sort of return we'll get on our investment in each case. Right?

RICHARD Yes, we've still got a lot of research to do and feasibility studies to carry out before we can reach a decision. We'll need production forecasts for the two plants, of course.

CLAIRE Not only that. We'll have to take into account investment grants, and tax concessions.

JOLANTA We won't rush it, that's for sure. There'll be plenty of figurework. What I want to get clearly in my mind now are the broad arguments for each site. I know your opinion, Richard, you want us to set up the plant in Wakefield. Can you spell out for us why you favour this location?

RICHARD I'd be glad to. I say the arguments are *overwhelming* for having the plant here. Let's not forget, a few years ago, we were in a very serious financial situation. What was the problem? We weren't making the right goods at the right price. And, I might say, our staffing levels, and overheads, were too high. True?

JOLANTA I think we all accept your analysis. What are you leading up to?

RICHARD We got back on our feet by investing in the latest technology. Our productivity rose, and that helped to keep prices down. And we made a lot of other economies.

JOLANTA All right, we can certainly put down a lot of our success to pricing. And keeping costs low.

RICHARD Yes. We could do that because we have a first-class Research and Development Department at Head Office. They were pushing us to invest in more modern machinery. British-made machinery, I might add.

JOLANTA The Research and Development Department came up with the goods – no doubt about that. They were crucial to our recovery. We also had very tight financial controls on all our manufacturing plants.

RICHARD That's my point. Head Office provided the technical expertise, and the financial controls. We became a *centralised* organisation. And we still are one. That's what saved us from going under.

JOLANTA You're suggesting we should stay centralised. If we have a plant in Hong Kong, it's going to be more difficult for us to keep control of it.

RICHARD That's my main point. Let me remind you, also, our biggest sales area is the EEC. We need to have all our plants near the area. Think of the saving in transport costs, for a start . . .

JOLANTA OK, thanks . . .

RICHARD A final word, if I may. Just to point out, we've never run an overseas plant before. It's a new ball game for us – as the Americans say. Do we have the management skills for it?

JOLANTA Thanks a lot, Richard. Now, Claire, before you say anything, I might as well tell you, you'll have to make out a pretty strong case for Hong Kong.

CLAIRE I know that.

JOLANTA You all know why, too. My father was Polish. He came here after the war and settled. But he was more British than anyone born here. I'm the same. If we can, we'll buy British, and we'll provide work for British people – you know my feelings. So . . . Claire.

CLAIRE Look, you all know some of the advantages of having a plant in Hong Kong: cheap labour; lower corporation tax, no unions breathing down your neck, making life difficult.

JOLANTA All right, Claire, now tell us something new.

CLAIRE OK, I say we've got to be more *international* in our outlook. We must drop this 'little Englander' mentality. We're not going to expand sales for ever in the EEC. We'll need other markets. There are lots of opportunities for us in the Far East: in Japan, Malaysia, Singapore. We haven't touched those areas yet.

JOLANTA They're a long way away. Very tough to penetrate.

CLAIRE That's why the new plant's got to be in Hong Kong. It'd give us a base to attack those areas. We can compete with anyone – we've shown that already.

JOLANTA It would be a big step – into unknown territory.

CLAIRE I know your heart's in England, Jolanta. It's no time for sentiment. You must try to think internationally. Our future depends on it.

Key

Understanding the main points

1 1 True   2 False   3 False   4 False   5 True
   6 True
2 1 It helps to develop people – staff get more responsibility, make more decisions and so gain experience for later managerial positions.
   2 If an organisation is too centralised, people become robots, which is demotivating.
   3 It allows top managers to delegate jobs, giving them more time to work on setting goals, planning corporate strategy and working out policies.
   4 Decentralised companies are more flexible in competitive conditions, are better able to make quick decisions and adapt to change.

1
1 authority
2 recruitment
3 took over
4 founded
5 self-contained
6 bring up
7 delay
8 handing (it) over
9 authorised
10 autonomy
11 the 'buzz' word
12 demotivating
13 setting goals
14 flexible
15 balance
16 stresses
17 core values
18 initiative

3
1 functions
2 delegate
3 innovate
4 control
5 autonomy
6 innovative
7 authorised
8 initiative

4 A 1–c   2–e   3–d   4–b   5–a
   B 1 brought up   2 brought about   3 bring down
      4 brought, round   5 bring out

Understanding the main points

ADVANTAGES OF THE TWO SITES PROPOSED

WAKEFIELD

(i) Jolawear's recent recovery is due to the fact that they are a centralised company – Head Office provided the technical expertise (the Research and Development Department) and kept a very tight control on their manufacturing plants. It would be very difficult to remain centralised with a plant in Hong Kong.

(ii) Jolawear's biggest sales area is the EEC so it is better to have the plant near the area – Wakefield is nearer Europe than Hong Kong.

(iii) The company has never run an overseas plant before and may therefore not have the management skills required.

(iv) Jolanta would prefer to provide work for British people if possible.

HONG KONG

(i) Labour is much cheaper in Hong Kong.

(ii) Corporation tax is lower.

(iii) The company wouldn't have any unions making life difficult for them.

(iv) If the new plant was in Hong Kong, they would be able to penetrate new markets in the Far East – Japan, Malaysia, Singapore etc.

Vocabulary focus

1
1 return, investment
2 research, carry out, reach
3 into account
4 overwhelming
5 levels, overheads
6 invest in
7 controls on
8 keep, of
9 skills
10 out, case
11 expand
12 opportunities
13 step, territory

11 Communications

Tapescript

LISTENING

Gina Redman, a salesperson for a computer services firm, is talking to Donald Lester, her immediate superior, in his office. Lester is much older than Gina, is not an easy man to talk to but does have a lot of experience of the computer industry. Listen to their conversation.

LESTER Now, what did you want to see me about, Gina?

GINA I wanted to talk to you, to tell you about an offer I've had – for a job, that is.

LESTER A job offer? It's not unusual in our business. People move around a lot ... too much, in my opinion. Anyway, tell me about the offer.

GINA Someone called me, about a job in Paris. It involves running a business services outlet, providing computer systems to local businesses; consultancy work; on-site demonstrations; advising clients about software programmes; training their staff ...

LESTER The sort of thing we're doing, in fact – offering a complete package to firms, including reliable after-sales service.

GINA Yes, it's the kind of work I'm used to. I'd have no difficulty doing the job, I reckon.

LESTER Of course not. But, I thought you were happy here, Gina. Correct me if I'm wrong.

GINA I am happy here. I told you, someone phoned me, out of the blue. I didn't know him from Adam. I've no idea how he heard about me.

LESTER Oh, these headhunters have their sources of information ... it's flattering, isn't it, being head-hunted. I hope the offer was a good one.

GINA The salary was extremely tempting – 5,000 more than I'm getting here. And there were bonuses on top of it, depending on monthly sales increases.

LESTER Ha! And what about the car? A BMW, I bet you, or a Volvo perhaps?

GINA BMW.

LESTER Told you so. Listen, you've got to be careful about these job offers. Obviously, you're worth hiring. We've trained you, given you experience. You're a seasoned representative. Now the other companies are ready to cash in.

GINA I suppose so. On the other hand, I've worked hard for the business. I'm worth my salary. Otherwise I wouldn't have had the offer, would I?

LESTER Hm.

GINA I had the best sales record last year.

LESTER Huh, no one's indispensable, Gina. There are dozens of out-of-work computer salespeople. If we had to, we'd pay over the going rate to get someone to replace you.

GINA I didn't say I wanted to leave. But when you get an offer like this, well ... it makes you think.

LESTER I know. Paris ... it's exciting, glamorous. What about your husband? And your children? Do they want to go over there?

GINA We've discussed it. It wouldn't be easy for the kids. It's different for John, my husband. He works freelance: he's his own boss ... in the promotion field. He could do the same sort of thing in Paris, after he'd brushed up his French a bit.

LESTER   See, another problem – the language. What's *your* French like?

GINA   Fluent. Like my Italian.

LESTER   Oh ... oh yes, your mother's Italian, of course.

GINA   I didn't think you knew that.

LESTER   Really? I know a few things about you, Gina. I don't bury my head in the sand here, like an ostrich. You'd better think carefully about the job. Money isn't everything. Job satisfaction's important. And a sense of achievement.

GINA   Yes, that's what I think.

LESTER   Why move then, and uproot yourself and your family? Maybe the job won't be as interesting as you think.

GINA   Could be you're right.

LESTER   Paris is an expensive city. That salary they offered – it won't go far over there. I tell you, I was near the Arc de Triomphe recently, having a coffee. Do you know, it cost me over a pound. And they had the nerve to expect a tip.

GINA   I hope the service was good.

LESTER   Huh, service? You take my advice, Gina. Forget the job offer. I know I said no one's indispensible. I didn't really mean it. We all know you're a big asset to this company.

GINA   Thanks very much, Donald. Nice of you to say so. From you, that's a real compliment. Maybe I will think again about the offer. I'm glad I asked for advice – everything's much clearer now.

Key

READING

Understanding the main points
1   1–f   2–c   3–a   4–d   5–g   6–b   7–e   8–h
3   Because the subordinate misinterprets what the manager means.

Vocabulary focus
1 look into
2 tied up
3 below par
4 screw up
5 you're out
6 rush order
7 match
8 credentials
9 just your cup of tea
10 look it over
11 straighten (it) out
12 jointly

LANGUAGE STUDY

1   1 makes a point of
    2 comes to the point
    3 keep to the point/don't get away from the point/don't get off the point
    4 made a (very) good point
    5 up to a point
    6 point-blank
    7 on the point of
    8 pointed out

2   1 To back out of the contract.
    2 Someone with a background in the automobile industry.
    3 You would try to get the financial backing to put it on the market.
    4 By offering the customs official a backhander.
    5 Back-breaking.
    6 The owner feels that he/she has his/her back against the wall.
    7 You hope they have agreed to back-date the increase.
    8 Because you have broken the back of the job.

Understanding the main points

JOB WITH COMPUTEX IN PARIS

Position? *Manager of a business services outlet*

Duties? *Selling computer systems to Parisian companies; providing a consultancy service; giving on-site demonstrations; giving advice about software; training clients' staff.*

Salary? *£5,000 more than at present*

Bonuses? *depending on monthly sales increases*

Perks? *company car*

ADVANTAGES	DISADVANTAGES
much higher salary; *bonuses; company car (BMW); Paris would be an exciting city to live in; language no problem; John could work freelance, as he does now*	might not be as interesting as present job; *difficult for the children to adjust to life in Paris; John would need to improve his French; Paris is very expensive*

Vocabulary focus

1
1 move around
2 involves running
3 offering, package
4 Correct, wrong
5 being headhunted
6 cash in
7 going rate
8 freelance
9 brushed up
10 uproot yourself

12 Leadership

Tapescript

Most of the members of the Porchester Chamber of Commerce are business people. Each month, the Chamber of Commerce holds a luncheon. And afterwards, there is usually a speech by a well-known person. Today, the manager of the city's football club, Porchester United, is giving a talk on *Leadership*.

MC   Silence, please, for our Chairman.

CHAIRMAN   Thank you. Ladies and Gentlemen. It is my great pleasure to welcome today Frank Evans. He needs no introduction from me, I'm sure. Let me just say that, thanks to Frank here, Porchester United has won the League title *four* times in the last five years. His record as a manager is remarkable. And I wouldn't mind betting that, before long, he'll be running our England team. Frank Evans, Ladies and Gentlemen.

EVANS   Thanks very much, Bob. And good afternoon, everybody. I don't know about becoming manager of the England team. The selection committee seem to think that I speak my mind rather too often, but that's another story, isn't it?

Before I start, let me thank you for the magnificent lunch. I'll certainly feel the effect of it when I'm out on the pitch tomorrow with the lads. I hope that, when I've finished my speech, you'll think I deserved the lunch.

You know, when your Chairman asked me to talk to you, I was going to say 'No' at first. I said to myself, 'What can I possibly say to a group of business people that'll interest them?'

Then Bob says to me, 'Talk about leadership, Frank. There's no one knows more about it than you. Give them some tips on how to get the best out of people; how to get a winning team together.'

Maybe I do know something about leadership, Ladies and Gentlemen. When I took over at Porchester United, we'd been bottom of the league, or near it, for years. We didn't stay there for long, did we? And we didn't have to spend millions buying players – like some teams I could mention.

What's the secret of leading a team, a winning team? That's the question, isn't it?

Now, first of all, and most important, you've got to make sure that every member in the team does his best, that he's performing to his maximum potential. How do you do that?

My advice is, use a bit of psychology with people. Now, in a football team, you've got eleven players, and they're all different. So you treat them differently. Some of them, you've got to *push* them to do their best. Shout at them, be hard on them. Bully them if you have to. Then they perform well. But if you're nice to them, they ... walk all over you. With other players, you've got to be nice to them – super nice – if you want them to play well. You praise them as much as possible. Tell them how wonderful they are. Flatter their egos. Right? And then there are some players, well, you leave them alone, let them get on with it.

What I'm saying is, if you're a leader, change your style to suit the person. Be flexible. And treat people as individuals.

And now my second point. If you're a good leader, you don't tell people what to do all the time. You listen as well. When I want to try a new move in a match, a tactic to surprise the other team, the players practise it first in training, of course. And then I ask some of them,' Charlie, do you think the move will work?', 'Harry, what do you think?' If they say 'No', I probably won't use it. So remember, Ladies and Gentlemen, if you're leading a team, let the members *participate*. Listen to their opinions. They often know better than you do.

Finally, a little story. We got to the F.A. Cup Final in my first year as manager. Remember? I wanted to win that match very much. So I thought up a clever move. A bit complicated, but clever. 'It'll be a match winner,' I thought. Well, it *was* a good move. And it *almost* won us the match. The trouble was, Charlie Parker wasn't in the right position to put the ball in the net. 'Where the hell were you?' I asked Charlie after the match. 'Sorry boss,' he says, 'I didn't understand the move. And I still don't.'

The lesson is, Ladies and Gentlemen, don't make things

too complicated. Try to explain things simply and clearly to the people who work for you. Keep it simple. If I'd done that, Porchester United would probably have won that cup final.

I hope you've found this little talk interesting. I've tried to 'keep it simple' as well. A final word. Most of you here are business leaders. Let's see some better performances from English companies in the future. It's high time our manufacturers got back their position as world leaders. Like in the old days. Thank you very much, Ladies and Gentlemen.

Key

Understanding the main points

1   1 ... many people who had these typical traits did not become leaders and also that many leaders did not have these traits.
    2 ... to get the job done.
    3 ... to be admired and liked by their subordinates.
    4 ... measure their leadership style to find out whether they are *relationship-motivated* leaders or *task-motivated* leaders.
    5 ... both styles of leadership could be effective in appropriate situations.

2   1 being 'visible' – making their presence felt by keeping in close contact with employees; showing their employees that they were personally interested in them
    2 providing a 'clear mission' – keeping all their staff informed about where the organisation is going and what it hopes to achieve in the future
    3 constantly reminding their staff what the organisation's values are

Vocabulary focus

 1 in which direction the company is moving
 2 an example of the position staff could rise to in their own working lives
 3 not as good as expected
 4 shown to be of doubtful value
 5 instructions
 6 main concern
 7 successfully completing the task
 8 primarily concerned with people
 9 set a value on
10 was likely to be
11 thoughtful of other people's feelings
12 vitally important
13 kept the employees alert
14 travels down the company hierarchy

LANGUAGE STUDY

1   1 self-explanatory   8 self-evident
    2 self-made   9 self-confidence
    3 self-reliant   10 self-control
    4 self-discipline   11 self-addressed
    5 self-appointed   12 self-confident
    6 self-satisfaction   13 self-educated
    7 Self-employed

2 1 market study/survey
2 market share
3 the stock exchange
4 marketable
5 on the market
6 If it goes 'up-market' it produces better-quality and more expensive goods. If it goes 'down-market' it makes cheaper, lower quality goods.
7 black market
8 A 'seller's market' is a market in which the demand for goods is greater than the supply and sellers can influence the price. In a 'buyer's market' supply exceeds demand and it is the buyers who can influence price.
9 We mean that there is no room for any new products.
10 onto
11 value

3 A 1–j   2–h   3–c   4–d   5–g   6–i   7–a
        8–e   9–b   10–f
    B 1 1 turnover   2 turn out   3 turning point
            4 turned round   5 turnover
        2 1 turn up   2 take turns   3 turned down
            4 turned against   5 turned over

LISTENING

Understanding the main points

HOW TO BE A WINNER

... In the previous five years *Porchester United had won the League title four times.*

... He said he did not expect to become manager of the national side because *he speaks his mind too often.*

... Then he thanked the Chamber of Commerce for the splendid lunch, saying that *he would feel the effects of it when he trained with his players the next day.*

... To do that a leader had to *change his/her style of management to suit the person, in other words to treat people as individuals.*

... His second point was that leading a team was not just a question of giving orders. *A manager should also listen to the opinions of his subordinates.*

... It appears that during the 1982 Cup Final Parker made a bad mistake: *he wasn't in the right position to put the ball in the net because he hadn't understood the move.*

... The point of the story was that a leader *should not make things too complicated but should explain things clearly and simply to the people who work for him/her.*

... Frank Evans ended his speech with a 'pep talk' to his audience. He thought it was high time *British manufacturing companies got back their position as world leaders.*

Tapescript

Harold Goodman is Chief Executive of a subsidiary of a multinational shoe company. The subsidiary is in a South American country. One of the firm's most senior directors is Carlos Hernandez. It is six o'clock in the morning. Harold Goodman receives an unexpected – indeed frightening – phone call.

Section 1

MRS GOODMAN	Oh no, who on earth can that be? You take it, Harold – it must be for you.
HAROLD	All right, dear. Hello, Harold Goodman here.
TERRORIST	Listen to me carefully, Mr Goodman. Do not ask questions.
HAROLD	What? Who is it?
TERRORIST	We are the National Freedom Movement. Listen. We have taken your Vice-President, Hernandez. We will KILL him if you don't do what we say. You understand? HERNANDEZ WILL DIE.
HAROLD	But ... what do you want?
TERRORIST	Thirty million dollars. Thirty million. You have one week to get the money. If you don't, you will never see Hernandez again.
HAROLD	Angela!
MRS GOODMAN	What's the matter, dear?
HAROLD	I don't know if it's a joke or something. It sounds as if Carlos has been ... kidnapped. They've asked for a ransom. Thirty million dollars! Can you believe it!
MRS GOODMAN	Good Heavens! Poor Carlos.
HAROLD	I'd better phone the Chief of Police. Right away.

Section 2

It is three days later. Harold Goodman is talking to the Minister for Internal Security at Government House.

MINISTER	These people are terrorists, Mr Goodman, not freedom fighters. They want to take over the country. And they'll stop at nothing to do it.
HAROLD	So I hear. I believe they live in the jungle area, don't they? And cause a lot of trouble for your troops.
MINISTER	Yes, they're difficult to flush out of the areas. Most of them were born there. They know the jungle like the back of their hand. We've lost a lot of troups going after them. Ambushes, mostly.
HAROLD	I talked to your head of security. He's advising me what to do – about Hernandez.
MINISTER	Good. You must do as he says. And trust him.
HAROLD	Of course.
MINISTER	Let me explain something to you. Officially, our government's attitude will be: no compromise with the rebels. We will never meet their demands.
HAROLD	You take a tough line, uh?
MINISTER	A government can never be seen to be negotiating with terrorists. It would encourage other kidnappers.

HAROLD	But, unofficially, you're more . . . flexible?
MINISTER	Yes. What happens next is that the terrorists will contact you again, and suggest an intermediary. A messenger between you and them. It'll probably be a university professor – someone sympathetic to their cause.
HAROLD	When they call me, I'll have to offer *some* money. I've talked to our board in New York – I'm in constant contact with them – they say, don't put Hernandez's life at risk – whatever happens.
MINISTER	When the terrorists call again, offer them a million dollars. No more, you understand.
HAROLD	They won't accept it.
MINISTER	So . . . play for time. Say you have to contact your board again, to see if they'll offer more.
HAROLD	Stretch out the negotiations, you mean.
MINISTER	Exactly. Bargain with them. They'll threaten to kill Hernandez but . . . they'll only be bluffing.
HAROLD	How can you be so . . . sure?

Section 3

MINISTER	You must stay calm, Mr Goodman. We'll be watching every move you make. And we'll be searching for the terrorists. All the time.
HAROLD	It's difficult to haggle when a man's life is at stake. I have authority from my board to offer ten million dollars – they think the terrorists will accept that amount.
MINISTER	No secret deals, please, Mr Goodman. Don't go behind our backs. A company tried to do that two years ago, pay a big ransom, against my orders.
HAROLD	Oh? What happened?
MINISTER	They got their director back. He was found in the trunk of a parked car.
HAROLD	Dead?
MINISTER	Two bullets through the head.
HAROLD	Really?
MINISTER	It was a dirty business. If only they'd listened to us! So remember, no secret deals. Offer a million dollars, and no more.
HAROLD	You can take my word, Señor Gomez, that my board will rely on your experience in this matter. Tell me, what are the chances of Hernandez coming out alive?
MINISTER	Who knows? It's in the hands of God. Let's just pray for him. And his family. And hope that we can save him.

Key

DISCUSSION

A Many people in Brazil were upset because the word 'rendezvous' in Portuguese means a room which is hired for love making!

B The picnic did not improve the relations between the US managers and the Spanish workers. The lower level workers stayed in their own groups and did not want to be served by their bosses. The Spanish have strong views on class distinctions and social groups. Many Spanish people do not believe in workers socialising with executives.

C The advertisement did not truly reflect French–Canadian life and customs. It was not usual for wives to play golf with their husbands. Nor was it socially acceptable, at a high-class golf course, for women to be seen wearing shorts. Finally, French–Canadians did not serve that type of fish as a main course at dinner.

D The US manufacturer did not consider local distribution characteristics. In France, most cosmetic manufacturers give franchises for their products to a few local retailers, known as 'perfumers'. These are mainly small shops, but they have a lot of influence in the perfume trade, and on customers. It is important for a manufacturer to have good relations with these perfumers if its cosmetic products are to sell well. Because it ignored these important outlets, the company's marketing approach failed.

E The foreign buyer did not understand the behaviour of a Japanese person when negotiating a deal. A Japanese businessman will often sit back and think for some time when he is made an offer. The foreign buyer did not realise this and thought he had to make a better offer.

F When an Englishman shakes his head up and down, this does not always mean that he agrees with the other person. It could simply mean that he hears you or understands the point you are making!

READING

Understanding the main points
1 (i) It should operate in at least six countries.
  (ii) It should have no less than 20% of its sales or assets in those countries.
2 British Petroleum.
3 Because it takes away business from other potential suppliers based in the foreign country itself.
4 It must allow a certain percentage of the subsidiary's equity to be owned by local investors.
5 To warn its readers against making the same or similar mistakes as those given as examples in the book.
6 Because they felt that the Americans had an attitude of cultural and intellectual superiority and because they tried to impose their way of life on local workers.
7 It might cause them to react in the wrong way to long silences during negotiations so that they lose ground in the discussions by making concessions or by being over-eager.

Vocabulary focus
  1 everything that belongs to a company, and that could be sold in order to pay a debt
  2 stop production, shut completely
  3 pressurise, attempt to make somebody do something by means of forceful demands
  4 begun to do business, begun production
  5 get it established
  6 money earned, revenue
  7 disagreement and bad relations caused by differences of opinion
  8 shares
  9 displeased, annoyed, hurt somebody's feelings
10 speak about the most important part of a subject
11 avoid coming to the point
12 without gaining anything

2
1 investment
2 equity
3 shareholding
4 negotiate
5 counter-proposals
6 concession
7 compromise
8 inflexible
9 stalemate/deadlock
10 withdrawing/pulling out
11 agreement
12 deal

3
1 ... has put its foot down ...
2 ... we've got a foot in the door.
3 ... fell on my feet ...
4 ... put my foot in it ...
5 ... got cold feet.
6 ... got back on its feet again.
7 ... we've got a foothold ...

4 A
1 making
2 two
3 bear/keep
4 To
5 one
6 open/broad, narrow
7 good
8 crossed

B
1 Please note.
2 It doesn't matter.
3 forgetful
4 tell her angrily what I think of her
5 I've been thinking about it.

5
criticise (sb.) *for*
focus *on*
responsible *for*
agree *to/on*
praise (sb.) *for*
congratulate (sb.) *on*
famous *for*
set one's heart *on*
gamble *on*
succeed *in*
approve *of*
accuse (sb.) *of*
chance *of*
in favour *of*
object *to*
think *of/about*

1 Some people have *criticised* multinationals *for not training* enough local staff.
2 'Today, we shall *focus on* the problems of multinationals,' said the television presenter.
3 *We did not agree to* their proposal.
4 IBM *is famous for making* high-quality products and *for giving* good service.
5 *He is responsible for* several local firms *going bankrupt.*
6 *I've set my heart on working* in our Los Angeles plant for a year or two.
7 *Is there any chance of you/your being* transferred abroad?
8 *We are gambling on* the host government *making* concessions.
9 Some governments *object to the fact that* multinationals dominate/*object to multinationals dominating* key industrial sectors.
10 They *succeeded in persuading* the government to offer more favourable conditions.

Understanding the main points
1 He has been kidnapped by the National Freedom Movement.
2 Because they live and operate in the jungle area, which they know much better than the government troops.
3 It gives the public the impression that it is not going to give in to their demands, but privately it negotiates with them.

4 It is prepared to offer the terrorists ten million dollars because it feels they will accept it in return for Hernandez's life.
5 To offer the terrorists a million pounds only.
6 He was murdered by the terrorists because his company made a secret deal with the terrorists without the government's approval.

Vocabulary focus
1 'They want to take over the country.'
2 '. . . they'll stop at nothing . . .'
3 '. . . they're difficult to flush out . . .'
4 'They know the jungle like the back of their hand.'
5 'We will never meet their demands.'
6 'Stretch out the negotiations, you mean?'
7 '. . . they'll only be bluffing.'
8 '. . . when a man's life is at stake.'
9 'Don't go behind our backs.'
10 'You can take my word . . .'

14 *Social responsibility*

Tapescript

LISTENING

Margaret Springfield is an executive for a firm of interior designers in the East End of London. The Managing Director of the company is Alexandra Leslie. One day, Margaret is told that Alexandra would like a word with her. Listen to their conversation.

ALEXANDRA   What about that estimate for Jock Smith, Margaret? What happened to it?

MARGARET   I'm sorry. I've almost finished preparing it. I've been so busy lately.

ALEXANDRA   It's over a week late, the estimate. The deadline was last Wednesday. Jock just called me. He said he tried to get you three times last week. You were never in your office.

MARGARET   Oh dear. Jock's one of our best customers. I wouldn't want to upset him for the world.

ALEXANDRA   It's not like you, this. I was talking to Dave this morning. He was complaining about you. He said you never give him enough work to do. Funny. Some time ago, he used to call you a 'slave driver'. What do you make of that?

MARGARET   I don't know – I've got a lot on my plate at the moment. Like last week. I was with the Education Committee all Tuesday. And on Wednesday, I was working on the Community Businesses Project – you know, helping immigrants to start up their own firm.

ALEXANDRA   All these community activities. You're on so many outside committees these days. No wonder your work's suffering.

MARGARET   You don't think that, do you?

ALEXANDRA   I know I encouraged everyone in this firm to take part in outside activities. Community projects. After all, it's good for our image. But I didn't expect you to get so involved, Margaret. Not you.

MARGARET   It's true – I do like the work. It's fascinating, and it's paid off for us too. That Education Committee now. Because of it, I've established good relations with the colleges. We got Sheila and Clive from the Polytechnic because of my contacts. You're pleased with their work, I know.

ALEXANDRA   Mm, yes, they're both talented designers. And they've got business skills – they're better than most of our university graduates.

MARGARET   I hope you won't criticise me for the work I'm doing on the Community Businesses project. Two of those people placed orders with us. £30,000 worth, wasn't it?

ALEXANDRA   I'm beginning to wish I'd never brought up the subject. Your outside work has been useful, I grant you. Maybe you're overdoing it a bit, Margaret. Putting all your energy into community work. Not leaving enough for us. We're your bread and butter, don't forget.

MARGARET   I do enjoy the work. It seems to be the way I'm moving now.

ALEXANDRA   Eh? How do you mean? *More* community work?

MARGARET   No, I mean I really like that sort of work – service to the community – it's challenging, rewarding. Not financially. It gives you a sense of . . . accomplishment, know what I mean?

ALEXANDRA   Mm. You're not thinking of leaving us, are you?

MARGARET   Leaving? No. Not really. I did have an offer recently. From someone I met on the Education Committee.

ALEXANDRA   I see.

MARGARET   It was to run a charity. Full time. Very well paid.

ALEXANDRA   You turned it down, I hope.

MARGARET   Yes. But if I can't continue my community work, I might be . . . tempted.

ALEXANDRA   Margaret, you know jolly well we don't want to lose you. You've been here years. I can't do without you. If I have to, I'll move you to another position, so you'll have time for your outside work.

MARGARET   Oh, don't worry . . .

ALEXANDRA   I remember now, we'd never have got planning permission for our new office if it hadn't been for your contacts.

MARGARET   It's sweet of you to say that, Alexandra. I don't want to leave here, really. Let me see how I can cut down on the outside activities. I have been getting a bit carried away, lately. Even my boyfriend's started complaining!

Key

Understanding the main points
1 True   2 False   3 False   4 True   5 True
6 True   7 True   8 True

Vocabulary focus
1 ethical standards
2 bribe
3 environment
4 opposed
5 boycotting
6 deception
7 fraud
8 create wealth
9 in the long run
10 critical

1 1–i   2–c   3–e   4–a   5–b   6–j   7–f   8–h
   9–g   10–d
2 1 1 of   2 for   3 by
   2 1 out   2 from   3 against
   3 1 in   2 from   3 with
   4 1 to   2 to   3 on   4 to
   5 1 in   2 from
3 A 1 ... We're *running out* of time.
      2 Can we *run through* the plan ...?
      3 ... The Design Department have *run up* against some
        technical problems.
      4 Our firm is gradually *running down* its marketing
        operation ...
      5 This contract *runs out* next month ...
      6 They have *run up* so many debts ...
   B 1–e   2–g   3–b   4–h   5–c   6–d   7–f   8–a
      1 running order   4 run-down
      2 in the running   5 runner-up
      3 run off their feet   6 run-up

Understanding the main points
1 ... his estimate was over a week late.
2 ... she spends so much time on outside activities such as
  community projects.
3 ... the company has good relations with the colleges and got two
  of their designers through Margaret's contacts with the
  Polytechnic.
4 ... two of the people involved later placed orders worth £30,000
  with them.
5 ... the work is both challenging and rewarding.
6 ... the company doesn't allow her to continue her community
  work.

Vocabulary focus
1 1 on, plate   6 overdoing
   2 start up   7 bread, butter
   3 good, image   8 down
   4 paid off   9 without you
   5 grant   10 down on